Mark,

I enjoyed you tonight at the moon and back program.

- The science of laws will improve our system of governance. Let's make this happen!

David G Schrunk

June 23, 2016

www.scienceoflaws.org

THE 𝓔ND OF 𝓒HAOS
QUALITY LAWS AND THE ASCENDANCY OF DEMOCRACY

DAVID G. SCHRUNK
Founder and Chairman
Quality of Laws Institute

Quality of Laws Press
Poway, California

THE END OF CHAOS
Quality Laws and the
Ascendancy of Democracy

By David G. Schrunk

PUBLISHED BY:

Quality of Laws Press
Post Office Box 726
Poway, CA 92074
www.qlpress.com

©2005 David G. Schrunk

ISBN 0-9770660-0-2

Library of Congress Control Number 2005905601

To Sijia and to Erik and Brigitte,
with all my love

TABLE OF CONTENTS

Figures

Tables

One of the most frustrating of my tasks over three decades of teaching political science at the college level has been to rationalize the process of legislating—to explain to my students *how* and *why* lawmaking is so chaotic, so irrational and counterproductive (not to mention corrupt and cynical) and yet to instill in them, somehow, a trust in our democratic governance.

I've been forced to conclude that *all* democracies are doomed to muddle along, at best, burdened by the tendency of power to corrupt and by the inevitable acquiescence of lawmakers to the influence of interest groups. Despite all our scientific progress in applying human reason in the quest to uncover nature's secrets and live more purposefully in our society, our lawmaking institutions continue to reveal the fatalistic ignorance more reflective of the early medieval era—aptly called the "Dark Ages."

Now comes a beacon to penetrate this darkness and this debilitating process—a plea to *apply the processes of science to the making of the laws* on which civilization depends. I am fortunate to have known David Schrunk for over twenty years, and have come to appreciate the vision behind this proposal—his contribution to the attainment of a more efficacious and just society.

Dr. Schrunk's experience in the medical field has proven to him personally the benefits of the scientific, quality methods whereby new medicines and procedures are created, tested, assessed and constantly re-evaluated based on their beneficial effects on patients' health. All the more understandable, then, has been his frustration at observing the vast wasteland of chaotic and counterproductive governmental laws.

According to the author, democratic government is obligated to serve the best interests of the people in terms of their liberty and well-being. Existing democracies have failed in this obligation, he argues, since their "traditional method of lawmaking" is based on anecdotes, opinions, deception and half-truths, and neither assesses risks nor evaluates the true effects of laws. Legislatures, capitulating too often to special interest groups and vote-trading pressures, create such an exploding complexity of laws that it is impossible for anyone to know or understand applicable statutes. The result is a bedlam of laws—an ever-expanding body of cumbersome, inane, useless and detrimental laws—which must necessarily be enforced selectively and arbitrarily. This conventional method of lawmaking is unprincipled, unreliable and irresponsible.

How should an enlightened society reverse this counterproductive chaos, weed out useless laws and create only those laws that will be truly effective, cost-efficient and user-friendly in the solution of societal problems? *The solution is to apply quality procedures in the design, implementation and evaluation of laws.*

Quality programs are essential for all other useful products and enterprises, such as pharmaceuticals, aircraft, nuclear reactors, automobiles and surgical procedures. Simply apply these universally respected methods to enhance democratic institutions and practices, aiming specifically at what the author calls "human rights, living standards and quality-of-life standards." Adopting quality programs for laws will lead inexorably to substantial economic gains and to greater respect by the public for laws and government.

Although some of Dr. Schrunk's corollaries and definitions concerning democracy and human rights have been a source of some minor differences between us, I have nevertheless returned again and again to the essential worthiness of his argument; this proposal is a truly valuable, overdue contribution to the evolution of democratic practice and deserves a serious place in American political philosophy. The premises are undeniable, as is the potential to contribute greatly to the efficacy of the legislative process—which is, after all, the primary function of government.

MICHAEL NEWBROUGH, PHD
Professor Emeritus of Political Science
Palomar College, San Marcos, California

I have always been fascinated with science. I witnessed the introduction of the polio vaccine, the definition of the structure of DNA and the orbiting of *Sputnik*. These and other equally dramatic achievements from the realm of science inspired me to study engineering and medicine and pursue a career in medicine.

During the years I practiced medicine, I was involved with ongoing quality programs such as patient surveys, diagnostic protocol reviews and medical education seminars. The objective of these quality programs was to make improvements in the delivery of health care so that only the most efficacious means were applied to the solution of medical problems. I also witnessed the advent of spectacular new medical technologies such as ultrasound and computed axial tomography. These imaging modalities enabled me to diagnose diseases with improved patient comfort and safety and with an accuracy that was several orders of magnitude greater than had been possible with previous technologies. My experience with quality programs and ongoing scientific advances accustomed me to the fact that progress of the human condition is a reality.

Although my work and studies focused on medicine, I followed government policies and activities with great interest. My informal observations made it apparent to me that the field of lawmaking, in contrast with the field of medicine, is not characterized by progress. Chronic societal problems such as homelessness, poverty and illiteracy, for example, have not been successfully solved or mitigated despite the enactment of thousands of new laws and the resulting commitment of substantial government resources. In fact some problems, such as the lack of health insurance coverage among a significant proportion of the population of the United States, have increased in size.

The disparity between the successes of medicine and the relative failure of laws led me to undertake an investigation of the design practices of laws (legislative drafting and the legislative process), codified legislative statutes, scientific reports of laws and the classical literature that relates to government and laws.[1] I also examined reports and opinions of laws and lawmaking from news organizations, "think tanks" and other sources. My studies uncovered several flaws and omissions in the traditional lawmaking process of governments:

- The lawmaking process is not a problem-solving process.
- The lawmaking process is based on dogma, not knowledge.
- The lawmaking process is primarily an exercise in rhetoric and dialectic.

---

[1] For my education and research , I relied to a great extent on the "Great Books" series (R. Hutchins, editor in chief, *Great Books of the Western World* [Chicago, IL: Encyclopaedia Britannica, Inc., 1952, 1990]), not because these works always have correct answers for the major concerns of society (they don't), but because they are comprehensive and have been so influential in the formulation of the structure and operations of governments.

- There is no institution that derives and organizes reliable knowledge of the structure and mechanics of laws (no science of laws).
- There is no institution that applies design expertise in the efficacious solution of societal problems (no engineering discipline of laws).
- There are virtually no quality programs for laws or lawmaking.

These findings were disconcerting but they explained why governments are grossly underperforming in terms of the net benefit they provide for the people by means of laws. In effect, the current method by which governments address societal problems—the traditional method of lawmaking—is foredoomed to failure as an effective problem-solving process because it ignores the knowledge-based analytical, modeling, simulation and follow-up procedures essential for the solution of complex problems. In any case, the objective of the traditional method of lawmaking is not to solve problems but to enact laws. Thus no matter how sincere their efforts and how elevated their goals or level of discourse, legislative assemblies will never be able to efficaciously solve complex societal problems by means of this method.

What can be done to correct the flaws and inadequacies of the traditional method of lawmaking so that governments can be successful in serving the best interests of the people? To answer that question, I investigated the potential role of quality programs for the design, follow-up evaluation and optimization of laws. My reasoning for this approach was that quality programs should be as successful for lawmaking as they have been for other productive human enterprises such as medicine. If that hypothesis proves correct, it follows that governments that apply quality methods to laws and lawmaking should not only *not fail* but should be highly successful in their efforts to solve societal problems.

It was evident from the beginning of my investigation that the poor performance of laws is a matter of concern for democracies, which are obligated to serve the best interests of the people, but not for authoritarian governments, which are under no such obligation. I therefore separated sovereign governments into two categories: authoritarian and democratic. I further subdivided authoritarian governments according to the nature of their ruling classes, and invented the term *ideocracy* to designate those governments that are controlled by the leaders of secular belief systems, or political ideologies. (Ideocracies are the secular equivalent of *theocracies,* which are authoritarian governments that are controlled by the leaders of religious belief systems.)

For the definition of democracy, I found that the frequently used definition—"the category of government in which leaders are selected by the citizens through periodic, competitive elections based upon universal suffrage"—was inadequate for my purposes. This procedural definition, in and of itself, can neither assure that a democratically elected government will uphold human rights nor prevent elected leaders from creating laws that are detrimental to the people. Instead I used the structural definition of democracy that has evolved over time: "A democracy is the category of government in which the citizenry is the sovereign." Since every government takes directions from and serves the interests of its sovereign, a democratic government, thus defined, must serve the best interests (i.e., the liberty and well-being) of the citizenry—the people as a whole. On the premise that every democratic government is worthy of the people it serves, it follows that the purpose of democracy is to accomplish the honorable objectives of the people by honorable means in the best interests of the people.

This definition of the purpose of democracy involves three considerations. First, it might seem that the purpose statement could be simplified to: "The purpose of democracy is to act in the best interests of the people." But that statement confuses the means and ends of government. The purpose of any activity is the objective that is sought, not the forcible means applied to reach that objective. (Appendix G discusses the relationship between means and ends.) Since "to act" is a statement of means—the force or action that is applied to achieve an objective—it cannot also be the purpose, or end, of democracy. A significant problem with substituting means for ends in the purpose statement is that a democracy could then satisfy its obligations by merely attempting to attain the objectives of the people rather than by accomplishing those objectives. To assure that democratic governments serve the best interests of the people, therefore, it is necessary that the statement of the purpose of democracy clearly refers to the objectives of the government. And those objectives must be the objectives of the sovereign: the people as a whole.

Second, democratic governments, in order to serve the best interests of the people and reflect their highest aspirations, are obligated to exercise integrity in both their means and ends. The purpose statement of democracy must therefore specify that democratic governments are limited to the attainment of the honorable objectives of the people, and only by honorable means.

Third, not every honorable objective is in the best interests of the people in terms of their liberty and well-being (i.e., their human rights, living standards and quality of life), and it is necessary to further restrict democracies to the attainment of only those honorable objectives that also serve the best interests of the people. For example, it would be, arguably, an honorable gesture for the federal government of the United States to erect a monument to the framers of the U.S. Constitution in Washington, D.C. To carry that reasoning one step further, it would also be honorable to have similar monuments erected in every other city that has a population of greater than, say, 20,000 people. But the erection of redundant monuments, while honorable, would waste the people's resources and therefore not be in their best interests. By this reasoning I derived the purpose statement of democracy: *The purpose of democracy is to accomplish the honorable objectives of the people by honorable means in the best interests of the people.*

In the satisfaction of the purpose of democracy, governments have three requirements: (1) Recognize the citizenry (people as a whole) as the sovereign of government, (2) secure the full complement of human rights of the people and (3) efficaciously solve or mitigate societal problems for the benefit of the people as a whole. Based on these requirements, I identified three levels of democracy: *electoral democracy* (first requirement of democracy fulfilled), *lib-*

eral democracy (first and second requirements fulfilled), and *true democracy* (all three requirements fulfilled).

The clear superiority of democracies over authoritarian governments in terms of the human rights, living standards and quality of life of the people has led to the *ascendancy of democracy*—the ongoing dramatic transition of authoritarian governments to electoral democracies and of electoral democracies to liberal democracies.[2] Unfortunately, the defects of the traditional method of lawmaking have prevented governments from reaching the status of true democracy because no government has yet discovered the means to satisfy the third requirement of democracy. The principal theme of this book is that quality programs for laws and lawmaking will correct the flaws of the traditional method of lawmaking and enable governments to become true democracies, thus completing the final step of the ascendancy of democracy.

For the discussion of knowledge as it relates to quality standards for laws, I distinguished between scientific knowledge and all other forms of knowledge. This simple division of knowledge into scientific and nonscientific categories was sufficient for my purposes. I leave an elucidation of the subtleties of epistemology, as those subtleties relate to knowledge of laws and lawmaking, to other investigators.

I also divided the field of science into creative and investigative branches and determined that the application of quality programs to the creation, follow-up evaluation and optimization of laws will require the establishment of two new sciences: the engineering discipline of laws (a creative science) and the science of laws (an investigative science). If these new sciences are successful, reliable knowledge related to laws and lawmaking will come into being, and it will then be possible to create and maintain bodies of laws that fully satisfy the purpose of democracy. With the aforementioned definitions and assumptions in place, I created a model for the ascendancy of governments based upon the advent of quality programs for laws and lawmaking, and the present book is the result of that effort.

I admit to being enthusiastic (perhaps overly enthusiastic according to more than one reviewer) in describing the defects of the traditional method of lawmaking. I wanted to point out that there are significant problems with this method, so I tended to emphasize the negative at the risk of alienating some readers. However, I acknowledge that a significant fraction of laws are highly useful to the purpose of democracy, and this book is not intended to be a general condemnation of government—quite the contrary. Furthermore, nothing I have stated should be misinterpreted as a denigration of legislators; I have a high regard for legislators and the office of legislator, and I expect and hope that quality programs will lead to greater public respect for legislators and the office they serve.

---

[2] See, for example, the chronicle of annual reports of Freedom House at www.freedomhouse.org.

The potential value of quality programs for laws and lawmaking is significant because laws, for the most part, are currently designed to advance political agendas and achieve special interest objectives rather than solve problems. When (not if!) quality programs are implemented, the entire approach to the design and disposition of laws will change. Nonproductive laws will be weeded out, with substantial cost savings, and new laws will be designed so that government resources are applied, on a priority basis, to the efficacious solution of societal problems in the best interests of the people. The result will be a marked improvement in the liberty and well-being of the people, and the flourishing of productive and creative enterprises.

I found that every time I reviewed the manuscript (an exercise in quality assurance), I discovered areas that needed further refinement (quality improvement). However, my principal concern was that the concept of quality programs for laws be presented in a relatively cogent manner and, rather than create a perfect document—which would take infinite time—I decided to publish the book in its present form. I am confident that readers will discover details of my book that need improvement and further explanation, and I welcome their feedback.

My largest source of cited materials was the "Great Books" collection, and excerpts were reprinted with permission from *Great Books of the Western World*, ©1952, 1990, Encyclopaedia Britannica, Inc. I also quoted extensively from *Legislative Process in a Nutshell*, 2nd edition, by Jack Davies, ©1975 and 1986, with permission from The West Group; and from *The Legislative Drafter's Desk Reference*, ©1992, by Lawrence Filson, with permission from the Congressional Quarterly Press.

The present work is the result of three decades of study and preparation. I consulted with a number of people who made generous and critical contributions to this effort (and who, on many occasions, expressed their reservations or concerns about my definitions, approach or conclusions).

In particular, I owe a deep debt of gratitude to the following individuals: **Arden Kelton, Ph.D.**, a physicist and entrepreneur who has in-depth knowledge of science and the scientific process. His advice to me on the structure and functions of science, especially as they apply to the proposed science and engineering disciplines of laws, was invaluable. He gave generously of his time and expertise in the preparation of the manuscript, and he is one of the founders of the Quality of Laws Institute. **Michael Newbrough, Ph.D.**, is a professor of political science and my former instructor. He reviewed and gave constructive criticisms of many evolving variations of my manuscript. He is also one of the founders of the Quality of Laws Institute. **Thomas Schrunk**, my brother, is a political consultant and an artist in lustrous materials. He provided me with many useful ideas and much feedback throughout this effort and introduced the concept of quality for laws into the political arena.

Special thanks are also due to **Victor Bolie, Ph.D.**; **Philip Harris, Ph.D.**; **Stuart Johnson, Ph.D.**; **Michael Kelly, J.D.**; **Donald LaRocque, J.D.**; **Ruth Lehr-Whitney, J.D.**; **Tom Miller, M.D., Ph.D.**; **Darryl Mitry, Ph.D.**; **Declan O'Donnell, J.D.**; **Tim Penny** (Senior Fellow of the Humphrey Institute); **Ramesh Rao, Ph.D.**; **William Shipley, M.D.**; **Wynn Volkert, Ph.D.**; **James Watt, J.D.**; and **Boyd Wilcox** for their critical advice, ideas and support.

For the preparation and design of the manuscript, I extend my sincere thanks to **Peter Stark** (Peter Barron Stark and Associates, Inc.); my editor, **Colleen Sharp**; and page and cover designers, **Annie Morley and Dena Demos** (Patera Graphic Design) for their exemplary skills and advice. Thanks also to **Jean Leasure** (Vaughan Printing) for her assistance and coordination of the printing tasks.

Finally, I wish to thank my wife, **Sijia Schrunk**, who aided my work from her background in education and statistics—and who endured, with immense patience, my years of research and time on the computer to bring this project to fruition.

Quality Programs for Laws: The Rationale

The laws of government may be counted among the most important works of humankind. They address the most significant problems of society and have a direct effect upon the human rights, living standards and quality of life of every person. However, laws have failed, for the most part, in their attempts to solve societal problems. High rates of crime, illiteracy, poverty, homelessness, etc. continue to plague every society despite the expenditure of enormous resources under the authority and direction of the laws of government. The relative failure of laws is of particular concern to democracies, which are obligated to serve the best interests of their citizenry.

Despite the historical lack of efficacy of laws, lawmaking assemblies continue to produce new laws that consume more resources and add complexity to people's lives but do little or nothing to improve their existence. The continued poor performance of the bodies of laws suggests that societal problems constitute the one area of the physical world that is beyond the ability of humankind to understand or control. It would seem that the people of every government must remain inured to the continued production of laws that are, at best, of marginal value. In addition, the increasingly complex bodies of laws threaten the stability of governments through the loss of public confidence and degradation of the rule of law.

However, the laws of government do not have to be mediocre or irrelevant in terms of the needs of the people; in fact, laws have the potential to be highly successful in accomplishing their problem-solving tasks. An investigation of the traditional method by which governments create laws reveals that this method—unlike the method used to design all other useful products—incorporates virtually *no* quality standards. It accepts unsubstantiated opinions, anecdotes, half-truths and known falsehoods as the basis for new laws; tolerates unscrupulous design practices; and foregoes elementary considerations such as problem definition and cost-benefit analysis. Furthermore, no provisions are made for the periodic and objective review of the performance of laws after they have been enacted, so ineffective and detrimental laws go unidentified and remain in force. In other words, the elementary quality principles that are routinely employed in the design and evaluation of other useful products are *conspicuously absent* in the traditional lawmaking process.

An opportunity presents itself: Since laws are humanmade products that are intended (in a democracy) to be useful to the people, why not apply quality programs to laws? The result will be that the usefulness of laws in terms of the purpose of democracy (i.e., in terms of the liberty and well-being of the people) will come to realize the patterns of success now observed in other useful products such as pharmaceuticals, transport aircraft and computers

What if proven quality methods are applied to laws and fail to be effective? Then the people will be subject to laws that are inadequate, useless and detrimental—but that is the very condition that already exists. In other words, the application of quality programs has the potential to substantially improve the performance of laws—hence governments—in their service to the people, and the risk of failure is exceedingly small.

Based on these observations, the logical conclusion is that quality design, quality assurance and quality improvement programs should be developed and implemented for laws. These programs will lead to the development of a new creative science, the engineering discipline of laws, which will derive competent design methodologies and apply them to the creation of laws that optimally serve the purpose of democracy. Quality programs will also necessitate the establishment of a new investigative science, the science of laws, which will generate reliable knowledge of the structure and mechanics of laws. The predictable outcome will be the eventual ascendancy of all governments to the status of true democracy, wherein governments serve the best interests of the people and reflect their highest aspirations.

The following chapters examine authoritarian and democratic forms of government; the laws of government; the traditional method of lawmaking; the threat that the traditional method poses to democracy; and the development and application of quality programs for laws. This examination leads to the conclusion that the implementation of quality programs for laws is a concept worthy of further investigation.

Government

The Structure and Purpose of Government

Every social organization requires a government to establish and enforce the rules, or laws, that define the structure and functions of that organization as well as the status and obligations of its members. For a small organization such as a family unit, the set of laws may be informally created and enforced. A large organization such as a sovereign nation has, of necessity, a highly structured government that creates, manipulates, enforces and interprets a written, codified body of laws. Without an enforced body of laws that defines the status and obligations of individuals and institutions, nations would collapse into chaos and no one would be secure. Thus governments are necessary for the stability and effective operation of social organizations, and laws are the means by which governments accomplish their tasks.

All governments[1] have a structure and a purpose. The structure of a government consists of the institutions and people that create, amend and repeal its body of laws (legislate), enforce its laws (administrate), and interpret and render decisions regarding its laws (adjudicate).[2] Since every government performs legislative, administrative and judicial functions, the structure of all governments is basically the same.

Although governments have a common structure, the purpose of governments varies widely. The purpose of a government may be to accomplish the objectives of, variously, a group of "aristocrats," a "royal" family, a secular ideology, a religion, or the people of the society as a whole. This variability of purpose among governments is due to the nature of the sovereign.

THE SOVEREIGN

Every government has a sovereign, the group of people who exercise supreme power and authority and who control the government's resources and actions. The sovereign uses the powers of government to manipulate the body of laws for the sovereign's own continued tenure and benefit. A government is thus an *implement* that is controlled by the sovereign and used to accomplish, by means of

---

[1] For the remainder of the book, the term *government* is used in reference to large governing institutions such as the federal government of the United States of America.

[2] J.Q. Wilson, *American Government: Institutions and Policies*, 2nd ed. (Lexington, MA: DC Heath and Company, 1983), chapters 10, 11, 12 and 13.

laws, the objectives the sovereign sets forth (see Figure 2-1). There are two categories of government, based upon the nature of the sovereign: authoritarian and democratic.

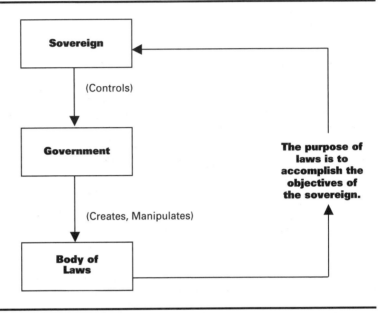

Figure 2-1. The Control System of Government: Every government is controlled by a group of people who constitute the sovereign. The government creates and manipulates a body of laws under the direction of the sovereign, and the purpose of government, i.e., the purpose of the body of laws, is to accomplish the objectives the sovereign has set forth.

AUTHORITARIAN GOVERNMENTS

In authoritarian forms of government, the sovereign is the ruling class, which is typically a small, "elite" group of people who direct the operation of government for their own benefit. The rest of the people within the jurisdiction of the government make up the ruled, or subject, class of people. Since laws are the means by which governments achieve their purpose, the ruling-class sovereign directs the government to create a body of laws that grants privileges to the ruling class and enables it to control the subject class. As John Stuart Mill explains in *Representative Government*, "The interest of the king, and of the governing aristocracy [the ruling class], is to possess, and exercise, unlimited power over the people; to enforce, on their part, complete conformity to the will and preferences of the rulers."[3] To minimize the negative effects of laws upon itself, the ruling class causes the restrictions and costs of the laws to be borne primarily by the subject class, as depicted in Figure 2-2.

---

[3] J.S. Mill, *Representative Government*, Great Books of the Western World, vol. 43, p. 366.

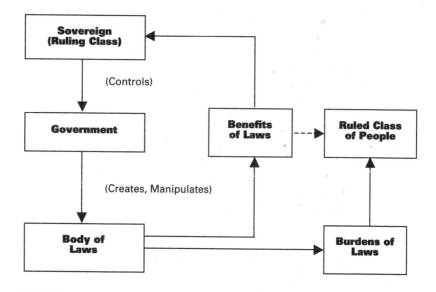

Figure 2-2. The Control System of Authoritarian Governments: The sovereign of an authoritarian government is the ruling class, which is typically a relatively small, "elite" group of people. The ruling class controls the government and is the principal beneficiary of the government's laws. The ruled, or subject, class receives some benefits from the laws, but is made to bear the burdens of laws.

There are four forms of authoritarian government, based upon the composition of the ruling class:

ARISTOCRACY. The sovereign is a group of "aristocrats" or "nobles" whose membership within the ruling class is based upon wealth, birthright, military rank or other arbitrary factor. The government acts, by means of its laws, to maintain the political power, wealth and privileges of the aristocracy.

IDEOCRACY. The sovereign consists of the leaders of a secular belief system or ideology (i.e., the leaders of a political party). The government is used to maintain the political power, wealth and privileges of the sovereign and to advance the secular belief system of the sovereign.

MONARCHY. The sovereign is a "royal" family. The leader of the royal family is the monarch who has the title of king or queen, emperor, czar, etc. The government maintains the political power, wealth and privileges of the royal family and assures continued control of the government by succeeding generations of that family.

THEOCRACY. The sovereign consists of the leaders of a religious belief system. The government is used to maintain the political power, wealth and privileges of the sovereign and to advance the religious belief system of the sovereign.

For the ruling classes of authoritarian governments, the position of sovereign endures as long as they can avoid being replaced by another political entity. When they come into power, they use the institutions of government to secure their permanent tenure as sovereign, employing four principal means to maintain and enhance their position of power and privilege. They (1) abuse human rights; (2) create large, complex bodies of laws; (3) impose economic sanctions; and (4) engage in wars of aggression.[4]

Abuse of Human Rights

The major threat to ruling classes is from rivals who may arise from the subject classes. To minimize this threat and maintain their position as sovereign, ruling classes neglect or deny the human rights of the subject classes (see Appendix A). They choose government leaders from among themselves; reject any competitive election process; control the media; and suppress or ban non-majority religions, opposition political parties and other potential sovereigns. In this effort to suppress political rights, they restrict legal rights and abuse substantive rights, often with harsh measures such as torture, mass starvation and summary executions. As Rousseau explains in *The Social Contract*:

> *The best kings desire to be in a position to be wicked, if they please, without forfeiting their mastery: political sermonisers may tell them to their hearts' content that, the people's strength being their own, their first interest is that the people should be prosperous, numerous and formidable; they are well aware that this is untrue. Their first personal interest is that the people should be weak, wretched, and unable to resist them.*[5]

Large, Complex Bodies of Laws

Large, complex bodies of laws help the ruling classes maintain and enhance their political power in four ways:

First, laws place restrictions on human activity. As increasing numbers of laws are imposed upon the subject class, the separation between the classes increases, to the benefit of the ruling class. With enough laws, the ruling class can totally dominate the activities of the subject class.

Second, laws can be designed to transfer wealth from a less favored group of people to a more favored group. Over time, the members of the ruling class can impoverish the groups of people they distrust or disdain while amassing wealth for themselves and their political allies and supporters.

---

[4] The classic reference work on the means for securing political power is *The Prince* by N. Machiavelli, Great Books of the Western World, vol. 23, in which Machiavelli provides advice to the head of the ruling class, the "prince," on the art of war and the use of any other means—including lies, flattery and deceit—to secure control of the reins of government.

[5] J.J. Rousseau, *The Social Contract*, Great Books of the Western World, vol. 38, p. 413.

Third, when the bodies of laws become sufficiently large, it is impossible to enforce every law, and the laws must then be enforced selectively. Arbitrary rule (the "rule of man") becomes possible; the ruling class can decide which laws to enforce and which laws to ignore, depending upon their temporal needs and circumstances.

Fourth, convoluted and vague laws may be variously interpreted (by the judicial branch of government that the ruling class controls) at different times and under different conditions so that the outcome always benefits the ruling class. In fact, the principal challenge for legislators of authoritarian governments is to design laws in a clever and subtle manner that seems to give deference to the subject class but actually transfers power and wealth to the ruling class.

Economic Sanctions

For authoritarian governments, poverty among the subject classes is a desirable condition because controlling an indigent subject population is easier than controlling one that is self-sufficient. When someone from the subject class manages to reach a position of affluence, that person no longer needs the largesse of the government and is therefore regarded as a potential threat to the ruling class. The economic challenge, then, for authoritarian governments, is not poverty of the subject classes but wealth. To solve this "problem," ruling classes use their hegemony over laws and lawmaking to confiscate and control, for their own benefit, major societal assets such as land, natural resources, transportation networks, communication systems and manufacturing facilities. In addition, they impose high income taxes, high inheritance taxes and limitations on property rights. Authoritarian governments also provide the subject classes with subsidies for goods and services (such as food and medical care) to make them dependent on the government. The result of these measures is that wealth is transferred to the ruling classes and the subject classes are reduced to a condition of economic servitude:

> The interest of a ruling class, whether in an aristocracy or an aristocratic monarchy, is to assume to themselves an endless variety of unjust privileges, sometimes benefiting their pockets at the expense of the people, sometimes merely tending to exalt them above others, or, what is the same thing in different words, to degrade others below themselves.[6]

Marx and Engels recognized these strategies and outlined the steps the ruling class ("the hands of the state") can take to suppress the subject class and secure its position of political power, wealth and privilege:

1. *Abolition of property in land....*
2. *A heavy progressive or graduated income tax.*
3. *Abolition of all right of inheritance.*
4. *Confiscation of the property of all emigrants and rebels.*

---

[6] Mill, p. 366.

5. *Centralization of credit in the hands of the state* [i.e., the ruling class] *by means of a national bank with state capital and an exclusive monopoly.*
6. *Centralization of the means of communication and transport in the hands of the state.*
7. *Extension of factories and instruments of production owned by the state....*[7]

Wars of Aggression

The fourth tactic ruling classes use to increase their power and wealth is war. Ruling classes divert significant government resources into the creation of armies and offensive weapons and then direct their armed forces to invade neighboring countries, especially those that are militarily weak. This strategy has two major benefits for the ruling classes: (1) It provides the opportunity to increase the size of the territory and subject populations under their control and to steal the resources and accumulated wealth of conquered nations; and (2) it encourages the subject classes to vent their frustrations on external "enemies" instead of their rulers. The history of civilization discloses that wars between nations have been a nearly continuous condition of humankind and that wars *always* involve participation by one or more authoritarian governments.[8]

Through the abuse of human rights, the creation of large, complex bodies of laws, the imposition of economic sanctions and the perpetration of wars of aggression, the ruling classes of authoritarian governments have used their position of political power to:

- Secure long-term control of governments.
- Control and exploit the subject classes.
- Imprison, persecute, exile or destroy real and imagined enemies.
- Impose their religious and secular belief systems upon the subject classes.
- Convert government resources to their personal wealth.
- Maintain the subject classes in a perpetual state of poverty and dependency.

The actions authoritarian governments take to maintain separate, unequal political classes have been and always will be associated with two self-destructive conditions. First, no group of people has ever expressed a desire to be the exploited underclass that serves a domineering ruling class. To mitigate their conditions of poverty and oppression, members of the subject classes frequently ignore or disobey laws; rebel against their government; or emigrate, if possible, to other countries that have greater freedom. Second, opposition political groups, including the ruling classes of rival authoritarian governments, are always seeking

---

[7] K. Marx and F. Engels, *Manifesto of the Communist Party*, Great Books of the Western World, vol. 50, p. 429. Marx and Engels were motivated by their dislike of the inequitable distribution of wealth they observed in capitalist economic systems. It is ironic that the result of their efforts for reform resulted in the establishment of more than a score of authoritarian governments (ideocracies).

[8] See, for example, W. Durant and A. Durant, *The Story of Civilization*, vol. I through XI (New York, NY: Simon and Schuster, 1935-1975); and J.F.C. Fuller, *A Military History of the Western World*, vol. I, II and III (New York, NY: Da Capo Press, 1956).

to replace the existing ruling class by means of coup or warfare. Authoritarian governments are thus inherently unstable; they have been noted throughout history by the discontent of the people under their rule and by an unending series of revolutions, coups and wars. The eventual collapse of authoritarian governments provides the people with the opportunity to establish the alternative category of government: democracy.

DEMOCRACY

As previously noted, all governments have the same basic structure that performs legislative, administrative and judicial functions. The principal—and significant—distinction between authoritarian governments and democracies is that the sovereign of a democracy is not composed of an "elite" subset of the population, but of the citizenry, as noted by Rousseau:

> The different forms of government owe their origin to the differing degrees of inequality which existed between individuals at the time of their institution. If there happened to be any one man among them pre-eminent in power, virtue, riches or personal influence, he became sole magistrate, and the State assumed the form of monarchy. If several, nearly equal in point of eminence, stood above the rest, they were elected jointly, and formed an aristocracy. Again, among a people who had deviated less from a state of nature, and between whose fortune or talents there was less disproportion, the supreme administration was retained in common, and a democracy was formed.[9]

The concept of government in which the sovereignty belongs to the people as a whole was also stated by Montesquieu in *The Spirit of the Laws*: "When the body of the people is possessed of the supreme power, it is called a democracy"[10]; by Kant in *The Science of Right*: "It is in the people that the supreme power originally resides, and it is accordingly from this power that all the rights of individual citizens as mere subjects, and especially as officials of the state, must be derived. When the sovereignty of the people themselves is thus realized, the republic is established..."[11]; by Madison in *The Federalist Papers*: "the ultimate authority...resides in the people alone..."[12]; and by Mill in *Representative Government*: "the ideally best form of government is that in which the sovereignty, or supreme controlling power in the last resort, is vested in the entire aggregate of the community."[13]

---

[9] Rousseau, p. 359.
[10] C. Montesquieu, *The Spirit of the Laws*, Great Books of the Western World, vol. 38, p. 4.
[11] I. Kant, *The Science of Right*, Great Books of the Western World, vol. 42, p. 451.
[12] J. Madison, *The Federalist Papers*, No. 46, Great Books of the Western World, vol. 43, p. 150.
[13] Mill, p. 344.

The Purpose of Democracy

Since every government is controlled by the sovereign for the benefit of the sovereign, democratic governments must define the conditions and goals that constitute the "public good"—the liberty and well-being of the people as a whole—and then take the prudent steps necessary to fulfill those goals. In other words, **the purpose of democracy is to accomplish the honorable objectives of the people by honorable means in the best interests of the people.** The concept of democracy, that governments are obligated to serve the public good, has been a major theme of political philosophers such as Plato ("The true art of politics is concerned, not with private, but with public good")[14] and John Locke ("These laws also ought to be designed for no other end ultimately but the good of the people)."[15]

It is important to note that the public good cannot be satisfied by "majority rule." Aristotle, when speaking of democracies in *Politics,* says that "the majority must be supreme, and…whatever the majority approve must be the end and the just."[16] Aristotle's statement is suitable only as it applies to the people's selection of the *leaders* of government, not as it applies to the *design of laws.* The problem with majority rule, or "the greatest good for the greatest number," is that the majority may use the government's laws to cause harm to minority groups for the benefit of the majority. As Mill points out, democracy requires that all citizens, not just the majority, be the beneficiaries of the actions of government: "…democracy must be so organized that no class, not even the most numerous, shall be able to reduce all but itself to political insignificance, and direct the course of legislation and administration by its exclusive class interest."[17] So, although a legislature's decision to enact a new law—or to amend or repeal an existing law—is usually based upon a majority vote, every law in a democracy must be designed so that it serves the best interests of the people as a whole.

Thomas Jefferson presented the basic principles of democracy in the Declaration of Independence, which pronounced "that all men are created equal" and have "certain unalienable [*sic*] rights" that include "life, liberty and the pursuit of happiness." Governments, according to Jefferson, are created "to secure these rights," and they derive their "just powers from the consent of the governed." He further stated that, "whenever any government becomes destructive to these ends, it is the right of the people to alter or to abolish it, and to institute a new government, laying its foundation on such principles, and organizing its powers in such form, as to them shall seem most likely to effect their safety and happiness." The Declaration of Independence was a milestone in political thought because it established, for the first time in the founding document of a new government, the

---

[14] Plato, *Laws,* Great Books of the Western World, vol. 7, p. 754.

[15] J. Locke, *Concerning Civil Government, Second Essay,* Great Books of the Western World, vol. 35, p. 58.

[16] Aristotle, *Politics,* Great Books of the Western World, vol. 9, p. 520.

[17] Mill, p. 381.

liberty and well-being of the people as a whole as the only justification for the existence of government.[18]

A basic assumption of democracy is that the citizens are worthy of their status as sovereign. This is in direct contrast with authoritarian governments, which presume that the subject peoples require loud direction from their governments. From their position of power and wealth, the ruling classes of authoritarian governments tend to view the subject classes as unsophisticated, indolent, credulous, ignorant, and in need of substantial assistance and direction. Democracies, on the other hand, regard their citizens as a whole to be industrious, resourceful, conscientious and responsible, and therefore able to exercise, through the rule of law, the greatest possible degree of freedom in the conduct of their affairs. The preservation and expansion of the liberty of the people is thus the ultimate concern of democratic governments[19]:

> *For law, in its true notions, is not so much the limitation as the direction of a free and intelligent agent to his proper interest, and prescribes no farther than is for the general good of those under that law....So that however it may be mistaken, the end of law is not to abolish or restrain, but to preserve and enlarge freedom.*[20]

> *It is therefore beyond dispute, and indeed the fundamental maxim of all political right, that people have set up chiefs to protect their liberty, and not to enslave them.*[21]

To accomplish their objectives, the people of a democracy (the sovereign) select the major leadership positions of government through competitive elections based upon universal suffrage. Democratic governments are thus representative governments (republics) in which representatives perform the legislative function. Significantly, the people, who are the sovereign, are also the governed who are required to comply with and bear the burdens of the laws, as depicted in Figure 2-3.

---

[18] T. Jefferson, the Declaration of Independence. Quotes are reprinted from Great Books of the Western World, vol. 43, pp. 1-3. Jefferson reinforced the concept of the supremacy and exclusivity of democracy: that, for the people of any nation, democracy is the only legitimate form of government.

[19] See the Preamble of the Constitution of the United States of America, American State Papers, Great Books of the Western World, vol. 43, p. 11: "in order to...secure the blessings of liberty to ourselves and our posterity."

[20] Locke, p. 37.

[21] Rousseau, p. 356.

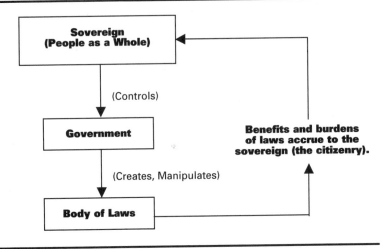

Figure 2-3. The Control System of Democracy: In a democracy, the sovereign consists of the citizens, who are the recipients of both the benefits and the burdens of the laws of government. A democratic government is obligated to ensure that the body of laws optimally serves the best interests of the citizenry.

Since laws place restrictions on human activities, democratic governments have an obligation to ensure that the bodies of laws contain the *minimum* number of laws that efficaciously satisfy the purpose of democracy, as noted by Mill: "The interest of the people is to have as little control exercised over them in any respect as is consistent with attaining the legitimate ends of government."[22]

The political equality of the citizens in a democracy means that the right of individuals to join or form associations (for example, special interest groups such as political parties) is guaranteed. In fact, special interest groups are important sources of ideas and advice on the best methods and goals for good governance. However, democratic governments do not need the involvement of special interests for the execution of the governments' proper functions. In contrast with authoritarian governments, whose ruling classes *are* special interests, democracies eschew the intervention of special interests in government affairs because the agendas of interest groups frequently conflict with the best interests of the citizens.[23] Also, democracies, as contrasted with authoritarian governments, encourage and welcome their citizens' economic self-sufficiency and restrict the use of military forces to those actions that protect the citizens from harm. The limitation on the use of military forces by democracies has led to the remarkable

---

[22] Mill, p. 366.

[23] See discussion of "factions" by J. Madison in *The Federalist Papers*, No. 10, Great Books of the Western World, vol. 43.

fact that democratic governments do not engage in war with other democracies.[24]
A comparison of authoritarian and democratic governments is presented in Table 2-1.

	Authoritarian Government	Democratic Government
Sovereign	the ruling class	the citizenry
Political Classes	the ruling (elite) class and the ruled, or subject, class	no political class divisions—all citizens are politically equal
Method of Selecting Leaders	selections made in secret by the ruling class	periodic, competitive elections by the citizens based upon universal suffrage
Use of Military Forces	to enhance the political power and wealth of the ruling class	to protect the citizens from harm
Desired Economic Status of the People	indigent	self-sufficient
Treatment of Human Rights	neglect, abuse or deny human rights if such treatment benefits the ruling class	guarantee the equal human rights of all citizens
Purpose of Laws	to maintain the political power of the ruling class (control people)	to satisfy the purpose of democracy (control problems)
Beneficiary of Laws	the ruling class	the citizenry
Burdens of Laws Borne By	the subject class	the citizenry
Attributes of the Body of Laws	large and complex	minimum number of efficacious laws

Table 2-1. Comparison of Authoritarian and Democratic Forms of Government: Authoritarian and democratic governments have significant differences. In essence, laws are written for the benefit of the ruling class in authoritarian governments and for the benefit of the people (citizenry) in democracies.

The Requirements of Democracy

Authoritarian governments have no obligations to their subject classes, and they provide essential services to the people only to the extent that such services maintain the privileged status of the ruling classes and the subservient status of the subject classes. In contrast, democracies are committed to the continued sovereignty, liberty and well-being of their citizens. To satisfy the purpose of democracy, a

---

[24] S.R. Weart, *Never at War: Why Democracies Will Not Fight One Another* (New Haven, CT: Yale University Press, 1998).

democratic government has three requirements: (1) Recognize the citizenry (people as a whole) as the sovereign of government, (2) secure the full complement of human rights of the people and (3) efficaciously solve societal problems.

FIRST REQUIREMENT: RECOGNIZE THE CITIZENRY AS THE SOVEREIGN OF GOVERNMENT. By definition, a government cannot be a democracy unless the sovereignty of that government is vested in the citizenry. To attain the status of democracy, therefore, a government must, at a minimum, allow its citizens to determine the major leadership of the government through periodic, competitive elections based on secret ballots and universal suffrage (see Political Rights, Appendix A). A government that meets this first requirement of democracy—voting rights—is termed an *electoral democracy*.[25] The recognition of voting rights by a government denotes a major distinction between democracies and authoritarian governments. By exercising their right to vote, the people can end the reign of tyrants and incompetent rulers by the ballot box rather than by coup or revolution.

SECOND REQUIREMENT: SECURE HUMAN RIGHTS. Because electoral democracies are obligated to serve the best interests of their citizens, they must recognize and guarantee, not only voting rights, but all other human rights as well (see Appendix A). A sovereign government that does not guarantee the human rights of its citizens has no legitimate purpose and, according to Thomas Jefferson, should either be altered or abolished and replaced. An electoral democracy that takes the additional step of guaranteeing the full complement of human rights of the people meets the second requirement of democracy and it is then termed a *liberal democracy*.

The most secure means by which the people can be guaranteed their political and other human rights is through a written constitution (the supreme law of the government).[26] According to Kant: "A constitution of the *greatest possible human freedom* according to laws, by which *the liberty of every individual can consist with the liberty of every other* is, to say the least, a necessary idea, which must be placed at the foundation not only of the first plan of the constitution of a state, but of all its laws."[27]

The written constitution of a democracy defines the structure, mechanisms and obligations of the government necessary to maintain human rights and the boundaries beyond which the government is not allowed to operate, thereby establishing the "rule of law." In effect, a constitution establishes a *limited* government. While authoritarian governments rely upon the "rule of man," democracies adhere to the rule of law, which limits the scope of government to the boundaries defined by law.

---

[25] The term *electoral democracy* is from Freedom House (www.freedomhouse.org), which defines an electoral democracy as a government that meets the standard of universal suffrage for competitive multiparty elections.

[26] See, for example, the Constitution of the United States of America, *American State Papers*, Great Books of the Western World, vol. 43, pp. 11-21.

[27] Kant, p.114.

The rule of law holds that the hierarchy of written, duly enacted and codified laws of government applies equally to all citizens, including government leaders, and is superior to any other directive of government. The major limitation of the rule of law is *quality*. A government that rigidly observes the rule of law can be no better than mediocre if its laws are mediocre. The challenge for democracies, therefore, is to establish a rule of law that comprises laws of the highest possible quality vis-à-vis the liberty and well-being of the people.

The guarantee of human rights by the constitution of a democracy establishes, perforce, the judiciary as an independent branch of government. To protect themselves from the possibility of abuse by the government, the people of a democracy—regardless of their ethnicity, religious preference, birthright, etc.—have the legal right to petition the government for an impartial disposition of claims or grievances against any party, *including that government*. For the citizens to be guaranteed equal and impartial treatment by the courts in such a petition, the judiciary (which upholds the law) *must* be independent from the other branches of government. Thus an independent judiciary, in which the loyalty of the judicial branch of government is pledged to the people and to their constitutionally guaranteed human rights, is one of the hallmarks of democracy. Conversely, a government in which judges are required to pledge their loyalty to an entity other than the citizens—such as a monarch, religion or political party—cannot be a liberal democracy.

Finally, the mandate to protect human rights also obligates the government to protect the citizens from destructive acts and wars of aggression by other nations ("protect from harm") and from domestic violence ("provide civil order").

THIRD REQUIREMENT: SOLVE SOCIETAL PROBLEMS EFFICACIOUSLY. As noted, a government becomes a liberal democracy when it guarantees its citizens the full complement of human rights. However, that guarantee, while *necessary*, is not *sufficient* for a government to accomplish the full objectives of the people in terms of their liberty and well-being. Thus liberal democracies, like electoral democracies, are incomplete democracies. Why? Because the observance of human rights alone does not prevent a liberal democracy from enacting laws that are detrimental to the living standards and quality of life of its citizens. For example, a government could meet the constitutional requirements of a liberal democracy and still enact a law that imposes a tax rate of 90 percent on the income of working people or that subsidizes illiteracy or pollution. Therefore, to satisfy the purpose of democracy, a liberal democracy must also meet a third requirement: to identify, set priorities for, and solve or mitigate, in an efficacious manner, the societal problems that degrade or threaten to degrade the liberty and well-being of the people. Since the solution of problems requires enacting and enforcing laws that consume and divert resources (see Chapter 3), the legislatures of democracies must create effective, cost-efficient, user-friendly and safe laws that solve or mitigate societal problems. Included in the problem-solving mandate of a democracy is the efficacious operation of essential services and facilities, such as public health administration, environmental protection and public utility infrastructures.

When a government is able to meet all three requirements of democracy, it fully satisfies the purpose of democracy and thereby achieves the status of a *true democracy.*[28] The citizens can then enjoy the highest levels of human rights, living standards and quality of life possible under the rule of law. The requirements of democracy are listed in Table 2-2.

First Requirement: Recognize the Citizenry as the Sovereign of Government.

The major leadership positions of government are selected by the people through periodic and competitive elections based upon universal suffrage.

Second Requirement: Secure Human Rights.

The full complement of human rights of the citizens is recognized by the government and is upheld by the independent judicial branch of government.

Third Requirement: Solve Problems Efficaciously.

The government creates and maintains a body of laws that optimally solves or mitigates societal problems for the benefit of the citizens as a whole.

Table 2-2. The Requirements of Democracy: A government is an *electoral democracy* if it meets the first requirement of democracy, a *liberal democracy* if it meets the first and second requirements, and a *true democracy* if it meets all three requirements.

Although many existing governments have been moderately successful in satisfying the first and second requirements of democracy, none of them has reached the status of a true democracy because none has been able to solve societal problems efficaciously. That is, despite the creation of large numbers of laws (instead of the desired minimum number of laws) and the expenditure and diversion of significant resources, existing democracies have been, and continue to be, grossly underperforming in terms of the third requirement of democracy. Since serious societal problems continue to plague the people of every government, existing democracies can only be regarded as incomplete democracies. The worthwhile goal of all democratic (and authoritarian) governments, therefore, in terms of the best interests of the people they serve, is to find the means to ascend to the status of a true democracy.

---

[28] The essential elements of a true democracy ("of the people, by the people, for the people") were stated by Abraham Lincoln in his Gettysburg Address. See *Abraham Lincoln: The War Years,* vol. II, by C. Sandburg (New York, NY: Harcourt, Brace & World, Inc., 1939), p. 469.

Laws

A *law of government* is defined as an order that is prescribed and enforced under the authority of that government. Laws are the basic elements of the control system a government uses to exercise its authority; they are the forcible *means* by which a government seeks its ends:

> *Law is a rule and measure of acts, by which man is induced to act or is restrained from acting....*[1]

> *...it is manifest that law in general is not counsel, but command.*[2]

> *A LAW, by the very meaning of the term, includes supremacy. It is a rule which those to whom it is prescribed are bound to observe. This results from every political association. If individuals enter into a state of society, the laws of that society must be the supreme regulator of their conduct.*[3]

The laws of government specify the rights and obligations of the people and institutions within the jurisdiction of a government and they deal with the most fundamental concerns of human existence, such as human rights, war and peace, and the financial stability of nations. The categories of laws include: constitutional (supreme) laws, statutes created by legislatures, regulations created by the administrative branches of governments, and common law (laws that originate in court decisions). Laws also have a hierarchy of authority: Constitutional laws are superior to statutory laws, which are superior to regulations and common law. In addition, the statutes of national legislatures are superior in authority to the statutes of state legislatures, which are superior to the statutes of municipal legislatures, etc.

Laws have many different names, including "rules," "regulations," "statutes" and "codes." The discussion of laws in the remainder of this book focuses on statutes that are enacted by legislative assemblies such as the state and federal legislatures of the United States of America. However, the definitions and conclusions apply equally to every other form of law of every government.

---

[1] T. Aquinas, *Summa Theologica,* Great Books of the Western World, vol. 20, p. 205.
[2] T. Hobbes, *Leviathan,* Great Books of the Western World, vol. 23, p. 130.
[3] A. Hamilton, *The Federalist Papers,* No. 33, Great Books of the Western World, vol. 43, p. 108.

The Premise of Lawmaking

The design and enforcement of laws is predicated upon two assumptions: (1) that human nature is predictable and (2) that laws, by their ability to manipulate human behavior, are effective means for attaining specific, desired governmental objectives. That is, the premise of lawmaking is that a *cause-and-effect* mechanism is brought into play when a law of government is enforced, as depicted in Figure 3-1. Under this universally accepted premise, governments expect that by creating and enforcing laws, they will achieve results that satisfy the needs of their respective sovereigns.

Figure 3-1. The Premise of Lawmaking: The premise of lawmaking is that a law (cause), when enforced, will produce a predictable societal outcome (effect).

Characteristics of Laws

Every law has the following characteristics:

LETTER OF THE LAW

A law is a written order—a set of instructions, or *software*—that provides directions for human behavior. The entire written content of a law is the *letter of the law,* which is nothing more or less than the fixed arrangement of its words and punctuation.

SPIRIT OF THE LAW

The spirit of any given law is the hoped-for change, or benefit, that the law will produce, from a less desirable condition to a more desirable condition, as predicted by the designers of the law. In a democracy, the spirit of the law is the intent to bring about an improvement in the natural order of things for the benefit of the people as a whole. Hence the purpose of laws in a democracy is the solution of problems. Since the purpose of the law is the very reason for its existence, the letter of the law is subordinate to the spirit of the law.

SANCTIONS

Laws are the *forcible means* a government uses to achieve its goals; they are coercions, restrictions, prohibitions or commands that attempt to regulate or change the behavior or status of the individuals and institutions subject to them. Laws must be obeyed if their purpose is to be achieved. To encourage individuals and institutions to comply with the law, each law has a mechanism of enforcement, or an authorized sanction (the "carrot" or "stick") that is applied to accomplish the intent of the law. Fines, subsidies and imprisonment are examples of mechanisms that may be used as sanctions.

COSTS

All laws consume and divert resources. Virtually the entire budget of a government is required for the research, design, promulgation, implementation and interpretation of its body of laws. To pay for these operations, governments create and enforce additional laws to raise revenue through taxes, fees, fines, etc.

Laws have seven principal costs: (1) the cost of research and development;[4] (2) the cost of the legislative process; (3) the direct disbursement of government funds from the treasury as specified by the letter of the law; (4) the costs incurred by the administrative and judicial branches of government to promulgate, enforce and interpret the laws; (5) the expense of compliance—the time, labor and funds expended by those required to comply with the laws; (6) the loss of opportunity for individuals and institutions to conduct alternative activities of high value, such as education or research, because the resources for those opportunities are applied instead to the creation, enforcement, interpretation and compliance of laws;[5] and (7) the costs required to assure and improve the quality of each law (quality assurance [QA] and quality improvement [QI]). Since governments do not now employ QA or QI programs for laws, those efforts do not yet contribute to the overall costs. (Of course, the benefits of those efforts are not realized either.)

SIDE EFFECTS

Laws, like all other humanmade creations, produce unintended side effects. In this respect, laws are analogous to medicines: In an attempt to produce a desired result, they produce unintended changes in the natural order of things. Medicines produce side effects in the form of disturbances in the normal operating parameters of the human body, such as heart rate, blood sugar concentration and level of consciousness. Similarly, laws produce side effects in the form of disturbances to the normal operating conditions of the body politic, that is, to the human rights, living standards and quality of life of the people (see Appendix A), any or all of

---

[4] See the discussion of research in the drafting of bills in R. Dickerson, *The Fundamentals of Legal Drafting* (Boston, MA: Little, Brown and Co., 1986), pp. 51-76.

[5] C.R. McConnell and S.L. Brue, *ECONOMICS: Principles, Problems, and Policies*, 14th ed. (Dubuque, IA: McGraw-Hill, 1999), p. 444: "The **economic cost**, or **opportunity cost**, of any resources used in producing a good is measured as its value or worth in its best alternative use."

which may be unintentionally and adversely disturbed when a law of government is enforced. For example, tariff laws that maintain high prices for products for the benefit of domestic industries have the adverse side effect of increasing the costs of those products for domestic consumers. Although side effects usually impose a burden on the people, some side effects may be beneficial. For example, a law may unintentionally reduce the incidence of a certain category of crime, to the benefit of the people. (If a side effect of a law is beneficial, its burden is assigned a negative value.)

The sum of the restrictions, costs and side effects (positive and negative) of laws make up the total burden of laws upon the citizens.

PERFORMANCE OF LAWS

Every law forces a change in the natural order of things, imposes restrictions, incurs costs and produces unintended side effects. The performance, or usefulness, of each law, in terms of its overall effect upon the well-being of the people, can be determined by comparing the measured problem-solving benefit of the law with the measured sum of its burdens (restrictions, costs and side effects).[6] The simplest description of performance is the *net benefit* a law confers upon the people, or the difference between the law's measured benefit and burdens (see Figure 3-2).

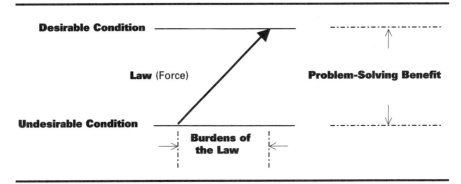

Figure 3-2. The Performance of a Law of Government: The performance of a law may be derived by subtracting the measured quantity of the burdens it imposes on the people (restrictions, costs and side effects) from the measured problem-solving benefit it produces (problem-solving benefit – burdens = performance, or net benefit).

Knowledge of how well laws perform is critical for the proper functioning of democracies. Any law that is found to be less than useful to the people must be repealed to protect their liberty and well-being. A *useful law* is defined as a law whose net benefit (benefit minus burdens) is positive (Figure 3-3); a *useless law* is a law whose net benefit is zero (Figure 3-4); and a *detrimental law* is a law whose

---

[6] The comparison of the benefits and burdens of laws requires that all parameters be described in equivalent units, e.g., dollars.

net benefit is negative (Figure 3-5).[7] By these definitions, only useful laws are capable of satisfying the purpose of democracy.

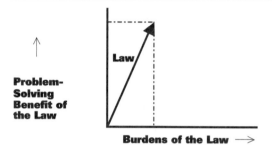

Figure 3-3. Useful Law of Government: A useful law is one that confers a positive net benefit for the people as a whole (problem-solving benefit – burdens > zero).

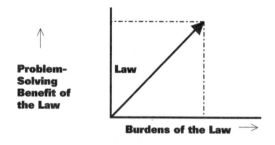

Figure 3-4. Useless Law of Government: A law is useless if its burdens are equal to its benefit, providing a net benefit of zero (problem-solving benefit – burdens = zero).

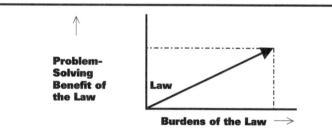

Figure 3-5. Detrimental Law of Government: A law is detrimental if its net benefit is negative (problem-solving benefit – burdens < zero). When the problem-solving benefit of a law is a negative value, e.g., when the law exacerbates the problem it is attempting to solve, it is doubly harmful to the people.

---

[7] The benefit of a detrimental law may be positive, zero (no benefit), or less than zero (a negative benefit means that the law exacerbates the problem that was being addressed).

FALLIBILITY OF LAWS

Every law is the product of human creative efforts and is thus susceptible to design imperfections. Laws may fail in their objective, become outmoded, incur excessive costs or produce unacceptable side effects. Fortunately, laws, like every other humanmade product, may by improved by design changes (amendments). In addition, they may be repealed when they are found to be less than useful. The characteristics of laws are summarized in Table 3-1.

- Laws are the means by which a government seeks to accomplish its ends.
- Laws are tools and, as such, are intended to be useful to the sovereign of government.
- Laws are the product of human creative efforts and are thus susceptible to design imperfections.
- Laws are produced by every branch of government. Statutes are produced by the legislative branch.
- Laws are the enforceable orders of government. The written words and punctuation of laws make up the "letter of the law."
- The intent of a law is the "spirit of the law." Every law in a democracy has the intent, or objective, of producing a positive net benefit for its citizens.
- Laws are restrictions, prohibitions or commands for action that incorporate an authorized sanction, or mechanism of enforcement.
- Laws produce changes in the physical world; they are a disturbance in the natural order of things.
- Laws have multiple costs; they consume and divert resources.
- Laws produce unintended side effects.
- The performance of laws can be determined.
- Laws can be amended to improve their performance.
- Laws can be repealed.

Table 3.1. Characteristics of the Laws of Government: Compare to Table E-1, Appendix E.

The Traditional Method of Lawmaking

The process by which the legislative assemblies of every government—authoritarian and democratic—currently design, amend and enact laws is termed the *traditional method of lawmaking*.[1] This method for designing laws is an immensely important process, since laws are the basis for the authority and operations of government and have a direct effect upon the human rights, living standards and quality of life of all people.

Although the traditional method has been successful in the production of laws, it has not been successful in solving societal problems, since it often creates laws that are purposeless, ineffective or even counterproductive. When these laws fail and problems persist, additional purposeless, ineffective and counterproductive laws are enacted, with the result that the bodies of law increase in size, but societal problems remain unsolved. McConnell and Brue highlight this problem:

> *Why are so many people disenchanted with—even distrustful of—government? One reason is the apparent failure of costly government programs to resolve socio-economic ills. For example, despite billions of dollars spent on the problem, widespread poverty in the United States remains. The U.S. farm programs were designed to save the family farm; instead, they have subsidized large corporate farms, which, in turn, have driven family farms out of business. While per-pupil spending has shot upward in U.S. public education, the academic performance of U.S. students on standardized tests compares unfavorably with that of students in many other nations.*[2]

As discussed in Chapter 2, purposeless, ineffective and counterproductive laws are acceptable to authoritarian governments as long as those laws regiment society and transfer wealth and power to the ruling classes. But for democracies, such laws are unacceptable because they do not serve the best interests of the people. The inability of the traditional method of lawmaking to prevent the creation of laws that are less than useful to the people invites a critical investigation of its structure and mechanisms. If defects can be identified, they can be corrected, and

---

[1] The traditional method of lawmaking as practiced by the federal and state governments of the United States of America is the primary focus of this text. However, the basic principle by which laws are created—from idea to bill to enacted law—currently applies to every government.

[2] McConnell and Brue, p. 643.

it may then be possible to create laws that consistently and efficaciously solve societal problems and thereby satisfy the purpose of democracy.

Analysis of the Traditional Method

The traditional method of lawmaking is a relatively simple process: Someone (e.g., a private individual, the representative of a special interest group or a legislator) conceives of an idea for a new law of government, or an amendment to an existing law, and transcribes that idea into a written petition, or bill. The author of the bill proffers the concept that, if enacted, the new law will produce a beneficial change in the existing order of things. After the bill has been written, it is introduced to the legislature by a legislator (its legislative sponsor), and the legislative process begins.

In the legislative process, a committee of legislators reviews the bill, gathers testimony regarding its provisions, and may change its design by means of amendments. If the committee approves the bill, it is presented to the full legislature, where it is reevaluated by means of rhetoric and dialectic in a debate format. (Simple or minor bills are occasionally enacted into law, or rejected, without formal debate.) Following the period of debate and additional amendments, if any, the members of the legislature vote to approve or reject the bill. If a majority of the legislators vote their approval, the bill is enacted into law and added to the existing enforceable, codified body of laws, thus concluding the lawmaking process.[3] In the U.S. federal and state governments, the approved bill must also be signed by the president or the governor of the state in which the bill will become law. The traditional method of lawmaking thus comprises two principal steps: (1) the initial design of bills (drafting) and (2) the legislative process (see Figure 4-1).

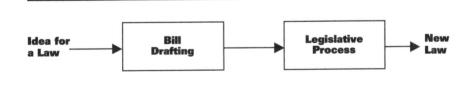

Figure 4-1. The Traditional Method of Lawmaking: The traditional method of lawmaking has two principal components for the creation of laws: bill drafting and the legislative process. It begins with an idea for a law of government and ends with the enactment of a new law. (Note that the traditional method operates without reference to the purpose of democracy.)

---

[3] See E. Willett Jr., *How Our Laws Are Made* (Washington, DC: U.S. Government Printing Office, 1990), p. 1; and http://thomas.loc.gov/.

Step One: Bill Drafting

The first step of the traditional method of lawmaking—the design of bills, or bill drafting—entails the transcription of an idea for a law into a written document. The individuals who convert ideas into written bills are the designers of laws.[4] In terms of the gravity of the societal problems addressed by laws and the scope of human activities affected by them, the level of design expertise brought to bear on their creation should be on a par with—or exceed that of—any other creative enterprise. However, a review of the related literature yields an entirely different picture: *There are virtually no quality standards for the design of laws.* This lack of quality design standards represents a gross defect in the traditional method of lawmaking and involves every aspect of the law-design process.

EDUCATIONAL REQUIREMENTS FOR LAW DESIGNERS

There are no educational or other substantive requirements for the designers of laws. This lack of qualifications is a significant and dangerous omission, since it allows individuals with no problem-solving credentials to play a major role in the design of bills, as noted by Davies:

> *Foremost among citizen participants in the legislative institution are the lobbyists. The hired lobbyists have no credential*[s] *as they arrive at the legislature, other than that somebody pays them to show up to represent a particular point of view. Hired or volunteer, lobbyists play a **major role** in the legislative institution. They prepare its bills, write amendments to those bills, advocate bills, and argue for amendments.*[5] (Emphasis added.)

IDENTITY OF LAW DESIGNERS

The process of designing new bills is a tedious and time-consuming task that is rarely if ever performed by legislators. According to John Kernochan, the author of *The Legislative Process,* "to a significant degree and for much legislation, Congress is not an initiator but is engaged in review and revision of proposals originating elsewhere."[6] And Davies agrees: "Legislatures work almost exclusively as boards of review to judge proposals brought forward by various groups. Legislators themselves seldom…draft…a bill….It is unrealistic to expect them to do so."[7]

Who, then, designs bills? To a considerable degree, bills are unsolicited proposals designed by special interests such as corporations, professional groups, trade unions, political parties and single-issue advocacy groups. Bills are also designed by employees of the legislative and administrative branches of government. However, the traditional method of lawmaking does not require that the identity

---

[4] *Law designers, bill drafters* and *lawmakers* are used synonymously in this text.
[5] J. Davies, *Legislative Law and Process in a Nutshell,* 2nd ed. (St. Paul, MN: West Publishing, 1986), p. 5.
[6] J. Kernochan, *The Legislative Process* (Mineola, NY: The Foundation Press, Inc., 1981), p. 8.
[7] Davies, p. 5.

of designers be made known. (A law usually lists the name of the legislator who sponsored it, but not the name of the person who designed it.) In fact, designers may prefer to remain anonymous so they can work without unnecessary interruptions. According to Lawrence Filson:

> *Because most professional drafters are subject to some requirement of confidentiality, they develop what is often described as a "passion for anonymity."…The legislative corridors are full of lobbyists and other partisans who will descend en masse on anyone they think they might influence; and professional drafting offices routinely try to keep their participation in particular legislative activities from becoming public knowledge.*[8]

A designer may also want to remain anonymous to avoid any responsibility for the preparation of a bill. As Bertram Gross explains: "A bill can serve as an ideal trial balloon for executive officials who are wary of taking a given course of action—particularly if the bill can be planted in Congress in such a manner as to leave the officials who originated the idea free from any responsibility for its preparation."[9]

The identity of the designers of bills (and, perforce, their qualifications and employers) is thus, for the most part, unknown. In this respect, Kernochan compares the design of bills to the composing of folk music: "As with folk songs, so many different persons and forces may have been involved over time with a particular proposal that its authorship is lost in the mazes."[10] This failure to require that the identity of bill designers be made known presents four problems for a democracy:

1. There is no way to know if the designer of a law is qualified—by education, experience or even citizenship—for the task of creating laws that satisfy the purpose of democracy. The obvious danger of unqualified designers is that they may create defective laws that harm rather than strengthen democracy.

2. No "paper trail" exists to indicate which designers created which laws. The lack of this information makes it impossible to employ continuing education and quality assurance programs to improve the performance of those designers who create useless or harmful laws.

3. Under the shield of anonymity, law designers from special interest groups can advance their own agenda at the expense of the general public. It is even possible for criminal groups and hostile agents from other countries to design laws.

---

[8] L. Filson, *The Legislative Drafter's Desk Reference* (Washington, DC: Congressional Quarterly, Inc., 1992), p. 15.
[9] B. Gross, *The Legislative Struggle* (New York, NY: McGraw-Hill, 1953), p. 169.
[10] Kernochan, p. 8.

4. Unnecessary secrecy causes the people to lose confidence in and distrust their government.

In democracies there is no need for secrecy in the design of laws. Lawmaking is the public's business and should be subject to the highest standards of accountability and transparency. Since the identity of law designers is not currently revealed, the implication—true or false—is that their work may not be in the public interest and that the government, at least to some extent, is not dedicated to the well-being of the people.

DEFINITION OF THE PROBLEM TO BE SOLVED

What is the purpose of legislators in a democracy? Since legislators are "lawmakers," the immediate response to that question might reasonably be: The purpose of lawmakers is to make laws. But that response would be incorrect because it confuses means and ends. While it is true that legislators enact laws, it is *not* true that their purpose is to make laws (see Appendix G). Rather, the purpose, or *end,* of legislators in a democracy is to attain the honorable objectives of the people in the best interests of the people. The *means* to that end is to create efficacious problem-solving laws. The first step a democratic legislature must take to satisfy its obligations, therefore, is to define societal problems so that they can be solved (see Appendix F). Once problems have been defined, they can be analyzed and given a priority for solution, including zero priority for irrelevant, unsolvable and nonexistent problems.

Unfortunately, the traditional method of lawmaking *omits* the essential definition, analysis and prioritization steps necessary for the solution of problems, and begins instead with an idea for a new law, as depicted in Figure 4-1. As a result, problems are not defined and most laws attempt to solve:

- significant problems of undefined size and complexity
- problems that do not exist
- problems that are trivial
- problems that are not relevant to the legislature's jurisdiction
- problems that cannot be solved

The lack of a requirement for the definition, analysis and prioritization of problems is a fatal flaw of the traditional method of lawmaking because it leads to the expenditure of resources on the attempted solution of low-priority or nonexistent problems instead of serious problems. It also prevents the traditional method from solving anything but the simplest problems that have a self-defined beginning and end. The result is that the traditional method cannot be an effective mechanism for the solution of societal problems.

STATEMENT OF PURPOSE

Undergoing any serious effort without a stated purpose is inane. It follows that the enforcement of a law that has no stated purpose is inane. If a statement of purpose is not included in a given law, those institutions and individuals who are required to enforce and comply with the law are forced to draw their own conclusions as to the spirit of the law, including purposes that may be completely at odds with the original public-benefit intent of the legislature. In addition, if the purpose of a law is not stated, it is impossible to derive objective measurements of its performance and, as a result, poorly performing laws cannot be identified and "weeded out."

What is the current practice regarding the declaration of a purpose in the design of a bill? Not only is a statement of purpose not required by any standard of the traditional method of lawmaking, the inclusion of a purpose statement in a bill is actually *discouraged*. For example, the Office of Legislative Counsel to the U.S. House of Representatives advises bill designers to *exclude* "findings and purposes" from their designs.[11] The practice of designing bills without a purpose statement has established, de facto, a precedent for the continued exclusion of purpose statements. Since purpose statements are regarded as optional, law designers may elect to use them solely as temporary expedients for political advantage.[12]

Laws that have no stated purpose are indefensible and are justifiably subject to derision. The people in a democracy are not intended to be automatons who blindly obey a law without knowing its purpose. In fact the people are the sovereign in a democracy and the government is obligated to inform the sovereign of the purpose of its laws—an obligation that the traditional method of lawmaking currently does not meet.

KNOWLEDGE BASE

In creating a solution to any problem, the mark of design excellence is a solution that is effective, cost-efficient, safe and user-friendly. Designs that meet these criteria approach the ideal and are referred to as "elegant." To consistently create elegant designs, a designer must collect and apply relevant, in-depth and reliable knowledge of the problem, possible solutions, optimization design techniques and the environment in which the solution will operate and interact, among other things. Any design practice that did not examine and utilize all reliable and relevant knowledge pertaining to the creation of a useful product would be regarded as irresponsible at best.

---

[11] See *Style Manual: Drafting Suggestions for the Trained Drafter* (Washington, DC: Office of the Legislative Counsel, U.S. House of Representatives, 1989), p. 25, section 325 (a). Also see discussion of law-drafting practices at http://leginfo.ca.gov/.

[12] Filson, p. 119; Davies, p. 176.

Using the same reasoning, the standards for the design of a bill intended to be an effective and just solution to a societal problem should require that the law designer acquire and utilize only relevant and reliable knowledge of the problem and the law-design process, including the predictable interactions of the law with its real-world environment.

However, the traditional method of lawmaking *does not* require the use of knowledge in the design of a bill. Aside from acknowledging changes that will be made to existing laws,[13] law designers are under no obligation to obtain or cite any factual material. Thus knowledge is regarded as an *optional* commodity in the design of a bill. Filson advises law drafters: "As statute law becomes more and more complex, you are almost *required* to develop a good working knowledge of the substantive field in which you are working."[14] (Filson's italics.) And Kernochan recommends: "The draftsman should master the existing law and experience of the jurisdiction which are pertinent to his proposal, just as an architect should study the site on which he must build."[15] But the fact is that architects *must*, not *should*, study the site on which they are planning to build. For architectural projects, unlike laws of government, quality design standards are mandatory, not optional.

In the traditional method of lawmaking, a law designer is free to write a bill first and conduct a literature search later. As Dickerson points out, one problem with this approach is that designers sometimes forget to conduct research:

> *The lesson for legal writing is clear. Unless his problem is simple, the writer does not try to do all his research first.... The one real danger in the write-early approach is that the writer may get so carried away with the beauties of his tentative results that he forgets to follow up with the research needed to verify them.*[16]

The treatment of knowledge as an optional commodity in the design of a bill means, simply, that laws may be based upon ignorance. One can thus design a tax bill without knowledge of economics; design a health care bill without knowledge of health care; design *any* bill without knowledge.

What is the hazard to the public from this failure to require that designers of laws obtain reliable and relevant knowledge of their subject matter? The same hazard that would exist if knowledge were not required for the design of any other important humanmade product. What, you might ask, would be the hazard to the public if the requirements for the design of nuclear reactors did not include knowledge of the means for properly handling radioactive materials? Or if knowledge of the harmful side effects of pesticides were eliminated as a requirement for their design? No responsible design process would allow knowledge to be

---

[13] See discussions of the Ramseyer Rule and Condon Rule, Filson, pp. 369-70.
[14] Filson, p. 30.
[15] Kernochan, p. 11.
[16] Dickerson, pp. 75-6.

optional in the creation of anything that affects public safety. It follows that the traditional method of lawmaking is not a responsible design process.

SELECTION OF APPROPRIATE SANCTIONS

Sanctions are the enforcement mechanisms, the "carrots" or "sticks" used to accomplish the purposes of laws. Examples of sanctions include fines, jail terms, subsidies and lawsuits. To be an effective mechanism in the solution of a problem, a sanction must be appropriately matched to the problem it addresses; that is, the force and size of the sanction should optimally match the severity and extent of the problem.

Suppose, for example, that a societal problem has been clearly identified and analyzed, such as the degradation of public health that results from the dumping of toxic wastes into rivers. The goal for the solution of the problem, i.e., the purpose of the law, is to meet established public health standards for river water. What sanction should be applied that would prevent individuals and institutions from dumping toxic wastes into rivers? Should fines or jail terms be employed? Or should the "carrot approach" be used, with sanctions such as subsidies, loan guarantees or tax credits that encourage the development of environmentally friendly ways to dispose of toxic wastes or of alternative production processes that do not generate toxic wastes?

The problem-solving approach to the selection of a sanction would be to first study the relevant knowledge-based literature that describes the performance of existing sanctions (see Appendix F). The sanction that most closely matched the size and severity of the problem would then be selected. Alternatively, various combinations of sanctions could be designed and tested in a solution-model that simulated the interaction of the sanctions with the defined problem. The results of the simulation testing would then predict which design would have the greatest likelihood of a satisfactory outcome in terms of the purpose of democracy—that is, effective correction of the problem with minimum burdens upon the people, individually and as a whole.

Unfortunately, no organized body of knowledge exists that describes the mechanics (causes and effects) of sanctions. Nor are there any comprehensive models for simulating the interactions of sanctions within a dynamic societal environment. The lack of knowledge of the mechanisms of sanctions makes it difficult for law designers to select appropriate sanctions. As Davies explains, "The drafter may have trouble finding the appropriate sanction to achieve the objective of the bill. The multitude of devices available, both to penalize and to reward, makes the selection difficult."[17]

---

[17] Davies, p. 144.

The result is that law designers must rely upon their personal set of beliefs ("I think"[18]) rather than knowledge ("I know")—an arbitrary, inconsistent and crude process that can lead to the selection of inappropriate sanctions that place the public at risk.

PERFORMANCE ENVELOPE

A critical consideration in the design of any useful product is its "performance envelope," or the internal and external boundaries of its range of operations, such as its allowable limits of costs, risks and side effects.[19] No new creation, however effective, is acceptable for public use if it is unsafe or generates unacceptable costs or side effects. But the traditional method of lawmaking does not require that the short- or long-term costs or side effects be taken into account in the design of bills, and these critical parameters are subsequently given little consideration or are ignored altogether.[20] In fact, the only current boundary of operations for laws is "constitutionality," which holds that a law must operate within the limits specified by the Constitution. Although the constitutions of existing democracies provide reasonable protection for human rights, they are inadequate for safeguarding living standards and quality of life (see Chapter 6.)

Costs

The lack of a requirement for a cost-benefit analysis for bills makes it possible for the advocates of a bill to emphasize its benefits while understating its costs—or ignoring them altogether.[21]

One manifestation of the de-emphasis on, or neglect of, the costs of laws is the creation of unfunded mandates. Unfunded mandates are laws that attempt to accomplish socially desirable goals but do not provide the funds to do so. For example, a legislature may pass a law that mandates an expansion of health care insurance coverage for working people, but gives the responsibility for funding that mandate to employers in the private sector. In this manner legislators can realize a favorable political outcome in terms of high approval ratings at the next election, since they can take credit for attaining a socially desirable goal without raising taxes in the short term. The problem with this "pass the buck" policy is that the costs (which may be significantly greater than the benefit) must eventually be accounted for through higher costs to consumers, higher unemployment, lower quality of services and/or, eventually, higher taxes.

---

[18] Filson, p. 34.

[19] In a democracy, the human rights, living standards and quality of life of the people define the performance envelope of laws (see Appendix A).

[20] An exception to this practice of ignoring costs in the U.S. Congress is the category of bills that require a large expenditure of funds from the treasury. These bills are typically directed to budget or appropriations legislative committees, and analysis of the cost of the laws to the treasury (the third cost of laws discussed in Chapter 3) is performed, e.g., by the Congressional Budget Office.

[21] Gross, pp. 200-01.

This lack of a requirement for cost accounting also allows law designers who are employed by special interests to create bills that provide legal competitive advantages for their employers but pass the costs on to the citizenry. For example, a law designer may draft a bill that establishes an artificially high price that the public must pay for a particular commodity. The special interest group that produces and markets that commodity will realize greater profits as the result of the law. The special interest will also be motivated to "reinvest" some of those profits in the form of gifts, e.g., campaign contributions, to the legislator(s) who permitted the measure to be incorporated into law. However, the higher price of the commodity will increase the costs to consumers. Also, a segment of the bureaucracy will be needed to monitor and enforce the law, adding to the costs of the law and diverting government resources away from productive programs such as environmental protection and crime prevention.

From the perspective of the "consumers" of laws—the people—the costs of laws are just as important as the benefits. To the extent that the traditional method of lawmaking allows bills to be designed without an accurate accounting of their direct and indirect costs, it operates against the best interests of the people, in violation of the purpose of democracy.

Risks and Side Effects

A major consideration for the design of any new product is the number and severity of its unintended side effects upon people, property and the environment. As Filson explains, "Bills do not exist in a vacuum; as often as not there are provisions of existing law that bear upon or would be affected by what your bill purports to do and that could result in consequences the sponsor didn't intend."[22] The regulatory agencies of the federal government of the United States, such as the Food and Drug Administration, devote substantial resources to screening and mitigating the risks of new products before permitting their use by the public. It is therefore ironic that high standards for the detection and elimination or mitigation of adverse side effects are mandated *by law* for the design of all useful products *except laws*. If anything, the standards for identifying and minimizing the side effects of proposed new laws should be more stringent than for any other humanmade product because the side effects of laws have a direct impact on the human rights, living standards and quality of life of the people.

However, the traditional method of designing laws does *not* require that side effects be evaluated. Rather, the investigation of the potential side effects of laws is regarded as an optional activity that can be dealt with, if necessary, after the bill has been enacted into law and its damaging effects become evident. As noted by Filson: "But if you [the law designer] are pressed for time and there is no obvious reason to suspect a problem, save your energy. Any collateral questions that do exist will surface eventually (and can be dealt with then)."[23] Davies also notes that

---

[22] Filson, p. 52.
[23] Filson, p. 54.

the consideration of side effects is an optional activity: "The one legislator in twenty who learns to foresee unfortunate secondary consequences of bills and to create amendments to avoid them should allocate available energy to doing that."[24] Note the use of the word *should*, not *must*.

This lack of due investigation into the potential side effects of bills is a fatal flaw of the traditional method of lawmaking, and it must be corrected if the purpose of democracy is to be satisfied.

DELIBERATE DECEPTION

In his noted work *The Prince*, Machiavelli advocated the use of deceit, lies, flattery and "faithlessness" for advancing the political power and fortunes of the "prince," the head of the ruling class of an authoritarian government:

> *...those princes who have done great things have held good faith of little account, and have known how to circumvent the intellect of men by craft, and in the end have overcome those who have relied on their word....But it is necessary to know well how to disguise this characteristic* [of faithlessness/lying/deception], *and to be a great pretender and dissembler, and men are so simple, and so subject to present necessities, that he who seeks to deceive will always find someone who will allow himself to be deceived.*[25]

The deceitful tactics of Machiavelli continue to dominate the design of laws under the aegis of the traditional method of lawmaking. When a law designer creates a bill that delivers a benefit to a special interest but imposes a net burden on the citizens as a whole, that designer must take special pains to conceal both the true intent of the bill and the burdens it imposes on the public. The challenge for designers who create special interest laws that are detrimental to the public is to sneak their suspect provisions into the body of laws without being caught. To that end they use deceptive techniques to hide their intentions from public scrutiny. According to Gross:

> *The drafting of a bill offers endless opportunities for deception. First, within the framework of a legislative proposal the simplest sentence composed of the simplest words is often far different from what it seems to be. Secondly, innumerable tricks of concealment are possible in the drafting of provisions amending previous acts or in incorporating parts of them by reference. When provisions of this type are inserted at the end of a long measure or buried within language that attracts attention for unrelated reasons, there are relatively few persons who will take the trouble to find out what they really mean. In addition to the standard tricks of the trade, the substantive ideas in measures are so complex as to provide endless opportunities for technicians to pull the wool over the eyes of laymen.*[26]

---

[24] Davies, p. 138.
[25] Machiavelli, p. 25.
[26] Gross, p. 216.

What are some of the "standard tricks of the trade" that may be used to slip noxious measures into bills? The various techniques vary in subtlety and cleverness, but they all have the same ultimate objective: Provide an advantage to a favored group and pass the burdens of that advantage on to the unsuspecting public.

The "Hairy Arm"

This is a diversionary tactic law designers use to draw attention away from the true nature of a bill. Davies expounds on this ploy:

> *A bill is sometimes introduced with some obnoxious feature. Critics pounce on that frightening "hairy arm" as the point of vulnerability in the proposal. Sponsors may defend the provision for a time, but before the critical vote they delete it. Opponents are left fighting the rest of the bill, which they may not have previously criticized or even studied. Inclusion of the provision may have been tactical from the beginning; deleting the hairy arm gives the appearance of compromising with the bill's critics.*[27]

The "Woodchuck" Technique

This ruse uses "housekeeping" bills to conceal dubious special interest legislation. A housekeeping bill is a seemingly innocent bill that corrects typographical and logical errors of previously enacted laws. Since housekeeping bills normally contain no substantive legislation, they are routinely enacted without scrutiny. As Davies explains:

> *A favorite legislative line is: "This is just a housekeeping bill." That tells legislators to let down their guard, to relax, to trust. But deep in a housekeeping bill some section may insert into the statute a few words with substantive implications worthy of careful thought. The housekeeping bill may hide—innocently or deceitfully—the wolf in sheep's clothing. (In some states victims of these provisions of hidden substance call them woodchucks, but terminology varies.)*[28]

Department Bills

Department bills are those created by government agencies. In some instances, they may serve as "fronts" for special interest legislation. Since they are created by government agencies, department bills may receive less scrutiny than would otherwise be prudent, and they are more likely to be enacted "as is." A lobbyist who can find a way to include special interest provisions in a department bill is assured of a high likelihood of passage:

---

[27] Davies, pp. 119-20.
[28] Davies, p. 193.

The department bill carries an aura of innocence much like the housekeeping bill, but that aura comes from the bill's origination in a public agency, rather than from its lack of substantive significance. The private lobbyist can occasionally take advantage of the trust between legislature and agency by persuading an agency to include in a department bill provisions of value to the lobbyist's clients. The agency more or less fronts for the private interest. To package a long-sought change of law in the homey wrapping of a department bill is a lobbyist's dream.[29]

Overly Long Bills

Another technique is to secrete a deleterious provision in a lengthy bill. The trick is to insert such a provision—not at the very beginning of a long bill, which may be studied on occasion—but somewhat back from the end, where the provision will have less chance of being spotted:

When a long bill is being reviewed, attention lags before review is complete. Since almost everyone reads bills starting at section one, closing sections are rarely read with the attention of a fully alert mind. The sponsor may take advantage of this fact by hiding a sensitive or unpopular section near the end of a bill, rather than putting it where logical organization dictates. Sometimes an alert reviewer finds the most significant provision in a bill in its last or next to the last section, where the repeal of some significant statute will appear.[30]

Omnibus Bills

With this strategy, a multitude of small, separate bills of loosely related topics are combined into one large bill. Omnibus bills offer the advantage (to special interests) of including questionable measures that would never become laws on their own merits. As Gross explains, "The omnibus approach also provides the opportunity to execute a hidden ball play. The broader the scope of the measure, the more chance there is of its carrying along to enactment provisions that would otherwise stand no chance of being enacted into law."[31]

Filson explains why the inevitable result of omnibus bills is confusion if not chaos: "These bills are always massive, they are invariably enacted under extreme time pressure, and they can include anything under the sun. And their lack of any rational order or stylistic consistency often makes it next to impossible to find what you are looking for even when you know it is there."[32]

---

[29] Davies, pp. 194-5.
[30] Davies, pp. 198-9.
[31] Gross, p. 209.
[32] Filson, p. 345.

Bills With Irresistible Titles

A bill that has an "irresistible" title is another conduit for the enactment of special interest legislation. Such a bill may develop strong support on the basis of its title alone. For "legislative opportunists," these bills are ideal for the attachment of "extra baggage" provisions that would never be enacted in their own right, as noted by Davies: "Strategically, an irresistible title situation is volatile, even dangerous; a bill so blessed can carry extra baggage without faltering. Therefore, legislative opportunists try to hitch onto the bill secondary propositions which could not be enacted by themselves."[33]

Intentional Vagueness

Law designers may also use vagueness as a convenient method of obscuring the true intentions, costs or side effects of a bill. Gross points out, "Sometimes the most elaborate facade of detail merely hides a tremendous blank-check delegation of power and resources."[34]

Davies advises that vague language may obscure the hazards contained within a bill so that they are easily overlooked by those who might be adversely affected by the bill's provisions, and also explains the use of vagueness by legislatures:

> ...vagueness may cause those affected to overlook some hazard in the bill. ...Intentional vagueness serves legislatures well and often. It may be adopted consciously, occur by oversight, or turn up as a compromise during negotiation. Legislators eagerly duck tough questions if answering them threatens the passage of a bill for which a consensus has developed.[35]

Like a law that has no stated purpose, a law that has a vague meaning is subject to various interpretations, and it may therefore produce spurious, harmful results that were not intended by the legislature. Leadership is the ability to establish goals and clearly communicate them. When a legislature tolerates the use of intentional vagueness to hide policies that are harmful to the public, it compromises its position of leadership and, worse, breaches the public trust.

The various techniques of deliberate deception in the design of bills are unethical, at best, and are completely contrary to the purpose of democracy. They are used to provide benefits for special interests at the expense of the public and they produce an overall deleterious effect, not only in their detrimental outcome, but also in the public's consequent loss of trust and respect for laws and government. The present tolerance of deception in the design of laws is in the best tradition of Machiavelli but it is totally unacceptable for democratic governments.

---

[33] Davies, p. 104.
[34] Gross, p. 204.
[35] Davies, pp. 191-2.

DESIGN IMPERFECTIONS

The public is accustomed to—and expects—high standards of design practices for the creation of useful products. For a product as important as a law, it would be logical to expect that the same quality of workmanship—for example, of thorough research, attention to detail and the application of accurate forecasting methodologies—would characterize each step of the design process. In reality, haste and shortcuts, with attendant design errors and omissions, are more accurate attributes of the design process for laws.

For example, if a legislator or special interest group wants to create a bill on short notice, the designer who is called upon to create the bill may be forced to sacrifice quality in the design of the bill so that a political accommodation can be reached:

> ...time pressures or needs for political accommodation or both may—more often than one would wish—prevent a draftsman from doing his job with the thoroughness and precision it deserves.[36]

> Unfortunately, the draftsman is often under time limitations that he cannot control, and he has to compromise accordingly...there will even be times when he has to draft impromptu. At such times, when he has to get it right the first time or not at all, he crosses his fingers and hopes that his past experience and a little luck will keep him from going too far astray....Some of these deadlines would be relaxed or dropped if it were explained to the client [the party that contracted the designer to create the bill] that either the time limit or the quality of the result must give way. The draftsman who is too easygoing about this winds up as a mediocre, short-order cook.[37]

The haste and compromises that typify the design of laws under the lax rules of the traditional method of lawmaking lead to the inclusion of flaws (technical shortcomings) in a significant percentage of bills, flaws that may result in "spectacular misfires" when the laws are enforced:

> And if all else fails and you [the designer] must simply do the best you can and hope for divine guidance, you should cling to the thought that you are not alone—most bills when introduced have gaps and flaws that have to be corrected later....A substantial percentage of the bills in Congress (and presumably in State legislatures) have serious substantive, legal, or practical problems in them when they are introduced, usually left there because of lack of time and with the knowledge of both drafter and sponsor.[38]

---

[36] Kernochan, p. 12.
[37] Dickerson, pp. 56 and 71.
[38] Filson, pp. 49-50.

…technical shortcomings are not very newsworthy (at least until the bill becomes law and some spectacular misfire occurs).[39]

So it appears that time constraints are a significant factor in limiting the quality of law design. But why the rush? Most of the current serious concerns of society, such as pollution and illiteracy, are long-term problems that require in-depth analyses and well-crafted solutions. The public would be far better served by a process that emphasizes quality of design over short-term political accommodation.

Legislative Sponsorship

After a bill has been designed, it must meet certain simple requirements before the second stage of the traditional method, the legislative process, can begin. For the U.S. Congress, the bill is required to contain:

1. a title that reasonably reflects the subject matter
2. a designation label, e.g., H.R. 12 (House of Representatives Bill Number 12)
3. an enactment clause
4. contents formatted in the accepted style of laws
5. a legislative sponsor[40]

Of these requirements, only the last one, legislative sponsorship, presents a significant challenge for the originator of the bill; if a sponsor cannot be found, the bill will not be reviewed by the legislature. Therefore the advocate of the bill must gain access to a legislator and use lobbying skills to persuade the legislator that the bill should receive priority over the bills of other petitioners. How does the advocate/petitioner of a bill gain access to a legislator and persuade him or her to sponsor a particular bill? Contributing money to a legislator's reelection campaign is the means petitioners most commonly use.[41]

Aside from the serious ethical quid-pro-quo questions raised by this practice, there is another significant problem: Nonpaying petitioners, whose bills may provide significant value to the public, may be unable to gain access to legislators. According to Davies, although an occasional "lone petitioner" with a sensible idea does manage to gain attention, "…few persons without an economic interest even try to gain access."[42]

After the petitioner gains access to the legislator, the next step is to convince the legislator to sponsor the bill, i.e., to endorse it and introduce it before the legislature. Sponsorship gives the legislator a certain degree of power over the fate of a bill, which—like the process of granting access—often results in offers of

---

[39] Filson, p. 35.

[40] See Willett, pp. 5-6; Kernochan, p. 16; *Style Manual: Drafting Suggestions for the Trained Drafter*; and http://thomas.loc.gov.

[41] M. Jewell and S. Patterson, *The Legislative Process in the United States* (New York, NY: Random House, 1977), p. 292; and Davies, p. 2.

[42] Davies, p. 60.

various inducements to the legislator from people who wish to amend, advance or retard the proposed law. As Gross explains:

> *The sponsor of a bill is often in the position of exercising a controlling influence over its future. Government officials, members of Congress, and leaders of private organizations will seek him out and ask for amendments. Many will offer various types of inducements to him to seek more rapid action on his bill or to try to hold up action.*"[43]

Since the legislator-sponsor of a bill does not usually have the time for a critical examination to determine the costs and benefits of the bill, he or she is forced to rely on the persuasive efforts of the bill's advocates for that information, as noted by Davies:

> *The effective petition is served on a silver platter as a soundly conceived and well-drafted bill. It is accompanied by supporting advocacy which convinces legislators that the bill is sensible and that they will not incur serious political vulnerabilities if they support it....Of course, good legislators try to fill the lobbying void with their own examination of each bill presented, but the sheer number of bills undermines this effort....The pace of most legislative sessions allows them* [legislators] *to do little more than judge the cases presented by advocates.*[44]

The problem with such persuasive efforts is that they are often unethical and are, in any case, unreliable as a means of understanding the issues involved. Also, when a given bill is designed by a special interest, the legislator who sponsors the bill assumes an advocacy role for the bill, and the special interest group becomes the legislator's client. The legislator now has two clients: the special interest that designed the bill and the legislator's constituents. Unless the bill provides a net benefit to those constituents, a clear conflict of interest exists. Thus the process by which legislators become sponsors/advocates of bills invites corruption, limits participation by the public and constitutes another serious flaw in the traditional method of lawmaking.

The typical characteristics of a bill that emerges from the first stage of the traditional method of lawmaking are listed in Table 4-1.

---

[43] Gross, p. 183.
[44] Davies, pp. 5-6.

- The bill was created by a special interest group as an unsolicited proposal.
- The designer of the bill, who is not named, wishes to remain anonymous.
- The qualifications of the designer of the bill are unknown.
- The societal problem that the bill addresses is not defined.
- The purpose of the bill is not stated.
- Problem-solving design expertise was not employed in the creation of the bill.
- Techniques of deliberate deception were used to conceal the true beneficiaries and costs of the bill.
- The potential side effects of the bill were not evaluated.
- The bill was written in haste and contains many design defects and omissions.
- Campaign contributions or other inducements were given to legislators by special interest groups in exchange for legislative sponsorship of the bill.
- The bill has no basis in knowledge.

Table 4-1. Initial Design Step of Laws—Typical Characteristics of a Bill: Based on current design practices, during the first step of the traditional method of lawmaking, these statements about a bill are either true or should be suspected to be true.

Step Two: The Legislative Process

The introduction of a bill before the legislature by a legislator-sponsor signals the beginning of the second step of the traditional method of lawmaking—the legislative process (see Figure 4-1). The legislative process is the dynamic, interactive component of the traditional method. During this process, legislators utilize a debate format to evaluate, redesign (amend) and enact bills into enforceable laws.[45] An idealist might expect that the flaws and inadequacies of bills that were generated in the bill-drafting step would be corrected during this second step. Regrettably, the performance of the legislative process is no better than that of bill drafting in the design of laws, and in many cases, bills are further degraded by amendments added at this stage. There are five troubling aspects of the legislative process that merit review: (1) debate, (2) committee hearings, (3) amendments, (4) voting and (5) follow-up evaluation.

DEBATE

The traditional method of lawmaking, which relies upon the process of debate—that is, of rhetoric (political oration) and dialectic (logical argumentation)—for making laws, has remained virtually unchanged throughout history. It was unfazed, for example, by the Renaissance, the Enlightenment and the Industrial Revolution. Its operating principles most closely approximate the tenets of medieval Scholasticism, which holds that everything that can be known has already been discovered and that the proper ordering of human affairs can be accomplished through philosophical musings and exercises.[46] According to this discredited belief, lawmaking assemblies need only use rhetoric and dialectic in the process of "open debate"

---

[45] See http://thomas.loc.gov/ and http://leginfo.ca.gov/ for a description of the legislative process.
[46] See "Medieval Universities and Scholasticism" in D. Kagan, S. Ozment and F. Turner, *The Western Heritage*, 2nd ed. (New York, NY: Macmillan Publishing Co., 1983), pp. 298-305, for a discussion of Scholasticism.

and compromise to create the just laws of government. But this approach is inappropriate and inadequate for the design of laws.

While proficiency in oration and expertise in logical argumentation are desirable skills for presenting and evaluating ideas and for making decisions in a debate, they are inadequate methodologies for the design of useful implements, including laws. Specifically, rhetoric and dialectic are incapable of performing the essential knowledge-based empirical and analytical steps of the problem-solving method (see Appendices E and F) and, in addition, they permit laws to be created on the basis of opinions, anecdotes, half-truths and falsehoods. In fact it is possible for a legislature—by means of duly observed parliamentary rules, eloquent oration and thorough and incisive debate and deliberation—to nevertheless create and enact seriously flawed laws that are harmful to the people. In other words, debate, which is the core operating system of the legislative process, is incapable of producing a body of laws that satisfies the purpose of democracy. The limitations of debate are discussed in Appendix J.

COMMITTEE HEARINGS

In the U.S. federal and state governments, a bill that has been accepted for consideration by the legislature is assigned to a legislative committee. If the committee decides not to review the bill, it "dies in committee" and must be reintroduced in the next legislative session to have a chance of becoming a law. If the committee deems a bill satisfactory "as is," it is advanced, or "reported," for review by the full legislature without amendments. If the committee decides to examine the bill in some detail, the committee conducts one or more hearings in which witnesses testify on the merits of the bill. Based on the outcome of the hearing(s), the committee may accept the bill as is, change its design with amendments (see following section), or allow the bill to die in committee. There are no fixed rules that a committee must observe for the examination of the efficacy of a bill; the subject matter, timing and purpose of hearings are at the discretion of the committee chairperson. In the ideal condition, committee hearings are used to assure that bills meet the highest-quality standards vis-à-vis the purpose of democracy. However, hearings are frequently used for purposes that have little or no connection to the bill under consideration:

> *But hearings are not always well managed to serve...*[an] *informational purpose and may be used to serve, instead or in addition, such other purposes as mobilizing public support or opposition, providing publicity for legislators, stalling the legislative progress of a bill, furnishing a "safety valve" for disturbances, and so forth.*[47]

> *From the point of view of the participants, hearings often serve purposes that have nothing to do with the legislation at hand.*[48]

---

[47] Kernochan, p. 25.
[48] D. Berman, *In Congress Assembled* (New York, NY: MacMillan Publishing Co., 1964), p. 155.

Since there are no rules for the conduct of hearings regarding the relevancy of bills to the public good, hearings can, in fact, be organized for the purpose of promoting a political agenda or other special interest objective. In that case, hearings are "choreographed" to exaggerate testimony favorable to a particular point of view, delay testimony or withhold unfavorable information altogether:

> *One way to ration* [committee time] *is to set up a schedule* [for committee hearings] *that favors friends and supporters. Occasionally long-drawn-out hearings are sought for the express purpose of delaying legislative action. …Sound strategy often calls for withholding testimony entirely or for delaying until the most auspicious moment.*[49]

Another troubling feature of hearings is that testimony is unreliable as a means of gathering relevant knowledge of the societal problem a bill addresses or of the benefit, risks and costs of a bill. Witnesses are inconsistent (ten witnesses may recollect ten different versions of the same topic or event); they often fail to recall all relevant facts; and their testimony is, in any case, anecdotal. Also, witnesses are sometimes misleading or even untruthful when giving testimony despite being under oath, and they are frequently spokespersons for special interests whose objectives are not in the best interests of the public:

> *They* [committee hearings] *provide a springboard for propagandist and pressure activities.*[50]

> *Except for Government witnesses, whose testimony is usually considered indispensable on bills affecting their jurisdiction, it is for the committee or subcommittee chairman to determine who will receive invitations to testify. In most cases, however, he will allow testimony to be offered by the representatives of any organizations with a substantial interest in the bill under consideration. The result is that the typical hearing is dominated by testimony from spokesmen for pressure* [special interest] *groups.*[51]

Even when relevant and reliable knowledge of a facet of a law under review is provided, such knowledge is often (if not always) rendered useless because it is combined with unreliable testimony that includes opinions, half-truths and falsehoods.

At the conclusion of a hearing, the participants may edit their recorded testimony. As a result, the committee report (the official summary report) of the bill is further degraded as a source of information on the subject matter of the hearing:

> *The information developed at a hearing is made available to members of Congress in the form of printed volumes which reproduce the testimony that was taken. Although these volumes appear on their face to contain verbatim transcripts, their contents often bear a somewhat distant relationship to what*

---

[49] Gross, pp. 287, 291 and 293.
[50] Gross, p. 284.
[51] Berman, pp. 152-3.

actually took place at a hearing. The reason is that committee members as well as witnesses are almost always given an opportunity to "correct" their remarks. In the absence of a rule that they must confine their editing to mistakes made in transcription and to matters of grammar, they often do a thorough job of rewriting. To diminish the value of the printed record still further, there is usually no subject-matter index to help one find at a glance the testimony that dealt with a particular point. Thus, from a practical point of view, the information obtained through a hearing is directly available only to members of the committee or subcommittee involved. Other congressmen, of course, would probably not have time to review it anyway, since they have their own committee work to keep up with.[52]

Thus, committee hearings usually provide only a collage of opinions, anecdotal information and advocacy—the sum of which is of little value, at best, in the construct of a body of laws that is effective in the solution of societal problems.

AMENDMENTS

Every bill and every existing law may be amended during the legislative process. An amendment is a design change that can produce substantial changes in meaning, as noted by Davies and Kernochan:

One amendment may sweep dozens (or thousands) more persons into or out of the ambit of the bill, or the amendment may change the impact from beneficial to troubling for one interest or another.[53]

The amendments offered may be and often are of such character as to change the bill substantially or weaken it drastically.[54]

Consider the following hypothetical tax law directive for corporations: *"Withhold an extra $2.00 from the weekly paycheck of all employees who are required to have a driver's license as a condition of employment."* For purposes of illustration, assume that company ABCD has 100 employees and that two of the employees are required to have a driver's license. In this instance, the company's accountant would withhold an extra $4.00 from the weekly payroll.

But suppose that the law is amended by placing a single comma after the word "employees." The tax law now reads: *"Withhold an extra $2.00 from the weekly paycheck of all employees, who are required to have a driver's license as a condition of employment."* The added comma causes the sentence to imply that all 100 employees are required to have a driver's license and that the company's accountant must now withhold a total of $200.00 from the weekly payroll (a fifty-fold increase!). As this example points out, the very simplest amendment can make significant changes in the meaning of a law.

---

[52] Berman, p. 156.
[53] Davies, p. 56.
[54] Kernochan, p. 41.

What are the present standards for making amendments to laws? Aside from rules of parliamentary procedures, there are none: Legislators may make virtually unlimited modifications, through amendments, in the design of laws. As a result, the amendment process is plagued with the same problems that afflict the bill-drafting process, including superficial evaluation, deliberate deception and lack of knowledge.

Superficial Evaluation

In the U.S. House of Representatives, a bill may be amended extensively at each stage of its review by committee and by the full membership of the legislature (which is termed *the committee of the whole house*). When a legislator offers an amendment during the "second reading" of the bill in the committee of the whole house, the evaluation of the amendment is limited by the "five-minute rule."[55] Under the five-minute rule, the amendment's legislative sponsor is limited to five minutes to speak in favor of the amendment, and one other legislator is given five minutes for a rebuttal. If the committee of the whole house approves the amendment, it is attached to the bill, and the amended bill may then be subjected to additional amendments.

The problem with this process is that amendments introduced at this stage cannot possibly be sufficiently evaluated for their benefit, costs and side effects. An amendment may be offered with good intentions but may be *seriously* flawed in a way that is not apparent during the legislature's superficial evaluation, thereby putting the public at considerable risk.

Deliberate Deception

Because of the lax rules for amending bills, law designers can create amendments that provide legal advantages (e.g., subsidies, trade restrictions, tax loopholes) to special interest groups, advance a political agenda and/or secure appropriations for political patronage, while passing the burdens of those amendments on to the public at large. When the burdens of an amendment on the people are greater than its benefit, deceptive practices (see earlier discussion of deliberate deception) are sometimes used to hide the true purpose and burdens of the proposed amendment. Gross notes that amendments lend themselves to deception: "Amendments, moreover, get less public attention....They are hard for the press or any outside observers to understand. Sometimes they pile up one on top of another in a manner that defies comprehension by anyone except a small handful of members of Congress, experts, and lobbyists."[56]

Amendments also receive less scrutiny when they are proposed at the last minute in a legislative session. The amending strategy of the legislative process thus includes surprise, whereby an amendment (e.g., one that is favorable to a

---

[55] Willett, p. 24.
[56] Gross, p. 218.

particular special interest) is deliberately added to a bill when there is insufficient time to evaluate it:

> *All who might want to advise the institution* [the legislature] *on the merit or demerit of an amendment would like to know that the amendment is to be proposed and when; without notice it is impossible to engage in timely lobbying. But advance notice of amendments need not be given. In fact, surprise is often a part of the amending strategy.*[57]

As a purported means of minimizing the addition of spurious amendments to bills, a "rule of germaneness"[58] is sometimes applied to amendments (in the U.S. House of Representatives, for example) to assure that they are relevant to the purpose of the bill. A major problem with germaneness is that a significant number of bills have no stated purpose and, for these bills, any amendment may be "germane." Another problem is that the meaning of the word *germaneness* can be very broadly interpreted: "...but you don't have to be a genius to recognize that 'germaneness' is a very slippery term. How far afield can you go before your amendment can be said to involve 'a subject different from that under consideration'?"[59] In the U.S. Congress, the germaneness rule is of very limited value because it applies only to those amendments that are added by the House of Representatives. The Senate has no germaneness rule, so an amendment attached to a bill in the Senate may address virtually any subject.

Under the lax rules of the legislative process that permit the use of deceptive practices, therefore, amendments that are harmful or of no value to the people are often added to bills without adequate evaluation.

Lack of Knowledge

Perhaps the greatest threat of the amendment process is that amendments do not need to be based upon relevant and reliable knowledge. A bill may contain many complex amendments that were added by legislators during spirited debate without the benefit of knowledge:

> *The preparation of a copy of the bill in the form in which it has passed the House is sometimes a detailed and complicated process because of the large number and complexity of amendments to some bills adopted by the House. Frequently these amendments are offered during a spirited debate with **little or no prior formal preparation.**[60]* (Emphasis added.)

> *A special and often offensive type of amendment that amends in form but not in substance is the amendment that begins with the words, "Notwithstanding any other law." What the words usually tell you is that the drafter is seeking a specific result, i.e., overcoming conflicting provisions, but has failed to integrate his*

---

[57] Davies, p. 56.
[58] Filson, p. 428.
[59] Filson, p. 429.
[60] Willett, p. 32.

amendment with other relevant statutes. In other words, he literally does not know what he is doing.[61]

...the opinions or private crotchets which have been overruled by knowledge always insist on giving themselves a second chance before the tribunal of ignorance. And when a Bill of many clauses does succeed in getting itself discussed in detail, what can depict the state in which it comes out of Committee! Clauses omitted which are essential...; incongruous ones inserted...; articles foisted in on the motion of some sciolist with a mere smattering of the subject, leading to consequences which the member who introduced or those who supported the Bill did not at the moment foresee, and which need an amendment act in the next session to correct their mischiefs.[62]

Incredibly, a single bill may contain *several hundred amendments* that produce substantial changes, may or may not be germane and have had little or no prior formal preparation. According to Willett: "On occasion there have been upward of 500 amendments [attached to a bill]."[63]

Although the amendment process is accomplished through the observance of traditional parliamentary procedures, the fact is that inadequate evaluations, deception and lack of knowledge render this seriously flawed process an ongoing threat to the people as a whole.

VOTING

The structure and operation of a government are defined and directed by its body of laws. A government may be efficient and just if its laws are efficient and just, but it can be no better than mediocre if its laws are mediocre. Because the legislature of a government controls the content of its body of laws, the legislators are ultimately responsible for the scope, direction and proper functioning of the government. In other words, it is the legislators who determine if the body of laws is characterized by efficacy or mediocrity. Therefore the vote to reject or enact a bill is one of the most significant responsibilities of a legislator.

The citizens of a democracy expect their legislators to base their voting decisions on wisdom, which is defined as knowledge combined with prudent judgment in the use of that knowledge (see Appendix L). However, wisdom in voting is not an option for legislators because wisdom requires reliable knowledge of the content and predicted outcome of bills, and such knowledge, for the most part, *does not exist.* As a result, legislators are thrust into the untenable position of making judgments and voting on hundreds or thousands of bills and their numerous and complex amendments without adequate knowledge:

---

[61] D. Hirsch, *Drafting Federal Law* (Washington, DC: Office of the Legislative Counsel, U.S. House of Representatives, 1989), p. 18.

[62] Mill, p. 359 (on a discussion of the lawmaking practices of the English Parliament).

[63] Willett, p. 43.

When a session adjourns, legislators look back on dozens of decisions which required more study and thought than they were able to give to them. Every legislator at every level is reminded of this time pressure by the stack of reports not read, by the bills voted on without adequate study....In many states, constitutional deadlines for adjournment turn the last days and hours of a session into a frantic drive to dispose of accumulated business. Legislators are so busy casting votes based on previously acquired information that they cannot take time to listen to additional evidence or argument.[64]

During the course of a [legislative] session, a congressman or state legislator must make a decision about a large number and variety of bills. Unless the bill directly affects his district, has come before one of his committees, or relates to some field in which he has specialized knowledge, he is likely to be poorly informed about the bill and proposed amendments that come to a vote. He has very little time to collect information about the bill from sources that he considers trustworthy.[65]

The fact is that the number and range of issues are so great that no one can safely rely solely on his own information and vote intelligently. Commented one lawmaker: "You have to take so much on faith on bills brought into the House; sometimes you get fooled."[66]

What sources of information are available to assist a legislator in making voting decisions regarding the fate of bills? Regrettably for the citizenry, the only readily available sources of information for legislators are lobbyists, committee reports and political parties.

Lobbyists

Lobbyists always have a special interest agenda and cannot be trusted to provide reliable information. They may in fact use their access to a legislator to *dissuade* the legislator from obtaining additional knowledge that may affect his or her vote:

While there may be a best time and place for most things, the only general rule about lobbying is to adjust to the circumstances. With some legislators on some issues, the best move is to step forward just before a vote and ask a relaxed question like: "You don't need any more information supporting our bill, do you? We haven't run across serious problems yet."[67]

---

[64] Davies, pp. 22 and 234.
[65] Jewell and Patterson, p. 410.
[66] C. Clapp, *The Congressman: His Work as He Sees It* (Washington, DC: The Brookings Institution, 1963), p. 146.
[67] Davies, p. 92.

Committee Reports

The second source of information available to legislators is committee reports, which provide an "official" summary of bills. As previously noted, there are serious problems with committee reports: While they provide an overview of testimony (i.e., anecdotal data) about bills, they do not reliably reveal the true intent and predicted consequences of bills or disclose significant distortions and omissions (which may have occurred as a result of staged hearings). Committee reports thus cannot be trusted to be a reliable guide to a bill's true purpose, benefit, costs and side effects. Also, reports are frequently not available in time to assist in decision making: "By far the most common congressional criticism of reports, however, is that too often they are not available in time to assist the legislator in reaching a decision. Frequently, they are issued just prior to a vote so that the congressman has little or no opportunity to study them."[68]

Political Parties

Uninformed legislators often defer their decisions to the research conclusions of political parties:

> As noted, bills that are regarded as non-controversial usually do not gain much attention from the heavily burdened legislators. The typical representative is virtually uninformed with respect to bills reaching the House floor...but in such cases his conscience is eased, for specific responsibility for ensuring that such bills are meritorious is delegated by party leadership to official party objectors whose job it is to screen the bills carefully.[69]

The problem with relying on a political party to learn if a bill is meritorious is that different political parties frequently have different interpretations of the definition of *meritorious*. The conclusions of one political party regarding a bill may in fact directly oppose those of another political party. Hence their recommendations are no more reliable than the urgings of lobbyists or the conclusions of committee reports. Also, political party investigators who screen bills for legislators always serve the best interests of the party but not necessarily the best interests of the people the legislator represents. A legislator who votes the "party line" thus serves the interests of his or her political party, but not necessarily of the people as a whole.

At the conclusion of the legislative process, each bill, with or without amendments, is submitted to the legislators for a vote. If the bill receives a majority vote in favor of enactment (despite legislators' lack of knowledge of the real meaning and potential consequences of the bill), and is approved to be a law (and "signed" by the chief executive of the government), it becomes a new, enforceable

---

[68] Clapp, p. 270.
[69] Clapp, p. 147.

law. The newly enacted law is then added to the existing body of laws and the two steps of the traditional method of lawmaking are thereby concluded.

FOLLOW-UP EVALUATION

In the traditional method of lawmaking, after a law is enacted, the legislature is done with its lawmaking task and has no further responsibility regarding the impact of the law on the people: "Once an act is passed, the legislature's job is done."[70] So who protects the people's interests by taking responsibility for the consequences of laws? The answer is, as yet, no one. Incredibly, the traditional method of lawmaking does not have a program of follow-up evaluation (i.e., quality assurance) for the laws it produces. Quality assurance (QA) is an essential feedback safety mechanism that maintains high-quality standards for products and services that have an effect upon the public well-being. The lack of a QA program for laws is another critical flaw of the traditional method of lawmaking. Unless the results of law enforcement are objectively measured and analyzed through a competent QA program, no one can know if any given law of government is beneficial, useless or harmful to the people—a condition of ignorance that is not tolerated for any other useful product or enterprise that has an impact on the public well-being.

A Seriously Flawed System

The traditional method of lawmaking has been used by governments throughout history to create the laws of government. However it has no quality standards and, rather than being an effective mechanism for solving societal problems, it is merely a lawmaking process that tolerates ignorance and deceit in the design of laws and does not account for the consequences of law enforcement. The traditional method of lawmaking is undisciplined, unprincipled, unreliable and irresponsible.

---

[70] Davies, p. 10.

Threat to Democracy

Democratic governments, by definition, must satisfy the purpose of democracy, and they are thereby obligated to serve the best interests of the people. Since government resources are provided by the people and are always limited, democracies must use these resources wisely to create and enforce their bodies of laws—and any process that impedes or detracts from this high purpose is a threat to democracy.

Given these considerations, the traditional method of lawmaking is a threat to democracy. Although in existing democracies the rules of periodic, honest and competitive elections are duly observed for major government offices, and legislators comply with established parliamentary procedures for introducing, enacting, revising and repealing laws, legislatures have not been able to create bodies of laws that satisfy the purpose of democracy. This is because the traditional method of lawmaking is not a problem-solving process but merely a *law-production* process that allows the enactment of laws that are less than useful in the solution of societal problems. In addition, the traditional method has no regular, reliable process for identifying and repealing such laws. Worse, as noted in Chapter 4, it permits the creation of laws that deceitfully provide advantages to special interest groups to the detriment of the people as a whole.

When societal problems are not effectively mitigated by existing laws, legislators enact more laws that are equally flawed, useless or detrimental. Since laws are not repealed (with rare exceptions), the growing bodies of laws increasingly restrict freedoms, waste the people's resources, undermine the rule of law and thereby threaten to cause the regression of democracies to authoritarian forms of government.[1] An urgent need of democratic governments, therefore, is to understand the threat that the traditional method of lawmaking poses to democracy. When this threat is understood and corrected, the full promise of democracy may be realized.

---

[1] The mismanagement of democratic governments has historically led to coups—for example, in Argentina in 1955, Chile in 1963 and Peru in 1992.

Misdirected Purpose of the Traditional Method

The traditional method of lawmaking is a classic feed-forward control system (see Appendix C) in which newly designed bills, *not societal problems*, constitute the driving force of legislatures, and newly enacted laws, *not solutions to problems*, are the output (see Chapter 4, Figure 4-1). Since the traditional method does not link laws to the solution of problems, it is not and cannot be a problem-solving process and, therefore, *it is unable to satisfy the purpose of democracy*. The traditional method substitutes its means (law creation) for its ends (problem solution), and it is entirely possible for a legislature to create thousands of new laws without solving one problem (see Appendix G).

However, the people of any given society do not need or want more laws for the sake of having more laws—they need solutions for problems. New laws that do not solve problems simply add complexity and restrictions to the human condition and divert resources away from legitimate needs. In other words, large and growing bodies of ineffective and less than useful laws not only fail to satisfy the purpose of democracy but also constitute an additional societal problem that needs to be solved. The misdirected purpose of the traditional method leads to waste, injustice, corruption and chaos, all of which undermine the rule of law and set the stage for a return to authoritarian rule.[2]

WASTE

The traditional method of lawmaking wastes government resources. As noted in Chapter 4, laws are currently designed without the benefit of design expertise or reliable and relevant knowledge, and they are frequently created and amended in haste, with attendant flaws and omissions. The result of a typical legislative session is therefore a mixed bag that includes inefficient, useless and detrimental laws (see Chapter 3, Figures 3-4 and 3-5).[3] Since government resources are limited, and laws are the conduits through which government resources are expended, wasteful laws degrade the ability of a democratic government to satisfy its purpose and are, therefore, a threat to democracy. Also, squandered resources must be made up through increased taxes and fees, which degrade living standards (see Figure 5-1).

Both government groups and nonprofit public interest groups currently investigate and report on wasteful programs authorized by laws.[4] However, although waste is identifiable, democratic governments currently have no ongoing, rigorous

---

[2] Authoritarian governments thrive on the perpetuation of a permanent underclass of people and therefore do not want laws to be successful in the solution of societal problems. The regression of a democracy toward an authoritarian form of government is evident when a government's body of laws increases in size and complexity while problems remain unsolved.

[3] For example, see www.loonylaws.com.

[4] For examples of inefficient, wasteful programs authorized by laws, see U.S. Government, www.gao.gov; American Enterprise Institute, www.aei.org; Brookings Institution, www.brook.edu; Cato Institute, www.cato.org; Citizens Against Government Waste, www.cagw.org; Common Cause, www.commoncause.org; Public Citizen, www.citizen.org; and Rand Corporation, www.rand.org.

mechanisms for repealing wasteful laws. Examples of wasteful laws are listed in Table 5-1.

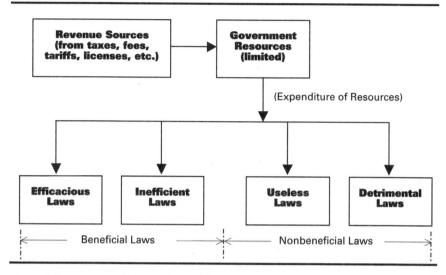

Figure 5-1. Sources and Expenditure of Government Resources: Laws are conduits for the disbursement of government resources. Nonbeneficial laws (laws whose net benefit is less than positive) are harmful not only because they are less than useful to the people but also because they expend limited government resources that must be replaced through taxes or other revenue sources. Inefficient laws (e.g., laws that are cumbersome, profligate, marginally effective) also diminish the effectiveness of democracy to the extent that they consume excessive resources in the completion of their problem-solving tasks.

Wasteful Laws	Examples
Inefficient Laws	• United States federal and state income tax codes
Useless Laws	• pork barrel spending projects (buildings, bridges, dams, etc.), authorized by law, which provide no net benefit to the public[5]
Detrimental Laws	• laws that fail in their purpose, such as tariff laws that increase rather than decrease unemployment

Table 5-1. Wasteful Laws: Laws that waste resources limit the ability of governments to carry out their legitimate function and are a threat to democracy.

---

[5] Pork barrel projects are political patronage programs whereby legislators authorize spending projects in their legislative districts for their own aggrandizement and to enhance their reelection prospects.

INJUSTICE

Every law provides a degree of justice to the people as a whole on a scale from positive (just) to negative (detrimental or unjust).[6] Democratic governments are obligated to dispense the highest positive levels of justice under the rule of law.

A significant problem for democracies is that the traditional method of law-making often produces laws that fail in their just purpose, i.e., that are less than useful to the people as a whole and are, therefore, unjust. For example, laws that impose tariffs on imported goods are frequently created for the purpose of preserving domestic jobs. However, if those tariffs cause an overall increase in unemployment, they are unjust because they exacerbate rather than mitigate the problem that they are attempting to solve. The injustice of such laws is compounded when they also increase costs to consumers and lead to retaliatory tariffs from other nations.[7]

CORRUPTION

The growing bodies of laws have made it difficult or impossible for individuals and institutions, including government institutions, to engage in productive pursuits without violating one or more laws. As a consequence, the temptation arises to offer bribes to government officials to overlook law violations or to facilitate license applications, etc. This form of corruption may temporarily benefit those who engage in it, but it negates the rule of law and leads to loss of respect for governments and laws. However, instead of engaging in the overtly illegal practice of giving bribes, special interests—such as businesses, trade associations and professional organizations—have the legal option, under the lax rules of the traditional method of lawmaking, of designing their own self-serving laws (e.g., tax breaks, "loopholes," tariffs and subsidies) and to pass the burdens of those laws on to the public.

As noted in Chapter 4, the design of a significant proportion of proposed new laws is not performed by legislatures but by special interest groups. If a special interest can convince a legislator to sponsor a bill it has designed (e.g., by means of donations to the legislator's reelection campaign), and if that bill is enacted into law, the special interest gains a legally sanctioned advantage over competitors. The leverage that a special interest gains from its self-serving laws allows it to make additional facilitating contributions to legislators and to design more laws in a never-ending cycle, as depicted in Figure 5-2.

---

[6] The parameters of justice for the people of a government are human rights, living standards and quality of life.

[7] See J. Francois & L. Baughman, "The Unintended Consequences of U.S. Steel Import Tariffs: A Quantification of the Impact During 2002," CITAC Foundation, Trade Partnership Worldwide, LLC, Washington, DC, Feb. 2003 (www.citac-trade.org).

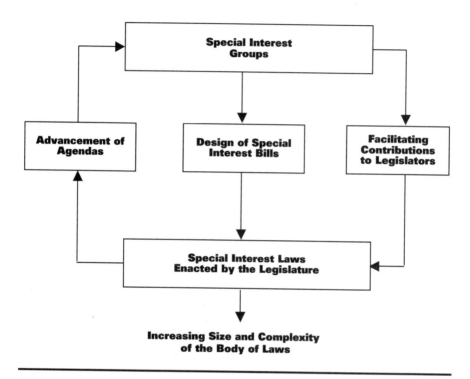

Figure 5-2. The Cycle of Special Interest Law Creation: By designing their own self-serving bills and persuading legislators to sponsor and enact their bills, special interest groups are able to create a favorable legal environment for themselves. As a result of this never-ending cycle, laws that are irrelevant to public needs are enacted, and the bodies of laws of government continually increase in size and complexity.

It should be noted that special interests are not inherently evil or corrupt—every individual, by virtue of his or her life circumstances, inevitably belongs to numerous special interest groups, and those groups have the right to petition the government regarding their matters of concern. However, the process by which special interest laws are presently designed, sponsored and enacted is associated with three major problems for democracies.

First, the donation of money by a special interest to a legislator's reelection campaign fund in return for the legislator's sponsorship of a given piece of legislation is a form of corruption. The problem with this practice is not that special interests support political candidates—a participatory activity that is a protected human right—but rather that the quid-pro-quo process leads legislators to enact laws that are harmful to the public. Legislators and their favored interest groups both benefit by realizing their separate ambitions, but at the cost of loss of the public's respect for the lawmaking process and for laws and legislators, particularly when techniques of deliberate deception are used in the design of bills.[8] Second, to the extent that laws are created by special interests, it is the special interests, not legislators, who "set policy" and, to that same extent, the government is not representative of the people. Third, the enactment of new special interest laws aggravates the problem of the increasing size and complexity of laws.[9]

For these reasons, the corruption that leads to the enactment of special interest legislation by the traditional method of lawmaking is a threat to democracy. When favored interest groups are allowed to create their own self-serving laws in collaboration with legislators, the government is "of the people, by the people and for the special interests." Such a government, which tolerates the misuse of public power for private benefit, can meet the requirements of an electoral or a liberal democracy but can never be a true democracy.

CHAOS

Democracies are obligated to provide order and to remove or mitigate conditions that degrade or threaten to degrade the liberty and well-being of the citizenry. When the traditional method of lawmaking causes more laws to be enacted with each legislative session (as depicted in Figure 5-2 and in Chapter 4, Figure 4-1), the liberty and well-being of the people are compromised by the disorder produced by the increasing size and complexity of the body of laws. Since laws are rarely repealed, the ever-growing body of laws imposes a cumulative burden on the people and becomes so large over time that no one can possibly "know the law" in its entirety. The result is the opposite of order—chaos:

> To the extent that one act is inconsistent with another, the latter act prevails. This allows legislatures to amend and repeal by implication; that is, legislative acts may gloss over past legislation and impose a new rule, yet leave the old, dead law on the statute books. Lawyers and other citizens may then be surprised to find that a statute, apparently relevant to some significant situation, has been superseded. Such negligent legislating leaves statute books in semi-chaos, full of inconsistencies that can be sorted out only by finding the date of each enactment and giving effect to the words last adopted. Sometimes a number of amendatory laws may have to be examined in detail to discover when the inconsistency came into the law.[10]

---

[8] Public opinion polls consistently find that legislators are held in very low esteem, as reflected by the public's ratings of "respected professions" and of "honesty and ethics in professions." See www.harrisinteractiv.com/harris_poll/index.asp.

[9] N. Byrnes & L. Lavelle, "The Corporate Tax Game," Business Week, Mar. 31, 2003, p. 81, on a discussion of the U.S. corporate income tax code: "Major companies can afford to hire high-powered lobbyists to push for tax breaks, creating yet more complexity with added loopholes and exceptions."

[10] Davies, p. 169.

Table 5-2 presents the results of the traditional method of lawmaking for the people of the state of California during the last decade of the twentieth century. The data disclose that the democratically elected federal (United States) and state (California) legislatures produced thousands of new laws (statutes) during that period of time, which, incidentally, is evidence that the previously existing laws were inadequate for their problem-solving tasks.

Year	Number of Enacted "Public Bills," Federal Government of the United States[11]	Number of "Chaptered Measures" (Newly Enacted Bills), Government of California[12]
1990	410	1,785
1991	243	1,374
1992	347	1,521
1993	210	1,430
1994	255	1,449
1995	88	1,086
1996	192	1,257
1997	241	1,087
1998	153	1,263
1999	170	1,166
	2,309 New Federal Statutes	13,418 New State Statutes

Table 5-2. The Chaos of Laws: During the 1990s, the people of the state of California were subjected to a total of 15,727 new federal and state statutes. (This figure substantially understates the total number of new laws because it excludes new county and municipal statutes as well as new case laws and federal, state, county and municipal regulations.) These new statutes were added to the tens of thousands of laws that had been enacted in the previous decades.

Even when each individual law produces a problem-solving benefit to the people, the combined benefits of the aggregate of laws are limited by the "law of diminishing returns."[13] That is, each law interacts with every other law and, beyond a certain point, each new law added to the body of laws produces proportionately less benefit than the preceding law. For example, one law that effectively addresses a certain category of crime, such as burglary, will produce greater societal benefits than no law, and ten anti-burglary laws may be more effective than one law. However, after the enactment of hundreds and then thousands of laws that deal with burglary, the marginal societal benefit of each additional law becomes immeasurably small (see Figure 5-3). As more laws are

---

[11] Source: http://thomas.loc.gov/.

[12] Source: http://leginfo.ca.gov/.

[13] McConnell & Brue, p. 447, on the law of diminishing returns: "as successive units of a variable resource (say, labor) are added to a fixed resource (say, capital or land), beyond some point the extra, or marginal, product attributable to each additional unit of the variable resource will decline."

created under the aegis of the traditional method, as presented in Table 5-2, a state of chaos ensues where no one knows for sure which laws apply to any given situation, and the enforcement of laws must be done selectively, which is, by definition, arbitrary rule. The stage is then set for the rise of demagogues who demand "emergency powers" to restore order and thereby ensconce themselves as the new ruling class of an authoritarian form of government.

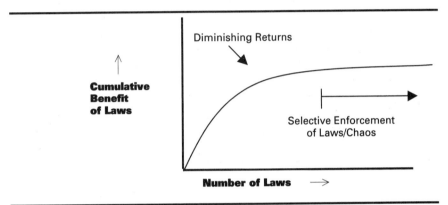

Figure 5-3. The Cumulative Benefit of Laws: As the traditional method continues to generate more and more laws, the incremental benefit of each new law approaches zero according to the law of diminishing returns. When the body of laws becomes so large and chaotic that the laws must be enforced selectively, the rule of law regresses to the rule of man.

Compounding the problem of the law of diminishing returns is the fact that every law restricts freedoms, incurs costs, diverts resources and produces unintended side effects (see Chapter 3). As the number of laws increases, the cumulative burden of laws upon the people also necessarily increases, and the oversized and chaotic body of laws itself becomes a problem. The relationship between the cumulative burden of laws upon the people and the number of laws is diagrammed in Figure 5-4.

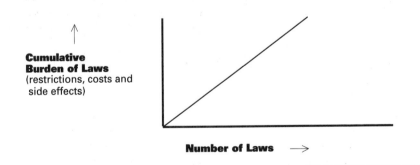

Figure 5-4. The Cumulative Burden of Laws: Every law restricts freedoms, incurs costs, diverts resources and generates unintended side effects. The cumulative burden of laws upon the people increases in proportion to the number of laws produced by the traditional method of lawmaking.

The Usefulness of the Body of Laws

The benefit of a given law is determined by measuring and analyzing the results of its enforcement. The usefulness or net benefit of the law is then derived by subtracting the sum of the burdens it imposes on the people from the benefit it provides. Similarly, for the body of laws as a whole, the relationship between the net benefit of laws and the number of laws can be derived by subtracting the curve of Figure 5-4 (the cumulative burden of laws) from that of Figure 5-3 (the cumulative benefit of laws). By this means, the relative usefulness of the body of laws to the people can be determined as shown in Figure 5-5, and the point of maximum usefulness of the body of laws in the service of democracy can be approximated (see Figure 5-5, condition B). Although it is doubtful that the exact number of laws for maximum usefulness can be derived for any given body of laws, the objective of democratic governments, which are obliged to serve the best interests of the people, is to cause the body of laws to approximate the optimum condition.

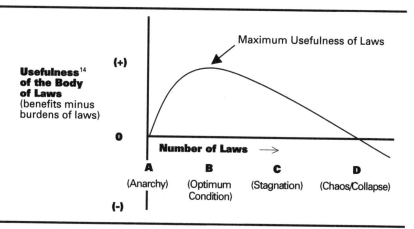

Figure 5-5. Relationship Between the Usefulness of the Body of Laws and the Number of Laws: (derived by subtracting the curve of Figure 5-4 from that of Figure 5-3). **LEGEND: A** = Anarchy: too few laws. **B** = Optimum Condition: the optimum number of laws for maximum usefulness to the citizenry. **C** = Stagnation: too many laws, unduly restricting the liberty of the people and consuming too many resources. **D** = Collapse of society: an overwhelming number of laws, forcing arbitrary law enforcement and the cessation of productive enterprises.

---

[14] The usefulness of the body of laws is measured in terms of the liberty and well-being of the people as a whole, i.e., human rights, living standards and quality of life.

Existing democracies now have far too many ineffective and less than useful laws. As the bodies of laws increase in size and complexity, they draw resources away from essential and productive enterprises and become a problem instead of an asset for the people. The integrity of the rule of law is compromised and the stage is thus set for the regression of democracies to authoritarian forms of government, where laws are arbitrarily enforced for the benefit of ascendant ruling classes. To eliminate this threat to democracy, the traditional method must be modified so that it facilitates rather than impedes the purpose of democracy.

Quality

Quality is defined as the degree of excellence that a given entity possesses. In every sphere of human activity, high quality is a desired commodity. For useful goods and services, quality consists of quantifiable properties—such as effectiveness, safety, cost and reliability—that can be measured empirically (see Appendix B). Since the laws of government are intended to be useful, they can be designed, evaluated and improved by the same generic quality methods and standards that apply to all other useful products. Quality standards for laws and lawmaking hold great promise because they will correct the defects of the traditional method of lawmaking, significantly improve the performance of laws and eliminate the chaos of laws.

Quality of Useful Products

For every institution that produces useful products, resources are limited. Since quality procedures entail planning and the expenditure of resources, those who create useful products exhibit a natural tendency to minimize or ignore quality procedures in an attempt to reduce costs. However, in the mid-twentieth century, investigators in the emerging field of quality debunked the idea that the costs of the design, production and maintenance of useful goods and services could be reduced (and productivity enhanced) by limiting quality.

Leaders such as Juran,[1] Deming[2] and Crosby[3] emphasized that applying quality procedures in the design, production and follow-up evaluation and improvement of goods and services actually *saved* resources by reducing the costs of replacement and redesign of defective products.[4] These leaders also pointed out that consumers prefer high levels of quality in goods and services. Therefore, enterprises that employ quality procedures for their products will have greater success through both lower production and replacement costs and greater customer satisfaction.

The result of the application of quality methods by productive enterprises has been that each new generation of useful products (for example, surgical implements and computers) is characterized by greater effectiveness, simpler operation and other measures of success. When such products occasionally fail or exhibit

---

[1] J.M. Juran, *Juran on Planning for Quality* (New York, NY: The Free Press, 1988).
[2] W.W. Scherkenbach, *The Deming Route to Quality and Productivity* (Washington, DC: CEE Press, 1988).
[3] P.B. Crosby, *Quality Is Free* (New York, NY: McGraw-Hill, 1979).
[4] D.V. Hunt, *Quality in America: How to Implement a Competitive Program* (Homewood, IL: Technology Research Corporation, 1992).

poor performance, the problems are identified through quality programs, and effective measures are taken to correct the problems. The result is that the trend of improved performance of useful products, based upon quality methodologies, is unmistakably positive.

Another significant result is the widespread acceptance of quality, which has produced a "quality culture" in which both producers and consumers have come to expect high quality in useful goods and services. The value of quality has been recognized by regulatory agencies of the U.S. government, such as the Federal Aviation Administration, Federal Drug Administration and Environmental Protection Agency. Their purpose is to ensure high levels of quality—in terms of safety, effectiveness, low environmental impact, etc.—in the design, use and final disposition of goods and services. Government regulations have thus contributed to the quality culture, that is, to the public's expectation of high quality in useful goods and services.[5]

An intriguing question arises: Since quality procedures have proven successful for other useful products, is it possible to develop quality procedures for laws—not only to correct the ineffectiveness and increasing chaos of laws but also to create much more efficacious bodies of laws? The answer to that question is, unequivocally, yes. All that is needed is to adapt well-established quality methods (quality design, quality assurance and quality improvement programs) to laws and lawmaking.[6] Through the application of quality standards, laws can be designed to solve societal problems for the benefit of the "consumers" of laws—the people as a whole. Inefficient, useless and detrimental laws can be identified and either amended to improve their performance or repealed, and the bodies of laws of government can therefore become much more efficacious in the service of democracy.

Existing Quality Programs for Laws

An argument can be made that quality review programs for laws already exist in the form of (1) judicial review of laws, (2) legislative oversight functions and (3) the periodic election of legislators (who defend their voting records in reelection campaigns). These procedures are important for democracies, but they do not meet the rigorous standards of a competent quality program for laws; in effect, quality programs for laws do not yet exist.

JUDICIAL REVIEW

In the United States, if a law is challenged in the courts and found to be in conflict with the Constitution, that law is nullified (repealed). While judicial review of the constitutionality of a law is a form of quality assurance, it is inadequate as a quality procedure because of its limited scope. First, it is a passive process; a law is

---

[5] The quality culture is exemplified by the competition for the annual quality-based Malcolm Baldrige Award (see www.quality.nist.gov).

[6] See, for example, American Society for Quality at http://www.asq.org; and international standards of quality at http://www.iso.org/

reviewed by the judicial branch of government *only* if it is challenged. If a law is unconstitutional but no one challenges it in the courts, it can remain in force indefinitely. Second, the judicial review process deals only with "constitutionality" and does not address a law's performance. Thus a law could impose ruinous economic sanctions on the people or significantly lower their quality of life without violating the letter of present-day constitutions, and such a law would never be repealed or even evaluated by the process of judicial review.

LEGISLATIVE OVERSIGHT

Legislatures have authority over the activities of the government agencies that enforce laws. As currently practiced, the oversight function of the legislature is primarily concerned with the performance of the agencies that carry out the letter of laws rather than with the performance of the laws themselves. Since the oversight function focuses on bureaucracies rather than laws, a legislature may find that a government agency is exemplary in following the dictates of a given law but fail to note that the law wasn't necessary in the first place. Also, as discussed in Chapter 4, legislative committees, where oversight functions take place, are not reliable as a means of deriving relevant knowledge of the performance of laws. So, although the oversight function of legislatures may be the logical beginning point for the initiation of quality programs, it currently has no value as a quality procedure for the evaluation of laws.

PERIODIC ELECTION OF LEGISLATORS

When legislators run for reelection in a democracy, they emphasize their voting record on the proposed new laws, and amendments to existing laws, that were presented to them in the previous legislative session. A legislator who convinces the public that his or her voting record is satisfactory has a reasonable chance of being elected to another term. If a challenger for the legislator's office promises to provide a "better" voting record than the incumbent legislator, the public may choose the challenger over the incumbent. Thus, in theory, the public, through the exercise of its voting rights, will be represented by the legislator whose voting record most closely reflects its needs and desires.

The problem with using a legislator's voting record as a guide for good governance, however, is that voting records are statements of *intentions*, not *results*. A legislator may be intelligent, articulate and charismatic and have a "perfect" voting record in terms of the votes he or she cast in favor of laws that *attempt* to solve societal problems. However, if those laws fail in their purpose (despite the good intentions of the legislator), not only will the resources of the government have been wasted on their enforcement but the societal problems will remain unsolved. The link between voting records and the quality of laws is tenuous at best, and periodic elections cannot be relied upon as an effective quality assurance program for laws.

Thus judicial review, legislative oversight functions and periodic elections are not adequate for the evaluation of laws. If laws are to be consistently effective in the service of democracy, entirely new, rigorous and comprehensive quality programs for laws must be established.

Quality Programs for Laws

Quality programs have significant value in that they seek the highest possible degree of excellence in the design, operation and outcome of products and processes. Quality programs will predictably have an identical effect on laws, resulting in the design and operation of efficacious bodies of laws that optimally serve the purpose of democracy. Quality programs for laws, as for all other useful products, will include (1) quality design, (2) quality assurance and (3) quality improvement programs.[7]

QUALITY DESIGN PROGRAM

The creation of useful products that have an impact upon the public well-being requires that standards of excellence be applied in the design process. High standards are applied to such design efforts both to achieve customer satisfaction (hence, success in the marketplace) and to minimize the risk of defective designs in accordance with government-mandated public safety regulations. In a democracy, that same logic should apply to the design of laws, since the citizens (the "customers" of laws) are the sovereign in a democracy and the government is obligated to serve the best interests of its sovereign. If anything, standards of excellence for the design of laws should be *higher* than standards for any other useful product, since the harm caused by failed laws is potentially far greater than the harm caused by the failure of any other humanmade product.

The problem with the traditional method of lawmaking, as noted in Chapter 4, is that virtually no quality standards exist for the creation or amendment (redesign) of laws. Law designers are currently free to base their law designs upon ideology (opinions), anecdotal data and even known falsehoods rather than reliable and relevant knowledge. No standards are applied to the definition of problems that require legislative solution, the definition of measurable goals or the creation of models that accurately forecast the costs and side effects of proposed new laws. The laws produced by this process are often of flawed design, and may be ineffective and even counterproductive in the solution of societal problems.

If the high purpose of democracy is to be achieved, rigorous standards of excellence must be developed and applied to the lawmaking process. Although laws, like every other product, are designed by fallible human beings, quality design (QD) standards have the potential to minimize human errors and omissions in the law-design process. For the initial QD program for laws, every new law design (bill) and every proposed amendment to an existing law should contain documentation, either in the law or in a summary report of the law, of the following items:

---

[7]   See, for example, D. Schrunk, "Lawmaking Standards for Space Governance," *Space Governance* (a publication of the World Space Bar Association), vol. 4, no. 1 (January 1997), pp. 44-7.

Name(s) of the Designer(s)

The names of the designers of bills and amendments should be made known to the public so that the designers' qualifications and any potential conflicts of interest are known, and assessments of their performance can be made. In a democracy, there is no situation in which the identity of a law designer should not be known to the public.

Identity of the Institution That Employs the Designer(s)

The name of the institution that employs the law designer(s) should be included to ensure that the institution is appropriate for the design task (for example, that it is not a hostile foreign government), and to minimize conflicts of interest between a designer's loyalty to his or her institution and the public at large through the application of effective safeguards.

Relevant Educational Qualifications of the Designer(s)

The educational background of law designers—specifically, their education in design expertise—must be made available to the public to assure that the designers are qualified to create laws. In today's democracies, law designers are not required by law to have an educational background in problem-solving design expertise, and a law designer could satisfy the requirement to list his or her qualifications in this area by stating "none." However, such an admission would be regarded, correctly, as unacceptable and would be expected to lead to a demand by the public for higher educational qualifications for law designers in the future (see Appendix K).

Definition of the Problem Addressed

The fundamental requirement of problem solution is that a problem must be defined before it can be solved; solving a problem that has not been defined is impossible (see Appendix F). Since the only valid purpose for laws in a democracy is to solve societal problems, it is essential that the size and nature of the problem be known before a law is created to solve it.

List of the Existing Laws That Have Failed to Solve the Problem

The existence of a persistent societal problem is *prima facie* evidence that the existing body of laws has failed to solve the problem. For the design of a new law, therefore, it is essential for law designers to first evaluate the laws that currently address the problem but have failed to solve it.[8] Knowledge of the existing laws that have failed to achieve their problem-solving goals will enable designers to avoid repeating the same errors that caused those laws to fail. Also, designers may learn that the problem can be solved by simply correcting the design faults of

---

[8] The objective analysis and reporting of the performance of existing laws is the task of the quality assurance program.

present laws (the task of the quality improvement program for laws) rather than going to the trouble of creating an entirely new law.

Priority of Each Problem Selected for Solution

Every legislature is presented with multiple societal problems in need of solution. Since government resources are limited, it is essential that the most serious problems be given the highest priority. Therefore, every problem must be given a designated priority for solution.[9]

Declaration of Purpose

Every law in a democracy must have a purpose for its existence vis-à-vis its usefulness to the people, as noted by Locke: "The public good is the rule and measure of all law-making. If a thing be not useful to the commonwealth, though it be never so indifferent, it may not presently be established by law."[10] If a law has no stated purpose, one cannot safely assume that the purpose is to benefit the public as required in a democracy. (In fact, the law may have been intended to benefit a special interest to the detriment of the public.) Also, the intent of a law with no stated purpose can be arbitrarily interpreted, by the people who enforce or comply with it, for purposes that are harmful to the public. In addition, it is impossible to determine, by means of quality assurance programs, the performance of a law that has no stated purpose. For these reasons it is critical that the purpose of every law be clearly stated.

Justification for the Sanction by Which the Law Will Achieve Its Goal

In a democracy, law designers must select sanctions for laws on the basis of the predicted optimum outcome for the people and, at the very least, on the principle of "do no harm." A statement that justifies the selection of the forcing mechanism for a new law design must therefore be provided. If the measured performance of a law is significantly different from the predicted performance, the design error(s) in the selection of the sanction must be investigated, documented and corrected through quality assurance and quality improvement programs.

Predicted Costs

An elementary consideration for the design of a law is an estimation of its total direct and indirect costs (see Chapter 3 and Appendix E). If the purpose of democracy is to be achieved, the short- and long-term costs of a law to the people, individually and as a whole, must be kept to a minimum and must be less than the benefit of the law. The designers of laws, for example, must account for the long-term consequences of their designs (and not just the impact on the next election cycle). An estimation of the costs of a new law is also useful for subse-

---

[9] One of the principal deliberative tasks of legislatures is to assign priorities to problems. For reelection purposes, the legislator's record on the selection of priorities for problem solution would be much more informative to the public than the legislator's voting record on the enactment of new laws.

[10] J. Locke, *A Letter Concerning Toleration,* Great Books of the Western World, vol. 35, p. 11.

quent investigations. If the actual costs of a law are significantly different from the estimated costs, the design errors (of the modeling process that was used to forecast costs) must be investigated, documented and corrected.

Predicted Side Effects

Enforced laws generate unintended and potentially harmful side effects upon the human rights, living standards and/or quality of life of the people. To satisfy the purpose of democracy, law designers must keep the number and severity of a law's side effects to a minimum. The design process must therefore include an effective means of assessing the risks to the people of each new law. A statement of the predicted side effects (as well as the methods that were used to assess these risks) will inform the public that the potential short- and long-term side effects have been examined and that they are projected to be within acceptable limits.[11] If the actual side effects of an enforced law are significantly different from the predicted side effects, the design error(s) of the model used to forecast side effects must be investigated, documented and corrected.

Methods for Monitoring the Efficacy of the Law

To ensure that a given law is just, the legislature must be able to determine that the enforcement of that law satisfied its intent in an effective, timely, cost-efficient, safe and user-friendly manner. To reach that determination, the designers of the law must include a statement of the effective empirical methods by which the performance of the law (e.g., the "benchmarks" or "milestones" of performance) will be monitored. Knowledge of the performance of laws will permit the legislature to repeal those laws that do not satisfy the purpose of democracy.

Citation of All References Used in the Law's Creation

Laws are often ineffective, and they occasionally fail. Reasons for the failure of laws include faulty design methods and databases, and it is therefore critical that designers cite all the references used in the design of the law. If the performance of a given law is found to be less than satisfactory, a review of the cited design methods and databases will disclose if irrelevant or unreliable information sources were mistakenly used in its design. The requirement for a citation of references will thus provide a guide, or "paper trail," for correcting design flaws and omissions.

To assure that the meaning of each new law design is clear, all of the aforementioned points must be organized and written in a simple and succinct manner, as recommended by Montesquieu:

> *The style* [of laws] *should also be plain and simple, a direct expression being better understood than an indirect one. There is no majesty at all in the laws of the lower empire; princes are made to speak like rhetoricians. When the*

---

[11] The summary statement of the competent investigation of the potential side effects of a law will be analogous to the environmental impact statement that is required for real estate construction projects.

style of laws is inflated, they are looked upon only as a work of parade and ostentation.... The laws ought not to be subtle; they are designed for people of common understanding, not as an art of logic....[12]

These initial QD standards will ensure that societal problems will receive an appropriate priority for solution and that the laws that address those problems will be created through competent design procedures.

QUALITY ASSURANCE PROGRAM

A quality assurance (QA) program for laws will inform citizens of the status of their democracy by answering the question: "How well are our laws performing?" By identifying less-than-useful laws, the QA program will allow legislatures to "weed out" the laws that degrade and threaten democracy.

The QA program will be a never-ending process that will conduct periodic, thorough and objective analyses of every law of government. If the QA program determines that a given law is a suitable problem-solving instrument in the service of democracy, the legislature will be justified in maintaining the enforcement of that law. If the QA program determines that a law is not an efficacious instrument of democracy, the legislature will have grounds to repeal the law or to amend it through a program of quality improvement to optimize its performance.[13] A QA program will give legislatures the knowledge needed to maintain an optimally performing body of laws that satisfies the purpose of democracy. QA standards apply to both the structure and the mechanics of laws.

Structure of Laws

For a given body of laws, the first and simplest step of a QA program will be to identify and repeal those laws that are structurally incapable of being useful to the citizenry. Laws that are found to have structural flaws in their wording and punctuation ("the letter of the law") will be submitted to the legislature for repeal or for referral to a quality improvement program. Structural defects of laws include:

FAILURE TO ADDRESS A SOCIETAL PROBLEM. A law that does not address a problem cannot serve any useful purpose in a democracy.

LACK OF PROBLEM DEFINITION. A problem that has not been defined cannot be solved, and it may be nonexistent.

---

[12] Montesquieu, pp. 266-7.

[13] QA and QI programs for laws can be expected to add at least 10 percent to the costs of laws, but those costs will be more than offset by the savings that accrue from the elimination of laws that do not accomplish their purpose and those that produce unacceptable costs or side effects.

OMINIBUS APPROACH. Omnibus laws (the compilation of multiple laws into a single large law) are unnecessarily complex and unwieldy, and the results of their enforcement, including their interaction with other laws, are difficult if not impossible to determine.[14]

LACK OF A STATED, MEASURABLE GOAL. The purpose of a law must be a goal that can be objectively and accurately measured by empirical methods. A goal that is ambiguous or nonquantifiable, such as "to enhance educational opportunities," is therefore unacceptable.

VAGUENESS. Vague and convoluted laws are subject to misinterpretations that can subvert the intention of the legislature and cause harm to the people.

FAILURE TO CITE REFERENCES. When a law does not cite references, the only safe assumption is that the law was designed without the benefit of knowledge—a condition that cannot be tolerated for any product that has an effect upon the well-being of the public. (The vast majority of laws currently do not cite references to reliable, relevant sources of knowledge—and they will need to undergo considerable design upgrades through the quality improvement program in order to meet QA requirements.)

Mechanics of Laws

The QA program will also evaluate the mechanics (cause and effects) of laws. Measuring the results of the enforcement of a law (problem-solving benefit, restrictions, costs and side effects) and comparing those results with the original intent of the law will verify the validity of each law in its service to democracy. The QA analysis of the mechanics, or performance, of each law will provide the legislature with the knowledge needed to determine if a law should remain in force, be repealed or be amended. The QA program of the mechanics of laws will recommend that laws be *repealed* by the legislature if they:

VIOLATE HUMAN RIGHTS. Laws that violate human rights are at direct odds with the purpose of democracy and must be repealed.

FAIL TO ACHIEVE THEIR STATED GOAL, OR PURPOSE. Laws that fail to satisfy the purpose of democracy are unacceptable for democracies. Also, if the specified goal of the law cannot be *measured* by empirical means, there can be no assurance that the law, no matter how well intended, has achieved its stated goal, and there is a possibility that the law is more harmful than beneficial. Therefore, laws whose results cannot be reliably measured must be repealed.

IMPOSE BURDENS THAT ARE GREATER THAN THEIR BENEFIT. Detrimental laws are contrary to the purpose of democracy.

ARE NOT ENFORCED. Laws that are not enforced cannot benefit the public.

---

[14] As noted in Chapter 4, omnibus laws are a means for enacting dubious special interest laws that have little if any value to the public at large—laws that would otherwise never be enacted. QA and QI programs for laws will ferret out these laws and designate them for redesign or repeal.

IMPOSE BURDENS THAT ARE EQUAL TO THEIR BENEFIT. A law whose problem-solving benefit is no greater than the sum of its costs and side effects provides a net benefit of zero to the people and is, by definition, useless. Since useless laws consume and divert resources and add to the confusion and complexity of the body of laws, they detract from the purpose of democracy.

HAVE NOT UNDERGONE A QA REVIEW WITHIN A TEN-YEAR PERIOD. Laws exist in a dynamic societal environment. Each law must periodically undergo a QA review to confirm that it continues to serve a useful purpose for the people as a whole. Any law that has not undergone a QA review within a ten-year period must be automatically repealed on the presumption that it has become outmoded. Application of this "sunset rule" will result in a body of laws that contains only those laws that have been currently and objectively demonstrated to be useful to the people.[15] If a given law is repealed by the ten-year sunset rule and it is subsequently determined, by reliable measurements and analyses, that the lack of that law is detrimental to the people as a whole, the law can then be reinstated. The automatic repeal of laws that have not undergone a QA review will also be a stimulus to the legislature to keep the QA program on schedule and to keep the number of laws to a minimum.

By leading to the repeal of defective and less-than-useful laws, a QA program will substantially enhance the performance of the body of laws in the service of democracy. The problem of the chaos of laws will be relieved and the resources that had been consumed by the repealed laws will be released for more useful purposes.

QUALITY IMPROVEMENT PROGRAM

The quality improvement (QI) program for laws will amend laws and thus enhance their performance in the service of democracy. (Amendments are *design* changes and, as such, must meet the previously stated quality standards for the design of laws. QD standards will prevent useful laws from being degraded by the amendment process.) The QI program will correct errors in the design of laws, enhance their performance and prevent them from becoming outmoded in a dynamic environment, as noted by Plato:

> And is not the aim of the legislator similar? First, he desires that his laws should be written down with all possible exactness; in the second place, as time goes on and he has made an actual trial of his decrees, will he not find omissions? Do you imagine that there ever was a legislator so foolish as not to know that many things are necessarily omitted, which someone coming after

---

[15] Legislatures occasionally insert a "sunset" provision into a law so that the law will expire after a given period of time unless it is reviewed by the legislature and reinstated. The ten-year QA provision will subject *every* law to the sunset rule.

him must correct, if the constitution and the order of government is not to deteriorate, but to improve in the state which he has established? [16]

The goal of these design changes is to create laws that approximate the ideal law (see Appendix I) by becoming more effective, cost-efficient and user-friendly Laws will be referred to the QI program if they:

HAVE STRUCTURAL DEFECTS. Laws that have structural defects but were not repealed by the QA program will be amended by the QI program to have their structural defects corrected.

HAVE ONLY MARGINAL USEFULNESS. Useful laws whose benefits are found to be only marginally greater than the sum of their burdens by the QA program must be amended to have their performance improved.

INTERFERE WITH THE PERFORMANCE OF OTHER LAWS. Laws often interact with one another. If the QA program determines that the enforcement of a given law degrades the performance of other laws, the interacting laws must be redesigned so that they do not interfere with one another. Ideally, the interactions of laws should be synergistic.

The QD program will channel design efforts into the creation of laws that optimally serve the purpose of democracy. However, the application of this program will not completely eliminate design imperfections. (Law designers and their methodologies will never be infallible.) The value of QA and QI programs will then become apparent because they will identify and correct design imperfections, and permit every law—through many cycles of QA and QI—to approximate the ideal law.[17]

It should be noted that with quality programs, as with every other government program, it is possible to have "too much of a good thing," and a significant proportion of a government's resources could be dedicated to quality programs for laws. Therefore, quality programs will also be subject to quality review. For example, QA procedures will be applied to the quality programs for laws to maintain their cost-effectiveness. The promise of quality programs for laws is that they will result in the creation of laws that are more efficacious in the service of democracy.

---

[16] Plato, p. 706.
[17] A QA program for laws will provide feedback to a legislature so that QI corrections can be made. A QA program will thus be the "feedback loop" that converts the lawmaking system of a government from a feed-forward control system to a feedback control system (see Appendix C).

CHAPTER 7

Quality Solutions for Societal Problems

Laws of government are essential for the liberty and well-being of the people, as John Locke pointed out in *Concerning Civil Government:*

> *For in all the states of created beings, capable of laws, where there is no law there is no freedom. For liberty is to be free from restraint and violence from others, which cannot be where there is no law; and is not, as we are told, "a liberty for every man to do what he lists." For who could be free, when every other man's humour might domineer over him? But a liberty to dispose and order freely as he lists his person, actions, possessions, and his whole property within the allowance of those laws under which he is, and therein not to be subject to the arbitrary will of another, but freely follow his own.*[1]

In meeting the requirements of democracy, governments use laws to address societal problems such as poverty, homelessness and illiteracy. But laws have either failed or had little success in their attempts to resolve these problems. Why? Because, as noted in Chapter 3, although laws have the characteristics of tools, they are presently designed without benefit of any formal engineering discipline—in stark contrast with all other sophisticated tools. To remedy this situation and improve the performance of laws in the service of democracy, quality design (QD) standards must be developed for the creation of laws. When quality programs are implemented, the process by which laws are designed and amended will become a new creative science, the *engineering discipline of laws,* and the corroborative study of the structure and mechanics of laws will be performed by a new investigative science, the *science of laws.* (See discussions of Engineering, Appendix E, and Science, Appendix D.)

---

[1] Locke, *Concerning Civil Government,* p. 37.

The Proper Role of Legislators

The authority to create, amend, repeal and enact laws is vested in the legislative branch of governments, and the office of legislator is one of the most powerful positions in government:

> *What is a power, but the ability or faculty of doing a thing? What is the ability to do a thing but the power of employing the means necessary to its execution? What is a LEGISLATIVE power but a power of making LAWS? What are the means to execute a LEGISLATIVE power but LAWS? What is the power of laying and collecting taxes, but a legislative power, or a power of making laws, to lay and collect taxes? What are the proper means of executing such a power but necessary and proper laws?* [2]

For the lawmakers of authoritarian governments, the task of lawmaking is as simple as issuing an order (which may be based on political expediency, whim, the enjoyment of exercising power, etc.) and having that order transcribed and enacted into a new law. The legislators of democracies, however, have the much more difficult task of creating the quality and quantity of laws that optimally satisfy the purpose of democracy. If legislators fail to create a sufficient number of effective laws, the public well-being will be adversely affected by crime and other social pathologies. But if, on the other hand, legislators create too many laws, the liberty of the people will be unduly restricted and the general welfare will be degraded by the diversion of limited resources into the enforcement of unnecessary laws (see Figure 5-5, Chapter 5). The challenge for the legislature of a democratic government, therefore, is to create a body of laws that serves the best interests of the people at all times. The problem is that legislators are unable to design laws that meet that challenge. Why? What are the qualities of the individuals who reach the position of legislator in a democracy? For the most part, legislators are respectable, responsible and likable, as noted by Davies:

> *Legislators come to their position through politics. Every legislator has some quality attractive to voters. That quality may be good sense; or it may be captivating friendliness and good humor. Or it may be impressive intelligence, irresistible ambition, utter decency, or some combination of these traits. By and large legislators are attractive, pleasant, and reasonably capable citizens selected by peers to hold positions of responsibility.* [3]

In addition, most legislators have one or more college degrees. However, while these attributes are admirable, they do not qualify legislators to be competent law designers. The fact is that legislators have the *power* to design laws, by virtue of their position in government, but they do not have the *expertise* to design laws that satisfy the purpose of democracy. This statement is not meant to deni-

---

[2] Hamilton, p. 107.
[3] Davies, p. 35.

grate legislators; *no one* currently has the expertise and tools required to design laws that satisfy the purpose of democracy. In any case, as pointed out in Chapter 4, legislators rarely, if ever, design laws themselves. Instead they rely upon others, such as special interest groups and government agencies, to create new laws.

The question arises: If the legislators in a democracy lack the qualifications to design laws and in fact rarely do so, what is the proper role of legislators? The answer is offered by Mill:

> *I know not how a representative assembly can more usefully employ itself than in talk, when the subject of talk is the great public interests of the country, and every sentence of it represents the opinion either of some important body of persons in the nation, or of an individual in whom some such body have reposed their confidence. A place where every interest and shade of opinion in the country can have its cause even passionately pleaded, in the face of the government and of all other interests and opinions, can compel them to listen, and either comply, or state clearly why they do not, is in itself, if it answered no other purpose, one of the most important political institutions that can exist anywhere, and one of the foremost benefits of free government.[4] [and]...it would soon be recognised that, in legislation as well as administration, the only task to which a representative assembly can possibly be competent is not that of doing the work, but of causing it to be done.[5]*

After legislators have discussed a problem and prioritized it for solution, therefore, they should *not* undertake the task of designing a law to solve the problem because they lack the requisite skills to do so. The legislators of a democracy are the representatives, or *trustees,* of the people; they are responsible for discussing important issues, making strategic decisions and delegating complex lawmaking tasks to those who are qualified to design laws.

The proper role of the legislature in identifying problems and delegating design tasks is illustrated by the 1985 decision of the U.S. Congress to proceed with the development of a new fighter airplane for the nation's defense. That decision was based on the collective perception of Congress that the lack of a new fighter aircraft would compromise the safety of the people of the United States. The Congress then authorized the government to sign contracts with two aircraft manufacturers to design and build prototype aircraft for a "fly-off" competition. The contractor whose aircraft won that competition would be selected to manufacture the aircraft. The conditions of the contracts were met, a fly-off competition was held, and the winning aircraft design for the officially designated F-22 was selected.

---

[4] Mill, p. 361.
[5] Mill, p. 360.

In this example, legislators were strategic decision makers: They decided, by means of debate and deliberation, that a fighter plane was needed; they awarded contracts for two competing designs; and they approved the production contract. But they played no role in the *design* of either aircraft. Although the legislators had the power to require that they should be the aircraft designers, they did not do so. Why? Because they did not have the knowledge or expertise needed to design fighter aircraft. And even if they did have superior qualifications as aircraft designers, they would not have undertaken the design task because their time was needed for their principal and much more important task: directing the solution of societal problems. Therefore the legislators made the decision to proceed with the design of a fighter aircraft but, as trustees acting in the best interest of the citizenry, they delegated that design responsibility to experts in aircraft design.

That same role for legislators—of making decisions about work to be done on a priority basis and then assuring that the work is performed in a competent manner in the best interests of the people—should also apply, for exactly the same reasons, to the creation and optimization of the laws of government. The problem with this scenario is that no individual or institution is now qualified to create laws that efficaciously solve the problems of society. Incredibly, no school provides an education in the subject of law design; in fact, the world's major universities teach design expertise for every utilitarian field (computers, communications, energy production, waste management, transportation, etc.) *except* lawmaking.

Many people assume that law schools educate future lawyers on the solution of societal problems through the creation of laws, but that assumption is incorrect. Law schools teach students how to create and interpret written legal contracts that assign tasks and responsibilities to various parties, but do not teach design expertise for the efficacious solution of societal problems. (This observation is not a criticism of law schools or lawyers—teaching design expertise for the solution of societal problems is not in the charter of law schools) Although a high level of design expertise is mandatory in other fields that create useful products, it is not required in the creation of laws (see Table 7-1). This poses a dilemma for the legislatures of democratic governments. Legislators now accept the law designs proffered by outside institutions, such as special interest groups, but they cannot be sure that such laws are in the best interests of the people.

How can legislators overcome the present lack of design expertise in lawmaking and create bodies of laws that satisfy the purpose of democracy? The competent design of useful products requires quality design standards, supporting sciences and a high level of relevant education for designers; in other words, it requires the methodologies and principles of engineering (see Appendix E). To satisfy these requirements for the design of laws, a new branch of engineering, the engineering discipline of laws, needs to be created.

Useful Products	Formal Design Discipline (University Degree Program)	Nominal Design-Expertise Education Requirement of Design Team Leader	Compliance With Quality Design Standards?	Supporting Science (Principal Base of Reliable Knowledge)
Transport Aircraft	aeronautical engineering	Ph.D.	yes	aeronautics
Treatments for Cancer	genetic (biomolecular) engineering	Ph.D.- M.D.	yes	cell biology
Laws of Government	none	none[6]	no[7]	none[8]
Biodegradable Plastics	chemical engineering	Ph.D.	yes	organic chemistry
Nuclear Power Reactors	nuclear engineering	Ph.D.	yes	nuclear physics

Table 7-1. Examples of Current Practices for the Creation of Useful Products: Design expertise, adherence to quality standards of design and reliance upon supporting knowledge bases characterize every responsible design field except lawmaking. These examples could be extended for hundreds of other useful products and design disciplines, and the same pattern would hold.

The Engineering Discipline of Laws

A problem-solving discipline for a given class of problems may be classified as a branch of engineering if it is consistently able to create efficacious solutions for that class of problems. The advent of quality design (QD) and quality improvement (QI) standards for laws, such as those discussed in Chapter 6, will lead to the development of the engineering discipline of laws and the emergence of competent law-design institutions whose specific task is to create laws that meet the requirements of democracy. Mill anticipated the need for competent law-design institutions by his call for a "Commission of legislation" that would have the charter and expertise to "make the laws":

There is hardly any kind of intellectual work which so much needs to be done, not only by experienced and exercised minds, but by minds trained to the task through long and laborious study, as the business of making laws....every provision of a law requires to be framed with the most accurate

---

[6] College courses that teach design expertise (e.g., modeling, simulation) in the solution of societal problems are not part of the formal curriculum of any school. The result is that problem-solving design expertise cannot currently be brought to bear on the creation of laws.

[7] There are no quality design standards for laws. The final version of a bill needs only to comply with the legislature's established style and format for laws. (See *Style Manual: Drafting Suggestions for the Trained Drafter.*)

[8] The design of laws is currently based on dogma and anecdotes, not reliable knowledge.

and long-sighted perception of its effect on all the other provisions; and the law when made should be capable of fitting into a consistent whole with the previously existing laws....Any government fit for a high state of civilization would have as one of its fundamental elements a small body...who should act as a Commission of legislation, [and] have for its appointed office to make the laws....[The Commission] should remain as a permanent institution, to watch over the work, protect it from deterioration, and make further improvements as often as required. No one would wish that this body should of itself have any power of enacting laws: the Commission would only embody the element of intelligence in their construction....No measure would become a law until expressly sanctioned by Parliament.[9]

Since the majority of individuals who now design laws are unable to meet quality standards for law design, the advent of standards will lead to a pressing need for qualified law designers. To satisfy that need, an engineering college curriculum that provides an education in law design will need to be established (see Appendix K).

EMERGENCE OF THE ENGINEERING DISCIPLINE OF LAWS

The new engineering field of law design will not become a mature discipline for decades even if QD standards are implemented immediately. However, the field can be organized in a relatively short time by assembling a scientific society of peers consisting primarily of engineers, scientists and related professionals with specialized knowledge of design methods and tools as those methods and tools pertain to the efficacious solution of societal problems (see Appendix H).

Since laws are software (see Chapter 3), the engineering discipline of laws will be a branch of software engineering. It will be separate and distinct from the institutions of government, and its principal obligation will be to create, maintain and improve design methods and standards of excellence for creating laws that satisfy the purpose of democracy. It will provide the forum for the exchange of ideas and will be the repository for knowledge of law design and associated methodologies. The emergence of the engineering discipline of laws will, in effect, cause the traditional method of lawmaking to be replaced by the problem-solving method (see Table 7-2) and will play a key role in the ascendancy of democracy.

---

[9] Mill, pp. 359-60.

	Traditional Method of Lawmaking	Problem-Solving Method[10]
Characterization of Problem	no requirement[11]	1. Identify problem. 2. Assign priority for solution. 3. Analyze problem.
Creation and Implementation of Solution	1. Generate ideas for solutions (ideation). 2. Create preliminary design of solution (bill drafting). 3. Participate in debate and propose amendments (legislative process). 4. Implement solution (enact bill into law).	4. Define measurable problem-solving goal. 5. Define allowable limits of operation for the solution. 6. Perform literature search.[12] 7. Generate ideas for solutions (ideation). 8. Create preliminary design of solution (modeling of solution). 9. Test, analyze and refine model of solution. 10. Implement solution.
Follow-Up Measures	no requirement	11. Evaluate solution performance. 12. Optimize design of solution.
Result	more laws	efficacious problem solution

Table 7-2. Comparison of the Traditional Method of Lawmaking and the Problem-Solving Method: The traditional method of lawmaking (idea → bill → law) is an opinion-based design process that is unable to meet the problem-solving requirements of democracy. The application of quality procedures to lawmaking will lead to the development of the knowledge-based engineering discipline of laws, which will employ the problem-solving method to create laws that satisfy the purpose of democracy.

---

[10] See Appendices E and F.

[11] Congressional hearings are occasionally held for the purpose of acquiring testimony about a given societal problem. However, there are no regular, competent processes by which the traditional method analyzes problems prior to attempting their solution by means of laws.

[12] Although a literature search (the search and retrieval of reliable knowledge/databases) is listed as a separate step, it is typically an ongoing process that involves the entire problem-solving exercise. If the literature search uncovers a suitable existing solution, that solution will be implemented and there will be no need to undergo steps 7, 8 and 9.

THE FUTURE LAW-DESIGN INDUSTRY

As quality programs are implemented and evolve, a new, competent, competitive, regulated and for-profit engineering law-design industry will supplant the present law-design industry. This new, evolving industry, which will employ the problem-solving method for the design of laws, will be marked by three important differences from the traditional method of lawmaking—differences that will dramatically improve the performance of laws in relation to the best interests of the people.

First, the legislature will conduct an open and competitive bidding process by which contracts for the design of laws will be awarded to law-design institutions. Bidding protocols will require that prospective contractors meet QD standards established by the legislature. In contrast with the undocumented practices of the present lawmaking industry, legislatures (hence the public) will know the names, affiliations, qualifications and potential conflicts of interest of the individuals and institutions that design laws. The advent of open, competitive bidding for design contracts—and the profits that ensue—will establish a link between success in the marketplace and laws that optimally solve societal problems. The practices of secrecy and deception now employed in the creation of legal advantages for special interests will be replaced by innovation and design expertise in the creation of laws that satisfy the purpose of democracy.

Second, the legislature will oversee the work of all law-design institutions to ensure that these institutions comply with the established QD standards. As a result, the public will have a much higher regard for the lawmaking process.

Third, quality standards will act as a filter that permits the enactment of only those laws that are designed to serve the best interests of the people (see Figure 7-1), and the connection between special interests and the enactment of laws favorable to special interests but detrimental to the people (see Figure 5-2, Chapter 5) will be effectively severed.

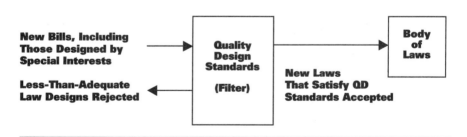

Figure 7-1. Design Standards—The Quality "Filter" for New Laws: Quality design standards will serve as a filter that accepts only bills that are designed to serve the purpose of democracy, thus blocking the enactment of nonproductive laws.

Special interest groups will still be able to design bills and make financial contributions to legislators (as a political right). However, only those bills that meet QD standards will have a chance of being enacted, and the donation of money to legislators by a special interest will not result in a new law favorable to that special interest unless, fortuitously, that law also happens to be beneficial for the people as a whole. As a result, the significant efforts and large amounts of money now expended by special interests to influence the design of laws will be to no avail and will, predictably, decrease dramatically. The ultimate goal of "campaign finance reform" will thus be reached, not by limiting the flow of money to legislators from special interests, but by simply applying QD standards to law-making. QD standards will also block the enactment of all other laws that are not designed to serve the purpose of democracy such as pork barrel legislation and laws that create gerrymandered congressional districts.

These measures will ensure that high standards, transparency and accountability will characterize the design of laws, and the present laissez-faire, undocumented law-design industry will be replaced by a regulated, competitive knowledge industry based on engineering standards and methodologies.

QUALITY DESIGN OF NEW LAWS

The proposed relationship between a democratic legislature and the engineering discipline of laws is illustrated by the following example. Suppose that a legislature, through the process of debate and deliberation, decided that the proportion of people who have no health insurance is a significant societal problem that needs to be solved by government action. To solve the problem in a manner that satisfies the purpose of democracy, the legislature would assign the problem a high priority for solution. It would then appropriate government funds for the solution of the problem and ask for bids from qualified law-design corporations to create a law solution that would substantially improve the access, affordability and range of options of health insurance for individuals while providing a net benefit to the people as a whole. The size of the law-design contract would likely be on the order of several billion dollars. (For comparison, the present cost of creating a new pharmaceutical in accordance with QD standards is on the order of $800 to $900 million.[13]) The legislature would review submitted bids for the design task from law-design corporations, select what it judged to be the best bid and award the design contract to the winning bidder.

To comply with law-design standards, the winning contractor would follow the steps of the problem-solving method. It would analyze the size and complexity of the problem and examine the reasons for the failure of existing laws to solve the problem. (The review of existing laws might reveal that some laws exacerbate the problem and that the repeal of those detrimental laws would help solve the problem; it might even disclose that the repeal of existing detrimental laws would eliminate the need for a new law.) The contractor would then proceed to set goals;

---

[13] C. Ezzell, "The Price of Pills," *Scientific American* (July 2003), p. 25.

gather relevant, reliable knowledge; explore and select ideas for the solution; and design and test models of a health insurance bill. The successful modeling and simulation of the dynamics of the bill—an enormous undertaking for the engineering discipline of laws—would rely to a significant extent upon university affiliations in the fields of computer and software engineering, economics,[14] sociology and statistics.

The proposed new law would be designed so that milestones of its performance could be measured accurately by empirical means and could be reached with a minimum of restrictions, costs and undesirable side effects upon the people, individually and as a whole. The law would also be designed so that, to the greatest extent possible, all the involved parties (such as insurance policy holders; patients; hospital administrations; public health officials; consumer representatives; health care providers; and insurance, pharmaceutical and medical equipment companies), acting in their own best interests, would be positively motivated to assure the law's success. (One of the strengths of the engineering discipline of laws is that it will account for the human impact of laws, thus correcting a major flaw of the traditional method of lawmaking.) After meeting all the design criteria, the contractor would submit the final bill to the legislature for review. If the legislature approved the bill, the bill would be enacted into law, and the enforcement and QA/QI phases of the problem-solving process would begin. (The designers would designate approximately 10 percent of the total budget of the law for QA and QI programs.)

If objective and reliable follow-up evaluations of the law disclosed design flaws or poor performance, such as a decline in affordability of health insurance or a decline in the quality of health care (a process that would take years or decades of study), the legislature would ask the original contractor to make design improvements. Alternatively, the legislature would hold a second bidding process to select another law-design corporation to improve the performance of the law.

QUALITY IMPROVEMENT OF EXISTING LAWS

When QA standards for laws are implemented, the laws that have design defects will be identified and will be either repealed or redesigned (amended) to improve their performance. The redesign of laws will be conducted by the law-design industry according to the same high-quality standards used to direct the design of new laws, as depicted in Figure 7-1.

An example of a body of laws in need of redesign to improve its performance is the tax code of the U.S. federal government. In engineering parlance, the tax code is a "Rube Goldberg" device, or "kluge" (the opposite of an elegant design); it is unnecessarily complex and requires an inordinate amount of effort to

---

[14] See, for example, McConnell and Brue; and S. Maurice and C. Thomas, *Managerial Economics*, 6th ed. (Madison WI: McGraw-Hill, 1999).

accomplish its purpose. Byrnes and Lavelle commented on the U.S. corporate income tax code:

> *...a tax code that has become ridiculously complex, a result of the annual welter of revisions from Congress and dogged work by an army of lobbyists....In 1913, one compilation of federal tax rules and regulations was 400 PAGES long. Today—with commentaries, interpretations, and many court cases—it weighs in at a staggering 54,846 pages: 16 FEET OF SOLID PAPER.*[15]

The trend of the traditional method of lawmaking to create bodies of laws that are increasingly complex and unmanageable is starkly contrasted with the rule of engineering, which holds that change in each new generation of engineering product is always characterized by improvement in terms of greater effectiveness, cost efficiency, user friendliness and other measures of success. When a QI program for laws is instituted, legislatures will contract with qualified engineering firms to optimize the design of laws (Table 7-2, item 12) so that laws will approach the design and performance parameters of the ideal law (see Appendix I). The rule of engineering will then apply to the laws of government and the present trend of the increasing chaos of laws will be reversed. The result will be increased productivity, under the rule of law, of all public and private institutions and, predictably, widespread socio-economic gains. Also, public respect for laws and government will increase when legislatures demonstrate that they are working to improve the performance of government for the people's benefit. The application and repetition of this general process will lead to the development of the engineering discipline of laws and a qualified law-design industry, which will work synergistically with legislatures to create laws that satisfy the purpose of democracy.

THE NEED FOR OBJECTIVE EVALUATIONS OF LAWS

The engineering process is not complete until a newly designed product (tool) has been evaluated to determine that it has attained its design objectives. If the evaluation program discloses that the product did not meet its goal, either the product is redesigned or an entirely new problem-solving effort is initiated. If the evaluation program discloses that the design goal has been met, the initial engineering process is then, and only then, complete.

To complete the design process of laws, therefore, the performance of each law must be evaluated, after its enactment, by a reliable and objective testing program. The validation of the performance of laws is a task for the QA program as described in Chapter 6. The QA program will inform the legislature—and the people—whether or not the purpose of democracy has been satisfied by the law's enforcement. If the QA program is unable to demonstrate that a given law pro-

---

[15] Byrnes and Lavelle, pp. 80-1.

vides a net benefit to the people as a whole, that law will be returned to the legislature for repeal or redesign. This process will eliminate the threat to democracy from useless and detrimental laws and reduce the expense, complexity, impediments and adverse side effects of the body of laws. A QA program is absolutely essential for the proper operation of a democracy (see Table 7-2, item 11).

A primary requirement for a QA program for laws is reliability, which entails accurate and thorough evaluations of laws. It would be tragic if the QA program proved unreliable and failed to identify useless and detrimental laws, or inadvertently caused the repeal of efficacious laws. The challenge in establishing and operating a QA program for laws, therefore, is to apply analytical tools and methods that are consistently accurate and thorough. The problem is that the requirement of reliability excludes virtually all the institutions that have traditionally investigated laws. For example, governments, political parties, "think tanks," trade unions, professional groups, corporations and news organizations have an interest in and routinely investigate selected aspects of various laws. However, these organizations are compromised by a number of factors including conflict of interest, actual or perceived bias,[16] lack of expertise or thoroughness, and/or political or self-serving agendas (see Committee Hearings discussion, Chapter 4).

An entirely new investigative organization that has none of the drawbacks of existing organizations is needed if an effective QA program is to be established for laws; and, to satisfy the requirement of reliability, that organization can *only* be a branch of science The immense value of science over every other field of inquiry is that it is, to the greatest extent possible, consistently accurate, thorough, honest and objective, i.e., *reliable*, in its evaluation and description of the structure and mechanics of the physical world (see Appendix D). Since laws produce profound effects upon the physical world, which is the domain of science, they are eminently suitable subjects for evaluation by science. A new investigative science, the science of laws,[17] which will derive reliable (scientific) knowledge of laws and serve as the foundation for the QA program of laws, is hereby proposed.

The Science of Laws

In a democracy, legislatures enact laws with the expectation that societal problems will be solved or mitigated to benefit the citizenry. However, after a given law is enacted, *no feedback process is currently employed* to determine if that law accomplished its goal. Thus legislatures and the people they serve are ignorant of the real-world effects of their laws and no one can know the degree to which the laws of present democratic governments are satisfying the purpose of democracy. This lack of knowledge is a serious problem because laws are as capable of producing harm as benefits. In fact some well-intended laws may actually be doing signifi-

---

[16] For example, see B. Goldberg, *Bias: A CBS Insider Exposes How the Media Distort the News* (Washington, DC: Regnery Publishing, Inc., 2002).

[17] D. Schrunk, "The Science and Engineering of Laws," *Proceedings of Space 2000* (Reston, VA: American Society of Civil Engineers, 2000), pp. 133-40.

cant harm to the people in terms of their human rights, living standards or quality of life—but no one knows because the effects of laws are not measured or analyzed. (Thus the mystery: We thirst for knowledge of every other aspect of the physical world—of whales, antibiotics, carbon nanotubes and galaxies. Why have we tolerated ignorance of our laws for so long?)

It is a matter of historical record that the worst human calamities—wars, gross abuses of human rights and the financial collapse of nations—have occurred under the authority and direction of the laws of government. The continued state of ignorance of the cause-and-effect mechanisms of laws can no longer be regarded as tolerable. Since laws are humanmade products that have a pronounced effect upon the physical world, this ignorance can be ended by simply expanding science to encompass the laws of government through the creation of the science of laws. (Although scholarly studies of laws are currently conducted under the heading of "jurisprudence," a *true* science of laws has never existed; a formal scientific society of peers, whose purpose is to derive, record, organize and promulgate scientific knowledge of the structure and mechanics of laws, has never been established. See Appendix H.)

The science of laws will accurately and objectively answer a critical question for every democracy: Is the government serving the best interests of the citizenry through its body of laws? The science of laws will verify or refute the legislature's *hypothesis* that each law is a worthy instrument of democracy. The conclusions of the scientific analyses of the structure and mechanics of laws will be subjected to peer review, and validated findings will be published in the international scientific literature, establishing a reservoir of scientific knowledge of laws. Scientific reports will be the basis of a QA program that will enable legislatures to repeal those laws found to be less than satisfactory in pursuit of the purpose of democracy. The result will be a substantial improvement in the performance of democratic governments.

HISTORICAL BACKGROUND

The concept of—and need for—the proposed science of laws is not a new idea. In 14 AD, Tacitus suggested that an investigation (a "fuller discussion") of the origins of laws was merited because of the undue burden that the laws of Rome placed on the people:

> ...and now the country [the Roman Empire] suffered from its laws, as it had hitherto suffered from its vices. This suggests to me a fuller discussion of the origin of law and of the methods by which we have arrived at the present endless multiplicity and variety of our statutes.[18]

Immanuel Kant expressed a desire for a process that would investigate the principles of laws and lead to the better design of laws:

---

[18] Tacitus, *The Annals*, Great Books of the Western World, vol. 15, p. 51.

It has been a long-cherished wish—that (who knows how late) may one day be happily accomplished—that the principles of the endless variety of civil laws should be investigated and exposed; for in this way alone can we find the secret of simplifying legislation.[19]

Roscoe Pound stated that the means for administering justice could be discovered through the process of observation (i.e., the process of science) rather than through "philosophical reflections":

...there is an idea of law as made up of the dictates of economic or social laws with respect to the conduct of men in society, discovered by observation, expressed in precepts worked out through human experience of what would work and what not in the administration of justice. This type of theory likewise belongs to the end of the nineteenth century, when men had begun to look for physical or biological bases, discoverable by observation, in place of metaphysical bases, discoverable by philosophical reflection.[20]

Hans Kelsen used the term *science of laws* to describe the means for understanding the mechanisms of laws:

The Pure Theory of Law is a theory of positive law. It is a theory of positive law in general, not of a specific legal order. It is a general theory of law, not an interpretation of specific national or international legal norms; but it offers a theory of interpretation. As a theory, its exclusive purpose is to know and to describe its object. The theory attempts to answer the question what and how the law is, not how it ought to be. It is a science of law (jurisprudence), not legal politics.[21]

Frederick Beutel wrote about applying the methodology of science to the study of laws and the lawmaking process:

A science of laws based on a rigorous application of the scientific method should be devoted to the study of the phenomena of law making, the effect of law upon society and the efficiency of law in accomplishing the purposes for which the law came into existence.[22]

Although the science of laws is not a new idea, it has not yet been established as a formal discipline. However it will, of necessity, come into being with the advent of quality assurance programs for laws.

---

[19] I. Kant, *Critique of Pure Reason,* Great Books of the Western World, vol. 42, p. 110.

[20] R. Pound, *An Introduction to the Philosophy of Law* (New Haven, CT: Yale University Press, 1922), pp. 29-30.

[21] H. Kelsen, *The Pure Theory of Law* (Berkeley, CA: University of California Press, 1967), p. 1.

[22] F. Beutel, *Experimental Jurisprudence and the Scienstate* (NJ: Fred B. Rothman & Co., 1975), p. 68.

A NEW SCIENCE

The science of laws will not be a study of human emotional/mental processes and behavior (psychology) or a study of human social interactions (sociology); these sciences of natural phenomena already exist. The science of laws, rather, will be a study of tools (laws) created by humans for the benefit of humans (see Appendix D). The new science of laws will have an enormous amount of material to explore: every law of government! Initially, only the least complex laws will be studied. As investigative methodologies advance, however, every law of every government, past and present, will be the subject of scientific evaluation.

The science of laws will seek to answer two questions: What are laws made of and what do they do? The first question will be answered by studying the *structure,* or "anatomy," of each law. Fortunately, the words and punctuation of a law constitute its entire structure, from which a scientific investigator may determine such features as the law's purpose and sanction. The official published legislative reports of the U.S. federal and state governments—which contain the majority and minority opinions and other historical information on the purpose, findings and testimony of individual laws—will also be helpful. The results of the study of the structure of laws will establish the basis for deriving the performance of laws and will be used to create a classification system for laws, analogous to the classification systems used in other sciences such as metallurgy and electronics.

Finding the answer to the question of what laws do is much more complicated. The answer will require investigators to *accurately and thoroughly* measure, analyze and record the sum of the consequences of the enforcement of laws. This process will be analogous to the testing and validation procedures now used to confirm the effectiveness and safety of pharmaceuticals or the airworthiness of a prototype aircraft. When the results of the enforcement of a law have been verified by the scientific process, it will be possible to derive a description of the law's *mechanics,* that is, of its cause-and-effect relationships. Whenever possible, the descriptions of the structure and mechanics of laws will be quantified so that mathematical models of their operations and performance may be formulated.

SCIENTIFIC ANALYSIS OF LAWS: STRUCTURE

The first and simplest step of the science of laws will be to derive knowledge of the structure of laws. A structural analysis is critical to establish a reference point for understanding the mechanics of laws. The letter, or structure, of a law is the *cause* that, when enforced, produces the *effects* that define the mechanics of the law—and that makes a QA/QI program for laws possible. The structural analysis of a law (see Chapter 6) will derive knowledge of the following:

1. title of the law and other identification information
2. name of the legislative sponsor
3. name, qualifications and employer(s) of the designer(s)
4. societal problem the law addresses
5. purpose of the law
6. forcible mechanism, or sanction, of the law
7. predicted costs and side effects
8. methods and materials the designer used to analyze the societal problem and create the law solution
9. references that document the databases and other sources of knowledge used in the law-design process

The structural analysis of laws will not be a simple task because most existing laws list only items 1, 2 and 6 of the above criteria. The other structural details are usually not included in a typical law and must be discovered, if they exist, by investigating the legislative history of the law. The legislative history of a law is the compilation of records of its development as a bill, including the various drafts of the bill, committee reports, documented congressional debates and other materials related to its design.[23] When the structural analysis of a law is concluded, the study of its mechanics can begin.

SCIENTIFIC ANALYSIS OF LAWS: MECHANICS

Physical changes in the real world are produced whenever a law of government is enforced (see Chapter 3, Figure 3-1). The effects of a law include the changes it makes to the problem it addresses and to the human rights, living standards and quality of life of the people. The science of laws will undertake a study of the mechanics of laws and determine the degree to which each law satisfies the purpose of democracy.

The task of gathering accurate data on the effects of a given law may be relatively simple for single-purpose laws but will be exceedingly difficult, if not impossible, for multipurpose laws such as omnibus laws (which is one reason why omnibus laws must be repealed). Also, since laws interact, the derivation of an accurate description of the relationship between a given law and an observed societal outcome will be a significant challenge when hundreds or thousands of interacting laws contribute to that outcome. A major task of the science of laws, therefore, will be to construct analytical methods that are effective in deriving knowledge of the mechanics of laws. The conclusions of scientific studies will be regarded as valid when those studies are accepted for publication in the peer-reviewed scientific literature.

---

[23] See, for example, www.lexisnexis.com, www.westlaw.com, http://leginfo.ca.gov/ and http://thomas.loc.gov/.

The knowledge derived will be used by law-design engineers to create more sophisticated and accurate models of laws that will predict the outcome of proposed new laws with increasing degrees of certainty. In other words, knowledge of the structure and mechanics of laws will permit, for the first time, the exercise of wisdom in the creation of an efficacious body of laws (see Appendix L).

Knowledge of mechanics will also be the key element of the QA program of laws, for which legislatures will have oversight responsibility. (However, to prevent a conflict of interest and to conform with the concept of checks and balances between the branches of government, the *administration* of quality programs should be the responsibility of the administrative rather than the legislative branch of government.) When the results of law analyses are derived and reported, legislatures can improve the performance of their bodies of laws by repealing laws found to be less than useful to the people. For example, if the analysis of a law discloses that it has no stated purpose or that it is detrimental to the people, the QA program will recommend that the legislature repeal the law. If the QA program recommends a given course of action, such as the repeal of a law that has no purpose, the legislature is not required to act on that advice and may in fact decide not to abide by it. However, since the legislatures of democracies are obligated to serve the best interests of the people, they must justify any action contrary to the findings of quality programs.

The legislature's implementation of a QA program will give rise to the need for individuals who can derive accurate and objective evaluations of laws. To satisfy this need, college curricula for the science of laws will need to be developed in parallel with the engineering discipline of laws (see Appendix K).

EMERGENCE OF THE SCIENCE OF LAWS

Although a separate, formal science of laws does not yet exist, scientific knowledge of laws *is now being derived.* An example of a scientific study that describes the mechanics of laws is found in the published scientific report titled "Efficacy of Mandatory Seat-Belt Use Legislation."[24] In October 1985 the legislature of the state of North Carolina began enforcing North Carolina Senate Bill 39: *An Act to Make the Use of Seat Belts in Motor Vehicles Mandatory.* The intent of the law was to reduce the incidence of morbidity and mortality from automobile accidents; the sanction was the imposition of a $25 fine upon individuals who did not use seat belts. The premise of the law was that individuals, in order to avoid the fine, would use seat belts and thus be protected from serious injury or death in the event of an automobile accident. In December 1988, three years after the seat belt law was enacted, a scientific report of the efficacy of the law was published in the peer-reviewed, scientific *Journal of the American Medical Association.* The report stated the methods and materials used for gathering and

---

[24] T. Chorba, D. Reinfurt and B. Hulka, "Efficacy of Mandatory Seat-Belt Use Legislation: The North Carolina Experience From 1983 Through 1987," *Journal of the American Medical Association (JAMA),* vol. 260, no. 24 (December 23/30, 1988), pp. 3593-7.

analyzing data and provided information about injury and fatality rates in automobile accidents as they related to the enforcement of the seat belt law. The report concluded: "This study indicates that the North Carolina law has reasonably achieved its legislative intent."

The scientific evaluation of the seat belt law, based upon observations of its real-world consequences, is an example of the inchoate science of laws. The structure and mechanics of the seat belt law were analyzed (although costs and side effects of the law were not studied in this example), and accepted analytical methods were used to compare the effects of the enforcement of the law with the original intent of the law. The results were subsequently published in the scientific literature after undergoing peer review by a scientific society. (Future scientific reports of the efficacy of laws will more appropriately be published in journals of the science of laws rather than in journals of the science of medicine.)

This scientific paper was valuable because it provided the feedback the North Carolina legislature needed to continue the enforcement of the law in the best interests of the people, and it provided knowledge that other state legislatures could apply to their bodies of laws. If the results had concluded that the premise of the law was a failed concept (see Appendix D, Figure D-4) and that the law was not useful to the purpose of democracy, the legislature could have used that knowledge as the basis for repealing the law, releasing government resources for more useful pursuits.

ACCUMULATION OF KNOWLEDGE

The initiation of the science of laws will have the subtle but momentous effect of converting laws from the dogma of authority to the "working hypotheses" of democracy. Although science is a human-directed (hence fallible) process that is limited by methodology, sampling techniques and degrees of certainty that are never absolute, the working hypotheses of science are continually refined in a self-correcting process that increasingly approximates the truth When laws become the working hypotheses of the science of laws, the same truth-directed evolutionary process will apply, and laws will become the increasingly useful implements of democracy.

The accumulation and organization of scientific knowledge and the application of knowledge to the design of laws will transform the traditional method of lawmaking into a knowledge-based, problem-solving discipline (see Table 7-2). Of significance, quality programs for laws, and the science and engineering disciplines of laws, can be established and can operate without disrupting the dynamic processes of democracy such as the election of legislators and the oversight functions of legislatures. To ensure that derived knowledge is not lost, the societies of the science and engineering of laws will publish their findings in peer-reviewed scientific law journals (see Appendix H).

The primary responsibility for the scientific investigation of laws will be delegated to nonprofit scientific institutions (e.g., universities). In contrast to law-design corporations, which will be primarily motivated by profits in a competitive marketplace, the nonprofit institutions assigned to the investigation of laws will be motivated by peer-reviewed government and non-government grants that support scientific activities and the prestige that comes from the derivation of scientific knowledge. (As a generalization, *creative* science is motivated by creativity, necessity and profits while *investigative* science is motivated by curiosity, prestige and grants.)

As a caveat, the science of laws, more than any other field of science, will be under pressure to reach conclusions that support special interest/political agendas. For this reason, the highest standards must be observed for the conduct of scientific activities to minimize, to the greatest extent possible, the influence from outside forces and from the constraints of dogma and tradition. Scientists must be free to follow the truth wherever it leads them. One safeguard would be to prevent governments from making grants directly to scientists, arranging instead for government research funds to go to independent scientific agencies. A panel of scientists within each agency would then award grants to scientists for the study of laws according to procedures analogous to those practiced by scientific foundations such as the National Science Foundation (www.nsf.gov/). The "arm's length" separation between the funding source and scientific activities would lessen the possibility of undue influence on scientific investigations. Another safeguard would be to require scientists to list (in their scientific publications) all the potential sources of conflict of interest in the conduct of their investigations.

Evolution of Quality Solutions

Quality programs for laws will generate the need to establish and develop the science and engineering disciplines of laws. As these new scientific disciplines evolve, reliable knowledge and the prudent application of that knowledge will replace dogma as the basis for the creation of laws. The patterns of success that now characterize existing science and engineering disciplines may then be expected to be repeated in the quality solution of societal problems by the science and engineering disciplines of laws. The result will be a substantial improvement of the performance of laws in the service of democracy.

C H A P T E R   8

The Ascendancy of Democracy

Democracies are far more advantageous to the people they serve than authoritarian forms of government, and the ongoing dramatic transition of authoritarian governments to democracies is a highly encouraging process. But despite their successes, existing democracies have been unable to ascend to the level of true democracy because they continue to rely on the inadequate and flawed traditional method of lawmaking. The result is that all existing (electoral and liberal) democracies are incomplete or "transitional," and are unable to fully satisfy the purpose of democracy. However, applying quality programs to laws and lawmaking will correct the deficiencies of the traditional method and initiate the final step of the ascendancy of governments to the status of true democracy.

The Emergence of Democracy

From the beginning of recorded history until the mid-twentieth century, the vast majority of the governments of sovereign nations were authoritarian. The rise and fall of these inherently unstable governments provided opportunities for experimentation with democracy. For example, limited trials with democracy were conducted in the city-states of ancient Greece, where all male citizens had the opportunity to participate directly in the formulation and enactment of laws.[1] Since the governments of ancient Greece excluded a major portion of the population (all women) from participation in affairs of state, these "democracies" were, in fact, authoritarian (aristocratic) governments. Nevertheless, the concept of equal participation by male citizens in the legislative process was a significant step in the evolution of democracy.

It was not until the eighteenth century that proto-modern democracies began to emerge and supplant authoritarian forms of government. One of the most notable and longest-enduring democracies to be formed at that time was the government of the United States of America. The U.S. Constitution, which was ratified in 1788, established a republican form of democracy that guaranteed the human rights of the citizens, including the right to participate in the government through elected representatives.[2] Since that time, an increasing number of

---

[1] See, for example, W. Durant, *The Story of Civilization Part II: The Life of Greece* (New York, NY: Simon and Schuster, 1966).
[2] The Constitution of the United States of America. The U.S. Constitution as originally designed had serious flaws, including its denial of voting rights to women and its tolerance of slavery.

governments have made the transition from an authoritarian form of government to democracy.

The process by which an authoritarian government becomes a democracy is simple. The government needs only to allow the people to vote for and thus select the leaders of government through competitive elections based on secret ballots and universal suffrage. By allowing the people to exercise their voting rights (see Appendix A), an authoritarian government recognizes the citizenry as the sovereign of government and it thereby makes the transition to an electoral democracy as depicted in Figure 8-1.

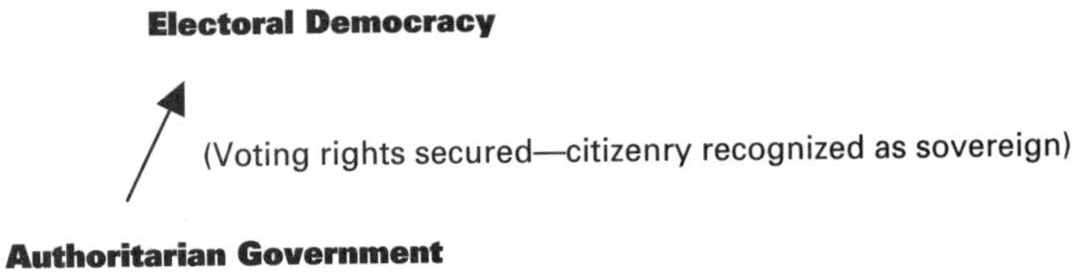

Electoral Democracy

(Voting rights secured—citizenry recognized as sovereign)

Authoritarian Government

Figure 8-1. The First Step of the Ascendancy of Democracy: An authoritarian government's recognition of the citizenry as the sovereign of government is the critical first step in the ascendancy of democracy.

The 1948 issuance of the United Nations Universal Declaration of Human Rights, a document that asserts that every person on earth has inherently equal human rights, including voting rights, added impetus to the transition of authoritarian forms of government to democracy. Of significance, Article 21 of the declaration states that the will of the people is the basis for the authority of government:

1. Everyone has the right to take part in the government of his country, directly or through freely chosen representatives.
2. Everyone has the right of equal access to public service in his country.
3. The will of the people shall be the basis of the authority of government; this will shall be expressed in periodic and genuine elections which shall be by universal and equal suffrage and shall be held by secret vote or by equivalent free voting procedures.[3]

By declaring the will of the people to be the basis of the authority of government, Article 21 affirmed that the status of sovereign is a political right for the people of *every* government. Since a democracy is the only form of government in which the people as a whole are the sovereign, the Universal Declaration of Human Rights thereby established the *right to democracy* as a human right that applies to all people.

---

[3] United Nations, Universal Declaration of Human Rights, General Assembly Resolution 217 A (III), 1948. See www.un.org.

Electoral democracies advanced from zero to 62.5 percent of all independent sovereign governments of the world during the twentieth century.[4] If the present trend continues, every sovereign government will meet the first requirement of democracy by the middle of the twenty-first century (see Figure 8-2).

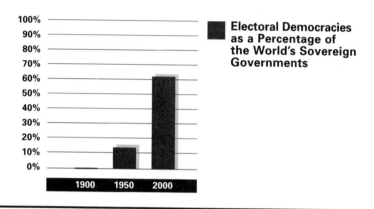

Figure 8-2. The Growth of Electoral Democracies: In 1900 there were no democracies in the world. By 1950, 14.3% of the governments of the sovereign nations of the world were electoral democracies, and by 2000, 62.5% (121 of the world's 192 governments) were electoral democracies.[5]

The transition from an authoritarian government to a democracy results in a subtle but significant change in the role of legislators. In authoritarian governments, legislators are "lawmakers" who have unrestricted power to create laws (resulting in the "rule of man"). While legislators in a democracy also have the power to create laws, they have the much more responsible and challenging position of *trustee*, and their exercise of legislative powers is therefore limited to the honorable means and ends that serve the best interests of the people.

A problem for electoral democracies is that they can easily regress to authoritarian governments, since the exercise of voting rights does not, of itself, assure that the legislators and other elected leaders will always serve the best interests of the people. In particular, the reliance upon voting rights alone lends credence to the "philosopher-king" concept, which holds that legislators who are charismatic, intelligent and benevolent will construct a body of laws that is beneficial to the people. According to this notion, the people will be assured of good government by the simple expedient of voting "good" men and women into office. This concept has two serious flaws.

---

[4] Strictly defined, democracies did not exist in the year 1900. The United States of America, for example, did not allow women to vote at that time and it therefore did not meet the universal suffrage requirement of democracy.

[5] The data for creating this graph were taken from Freedom House, www.freedomhouse.org, which defines a government as an electoral democracy if it meets the standard of "universal suffrage for competitive multiparty elections."

First, although charisma, intelligence and benevolence are desirable qualities for the leaders of government, they are, in and of themselves, *woefully inadequate qualities* for the task of designing laws that satisfy the requirements of democracy (see Engineering Design discussion, Appendix E). Second, philosopher kings and philosopher-queens often "go bad"—being human, they may become enamored with the exercise of power and use their hegemony over lawmaking to impose their personal belief system on the people and increase their wealth and power at the expense of the people, thereby causing the regression of electoral democracies to an authoritarian form of government.[6] So, although the exercise of voting rights by the citizens in the election of popular candidates to public office is an essential feature of democracy, it is not enough to accomplish the full purpose of democracy.

Since all governments serve the best interests of their sovereign and since it is in the best interests of the people to be guaranteed not only their voting rights but all other human rights as well, an electoral democracy is obligated to recognize and secure the full complement of the human rights of the people. When an electoral democracy takes this step, it meets both the first and second requirements of democracy and becomes a liberal democracy (see Figure 8-3).

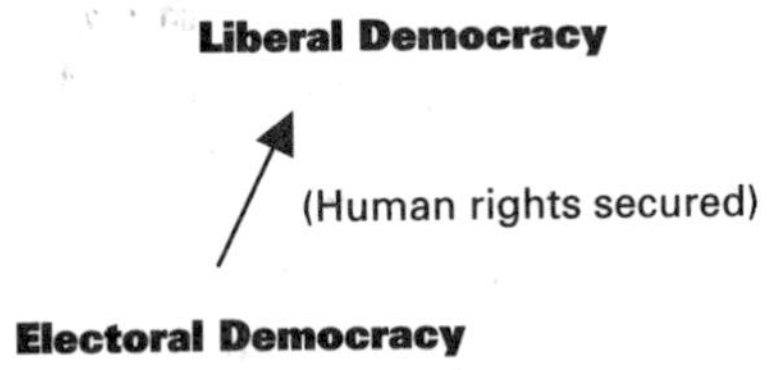

Liberal Democracy

(Human rights secured)

Electoral Democracy

Figure 8-3. The Second Step of the Ascendancy of Democracy: When an electoral democracy secures the full complement of human rights of the people, it becomes a liberal democracy.

Beginning in the mid-twentieth century, several organizations began to measure, compare and report the human rights records of the governments of the nation-states of the world.[7] The results of these ongoing periodic reviews indicate that:

---

[6] For example, Adolf Hitler became chancellor of Germany in 1933 following the legal democratic election procedures of the Weimar Republic.

[7] See, for example, Freedom House (www.freedomhouse.org); C. Humana, *World Human Rights Guide* (Oxford, England: Facts on File Publications, 1986); Amnesty International (www.amnesty.org); and Human Rights Watch (www.hrw.org).

- There is a significant variation in the performance of governments vis-à-vis their record of human rights.
- Both electoral and liberal democracies consistently have a better record of human rights (and living standards[8]) than authoritarian forms of government.
- The transition of authoritarian governments to democracies is an ongoing process.

The rate of transition of electoral democracies to liberal democracies suggests that liberal democracies will soon become the most common form of government in the world (see Figure 8-4). This trend is highly encouraging in view of the improving record of human rights, living standards and quality of life that accompanies the ascendancy of democracy.

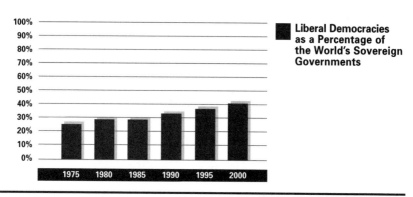

Figure 8-4. The Growth of Liberal Democracies: A liberal democracy is a government that meets the first and second requirements of democracy. If the present trend continues, every government will ascend to the level of liberal democracy before the end of the twenty-first century.[9]

However, liberal democracies can only be incomplete, or transitional, democracies. The problem with existing liberal democracies is that although they uphold the human rights of the people, they continue to create laws by means of the traditional method of lawmaking, which is incapable of solving problems efficaciously. The result is that liberal democracies have not been able to serve the best interests of the people at all times. To satisfy the third requirement of democracy and complete the transition to the status of a true democracy, liberal democracies must take the additional step of adopting the following quality programs for laws and lawmaking (outlined in Chapter 6):

---

[8] See *2000 Index of Economic Freedom* (New York, NY: The Heritage Foundation and *The Wall Street Journal,* 2001).

[9] Freedom House uses the record on human rights to rate sovereign governments as "Free," "Partly Free" or "Not Free." *Liberal democracy* in the present text equates to those governments that are rated as "Free" by Freedom House. See www.freedomhouse.org.

- a quality design (QD) program that requires law designers to create laws that meet the requirements of democracy
- a quality assurance (QA) program that leads to the repeal of less-than-useful laws
- a quality improvement (QI) program that maximizes the efficacy of laws vis-à-vis the purpose of democracy

Quality programs for laws and lawmaking will transform the traditional method of lawmaking into the problem-solving method (see Appendix F). Their implementation will dramatically improve the performance of laws in terms of the liberty and well-being of the people and will thus allow liberal democracies to complete the third and final step in the ascendancy of democracy (see Figure 8-5).

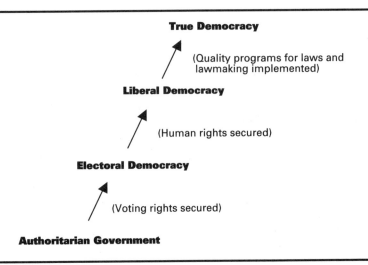

True Democracy

(Quality programs for laws and lawmaking implemented)

Liberal Democracy

(Human rights secured)

Electoral Democracy

(Voting rights secured)

Authoritarian Government

Figure 8-5. The Ascendancy of Democracy: The ascendancy of democracy is a three-step process. The first two steps are well under way and a majority of existing governments are either electoral or liberal democracies. To complete the ascendancy of democracy, governments must implement quality programs for laws and lawmaking.

Implementation of Quality Programs for Laws

Individuals and organizations that benefit from the present lucrative connection between special interests and laws and from the continued growth, inefficiency and complexity of the bodies of laws will undoubtedly resist the implementation of quality standards. Also, some legislators will be reluctant to endorse standards that prevent them from creating pork barrel laws and from drawing the boundaries of legislative districts for their own benefit (gerrymandering). Given these natural impediments to change, why would the legislatures of governments adopt quality standards for laws on the path to true democracy?

The answer is twofold. First, democracies are obligated to provide the highest possible level of governance for their citizens, and that obligation mandates that the legislatures develop and implement quality programs for laws. Second, even if governments do not readily adopt quality programs, the investigative and creative scientific disciplines of laws will derive and promulgate scientific knowledge of the structure and mechanics of laws and the lawmaking process (see Appendix H). History teaches us that as knowledge accumulates, means will be developed for applying it in ways that improve the human condition.[10] That is, the derivation and promulgation of scientific knowledge of laws and lawmaking will inevitably lead the public to *demand* the implementation of quality programs for laws.

QUALITY AS A POLITICAL ISSUE

Democracies hold periodic elections for the office of legislator. As the investigative and creative scientific disciplines of laws make scientific knowledge of laws and lawmaking available to the public, that knowledge will play a prominent role in the election process, and quality of laws will become a political issue. Suppose, for example, that a certain legislator voted not to repeal a number of laws that the science of laws had demonstrated to be detrimental to the citizenry. In the next scheduled election, that legislator would be vulnerable to any challenger who promised, if elected, to vote to repeal those detrimental laws. Similarly, the voting public, which embraces the concept of quality in consumer goods and services, will predictably be inclined to vote for any government office seeker who promises to adopt quality programs for laws and lawmaking—or to vote against those candidates who balk at the idea of quality programs. This reasoning applies equally well to the chief executives who have the power to endorse or veto legislative bills. A chief executive who endorses bills that fail quality design standards will be vulnerable to a challenger who promises to use quality as a guide for the enactment of laws. Thus the desire of individuals to be elected to the office of legislator (or chief executive) will lead, through many election cycles, to the development and application of quality programs for laws and lawmaking.

Another avenue for the introduction of quality methods is through the initiative or "direct democracy" process, in which a bill is submitted directly to the citizens for a vote, thus bypassing the legislature. For those governments that have a direct democracy process, an initiative that requires the legislature to develop quality programs for the design, follow-up evaluation and improvement of laws could be submitted directly to the voters. (Of course, the initiative would need to meet quality design standards—see Chapter 6.) Since quality measures for other humanmade products are overwhelmingly popular with the people, the majority of voters would most likely approve the development of quality measures for laws.

---

[10] C. Van Doren, *A History of Knowledge* (New York, NY: Ballantine Books, 1991).

THE FIRST QD STANDARDS FOR LAWS

To initiate QD standards for laws, accurate and succinct statements of the following items should be included in or attached to each bill submitted to the legislature:

- the identity of the law designer(s)
- the design expertise and other relevant qualifications of the law designer(s)
- the employer of the law designer(s)
- the definition of the societal problem the law addresses
- the magnitude of the societal problem the law addresses
- the purpose of the law in terms of a measurable objective that benefits the people
- the references used in the creation of the law

Note that these standards, while elementary and incomplete, will nevertheless dramatically reduce the number of (quality-challenged) bills now submitted to legislatures for review, and the agenda of advocates for legislative action will become limited to only those matters that concern the needs of the people as a whole. (As the effectiveness of simple design standards is realized, more comprehensive standards will be developed and implemented.)

THE FIRST QA STANDARDS FOR LAWS

The initial QA program for laws could consist of a simple evaluation of the *structural* characteristics of laws as outlined in Chapter 6. For example, those laws that are found to have one or more of the following structural defects would be recommended for repeal:

- laws that do not address a defined societal problem
- laws that have no stated purpose in terms of a measurable problem-solving goal
- laws that are open to different interpretations
- laws that have no citation of references

Conflict-of-interest concerns would prevent the QA analysis from being performed by legislative analysts employed by the legislative branch of government.[11] Hence the initial QA review of laws should be performed by non-government institutions, such as colleges of science. The fact that most laws are structurally flawed means that simply identifying and repealing structurally defective laws will produce a dramatic reduction in the size of the body of laws (see Figure 8-6). In addition, since laws place restrictions on human conduct and are the conduits for the expenditure of resources, the QA program will provide a net benefit to the people of a democracy by removing unnecessary legal impediments, releasing resources for more useful purposes and reducing taxation.

---

[11] See, for example, a description of legislative analysts of the state of California at www.lao.ca.gov.

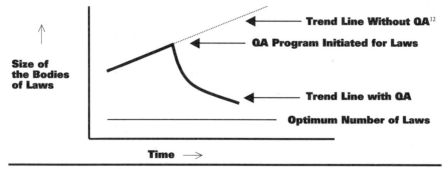

Size of
the Bodies
of Laws

Trend Line Without QA[12]

QA Program Initiated for Laws

Trend Line with QA

Optimum Number of Laws

Time →

Figure 8-6. The End of the Chaos of Laws: The legislatures of democratic governments, acting upon the recommendations of the initial QA program for laws, will "weed out" laws with structural defects. The first effect of a QA program will be a dramatic decrease in the size of the bodies of laws of governments, thus reversing the trend of the increasing chaos of laws. Over time, more comprehensive QA programs (for both the structure and mechanics of laws) will reduce the bodies of laws to the minimum size that optimally serves the purpose of democracy (see condition B, Figure 5-5, Chapter 5).

After the first QD and QA programs have been initiated, the public's expectation of high quality in laws will predictably lead to the demand for more comprehensive and sophisticated quality programs, including a QA program for the mechanics of laws (which would assess performance) and a QI program of laws. The implementation of QA and QI programs will result in an "S-curve" of increasing efficacy over time that is typical of knowledge-based technological development (see Appendix E), and the performance of laws will approach that of the ideal law (see Appendix I), as depicted in Figure 8-7.

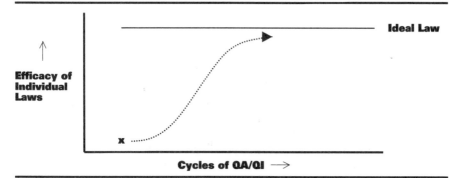

Ideal Law

Efficacy of
Individual
Laws

x

Cycles of QA/QI →

Figure 8-7. Impact of Quality Programs on the Efficacy of Laws: The introduction of quality programs for laws will yield an "S-curve" of enhanced efficacy that is typical of technological development. With each cycle of QA and QI, the efficacy of laws will improve so that their characteristics will approach those of the ideal law. The lack of quality programs currently prevents the performance of laws from improving beyond their original "x" position.

---

[12] See Table 5-2, Chapter 5, for a representative database. Also see H. de Soto, *The Other Path: The Economic Answer to Terrorism* (New York, NY: Basic Books, 1987), pp. 196-7.

The Role of Legislators in True Democracies

The transition of incomplete democracies to the status of true democracy will entail changes in the operations of government institutions. The most dramatic change will take place in the legislative branch of government, which will play the central role in the ascendancy of democracy. By implementing quality standards for laws, legislators will take increasing control of the disposition-of-laws process—that is, of policy—as the influence of special interests declines. However, QD standards will preclude most if not all legislators from being "lawmakers," and their role will become, exclusively, that of *trustee*. As trustees, legislators will:

- Assign priorities to societal problems that require legislative solutions.
- Oversee the QD, QA and QI programs of laws.
- Repeal laws that are less than useful to the purpose of democracy.
- Enact new laws that efficaciously serve the purpose of democracy.

True Democracy

The present method of lawmaking is a misdirected, incomplete, corrupt and fault-prone *feed-forward* control system that is driven by ideas for new laws and that produces more laws (see Figure 4-1, Chapter 4, and Figure C-1, Appendix C). When quality programs for laws are implemented, the operating system of government will be converted to a *feedback* control system (see Figure C-2, Appendix C) in which *efficacious problem solution* will be the independent variable that drives the operation of government, as illustrated in Figure 8-8. The human rights, living standards and quality of life of the people will then be added to the condition of "constitutionality" to define the allowable boundaries for the operation of laws, and wisdom will replace mere opinion as the basis for the origin and design of laws (see Appendix L). By these means governments will be able to satisfy all the requirements of democracy and ascend to the level of true democracy, as depicted in Figure 8-5.

What will be the result of the ascendancy of governments to the status of true democracy? A true democracy will always and honorably serve the best interests of the people, through the rule of law, and reflect their highest aspirations. Since quality programs will reduce and eventually eliminate the chaos of laws and will eliminate unnecessary legal impediments to productive enterprises, governments evolving into true democracies may expect substantial gains in productivity and, consequently, in their gross domestic product.

Among the beneficiaries of the ascendancy of democracy will be the significant proportion of the world's population that currently has insufficient means of procuring necessities such as food, shelter, medical care and

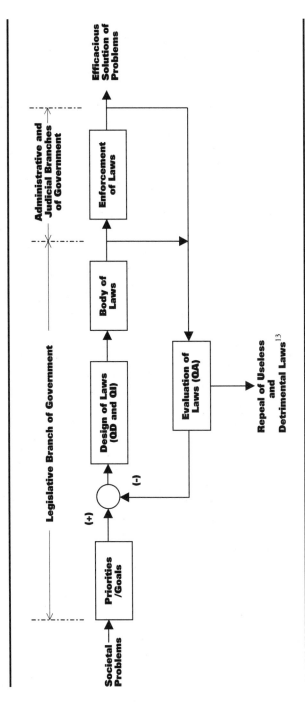

Figure 8-8. The Method of Problem Solution in a True Democracy (compare to Figure 4-1, Chapter 4): The application of quality methods (QD, QA and QI) to laws and lawmaking will transform the lawmaking process into a knowledge-based, problem-solving feedback control system that optimally serves the purpose of democracy.

---

[13] The judicial branch of government will also perform a quality assurance role through the process of judicial review.

transportation.[14] As pointed out in Chapter 2, the accumulation of wealth among the subject classes is regarded as a problem for the ruling classes of authoritarian governments, whereas poverty is regarded as a problem for democracies. As authoritarian governments are supplanted by democracies, therefore, poverty will replace wealth as a major focus of the problem-solving efforts of governments. In order to fulfill their obligations to the people, true democracies will recognize and enforce property and legal rights and will create bodies of laws that enable and encourage the people to attain economic self-sufficiency.[15]

A significant proportion of the world's people currently has an unacceptably low quality of life, for example from exposure to high levels of pollution and from lack of potable water and adequate sanitation.[16] However, most of these problems can be solved or mitigated through existing technologies. The ascendancy of democracy thus promises to make substantial improvements in quality of life on a global scale because true democracies, acting in the best interests of the people, will apply proven, effective means to the solution of public health and related problems. Since democracies have never gone to war with other democracies (see Chapter 2), the ascendancy of every government to the level of true democracy also holds the promise of permanent peace between nations, as suggested by Weart: "For if we can attain this [goal of universal democracy], we will at the same time attain universal peace."[17]

The ascendancy of democracy will not lead to utopia, but true democracies will establish and maintain a rule of law that enables the people to attain their goals with a maximum degree of liberty and the highest possible quality of life. The transition of authoritarian governments to democracy is well under way and, with the adoption of quality programs for laws and lawmaking, the final step in the ascendancy of democracy will be possible. The parameters that define governments and the ascendancy of democracy are outlined in Table 8-1.

---

[14] I. Serageldin, "World Poverty and Hunger—The Challenge for Science," *Science,* vol. 296 (April 5, 2002), pp. 54-8.
[15] See, for example, de Soto, chapter five, "The Costs and Importance of the Law," pp. 131-87.
[16] See "Global Water Supply and Sanitation Assessment 2000 Report," World Health Organization and UNICEF; and Serageldin, p. 54.
[17] Weart, p. 296.

	Authoritarian Government	Electoral Democracy	Liberal Democracy	True Democracy
Sovereign	ruling class	people as a whole (citizenry)	people as a whole	people as a whole
Means of Government	laws	laws	laws	laws
Guaranteed Human Rights	none	voting rights	all human rights	all human rights
Role of Legislator	lawmaker	lawmaker and trustee of the people	lawmaker and trustee of the people	trustee of the people
Purpose of Laws	enhancement of the power of the ruling class	solution of problems	solution of problems	efficacious solution of problems
Method of Lawmaking	traditional method	traditional method	traditional method	problem-solving method
Basis of Law Design	opinion/belief system	opinion/belief system	opinion/belief system	wisdom
Paragon of Law Design	none	none	none	ideal law of government
QD Program for Laws?	no	no	no	yes
QA Program for Laws?	no	no	no	yes
QI Program for Laws?	no	no	no	yes
Operational Limits of Laws	none	constitutionality	constitutionality	constitutionality, human rights, living standards and quality of life of the people
Composition of the Body of Laws	plethora of laws of unknown utility	plethora of laws of unknown utility	plethora of laws of unknown utility	optimum number of efficacious laws

Trend: $\longrightarrow$

Table 8-1. Parameters of the Ascendancy of Democracy: The ascendancy of authoritarian governments to electoral and then to liberal democracies is an ongoing process. The development and implementation of quality programs for laws will allow existing democracies to complete the last step in this process and thereby attain the status of true democracy.

C H A P T E R   9

Conclusion

Democratic governments are obligated to serve the best interests of their citizens. To satisfy that obligation, they have three requirements: (1) Maintain the citizenry in its status as the sovereign of government; (2) secure the full complement of human rights of the citizenry; and (3) efficaciously solve or mitigate societal problems for the benefit of the people. When a government meets these three requirements, it becomes a true democracy.

The overwhelming advantages of democracies vis-à-vis the best interests of the people have led to the large-scale conversion of authoritarian governments to democracies over the past century. Although this transformation is incomplete, the trend indicates that every government will become an electoral democracy (fulfilling the first requirement of democracy) or a liberal democracy (fulfilling the first and second requirements) before the end of the twenty-first century.

However, all existing democracies, while dedicated in principle to the well-being of the people they serve, have failed to fulfill the third requirement of democracy—and therefore have failed to reach the status of true democracy—due to the defects, inadequacies and misdirected purpose of the traditional method of lawmaking. The traditional method not only prevents democracies from creating laws that efficaciously solve societal problems but also threatens the people through its continuous production of more laws, including useless and detrimental laws. The result is chaos: The ever-growing bodies of laws have become so large and complex that it is impossible for anyone to "know the law" in its entirety, and laws are therefore enforced selectively. In the worst-case scenario, this increasing chaos will undermine the rule of law and cause existing democracies to regress to authoritarian forms of government.

The reason for the failure of the traditional method of lawmaking as an effective instrument of democracy is its complete lack of quality procedures for the design, follow-up evaluation and optimization of laws. A simple solution to the ineffectiveness and increasing chaos of laws, therefore, is for democratic governments to adopt quality programs for laws and lawmaking—the same quality programs that are now routinely applied to the design and evaluation of useful products in other productive fields such as medicine and transportation. By developing and implementing quality procedures for laws, governments will end chaos and create and maintain bodies of laws that optimally serve the purpose of democracy. The ascendancy of all governments to the condition of true democracy will then be possible, with the promise of substantial benefits for all humankind.

Human Rights, Living Standards and Quality-of-Life Standards

Democracies are governments that are obligated under the rule of law to serve the best interests—i.e., the liberty and well-being—of the people within their jurisdiction. To guide the governance activities of democracies and ensure that they are meeting their obligations, it is essential to define the measurable conditions that describe the people's interests. These parameters are human rights, living standards and quality-of-life standards.

Human Rights

Human rights are defined as the freedoms of action and freedoms from harm that every individual holds in equal quality and quantity with every other individual without regard to arbitrary distinctions such as race, religion, wealth, gender, nationality, etc. These rights are assumptions, or initial conditions, that are subject to additions and improvements based upon advances of knowledge.

Human rights are inalienable, and their scope is limited to the extent that the exercise of human rights by one individual cannot interfere with the human rights of another.[1] Another important feature of human rights is that they are the exclusive property of each individual; governments do not possess and therefore cannot "grant" human rights to anyone. Governments may give legal sanctions to groups of people such as corporations and trade unions, but such sanctions do not come under the heading of human rights; human rights pertain only to individuals.

Although they cannot *grant* human rights, democracies are obligated to *secure* the human rights of the people they govern. Human rights include the following substantive rights, property rights, political rights and legal rights:[2]

---

[1] Kant, *The Science of Right*, p. 401: "Freedom is independence of the compulsory will of another; and in so far as it can coexist with the freedom of all according to a universal law, it is the one sole original, in-born right belonging to every man in virtue of his humanity. There is, indeed, an innate equality belonging to every man which consists in his right to be independent of being bound by others to any-thing more than that to which he may also reciprocally bind them. It is, consequently, the inborn quality of every man in virtue of which he ought to be *his own master by right (sui juris)*." (Note that human rights apply to men and women equally.)

[2] These rights are derived partly from the Constitution of the United States of America and partly from the United Nations Universal Declaration of Human Rights (www.un.org).

SUBSTANTIVE RIGHTS

- right to life, liberty and security of person
- right to freedom from torture
- right to freedom from slavery
- right to freedom from interference with home, family or correspondence
- right to freedom from attacks upon reputation or honor
- right to freedom of thought, conscience and religion

PROPERTY RIGHTS

- right to purchase, own and dispose of property[3]
- right to copyright, trademark and patent protection

POLITICAL RIGHTS

- right of citizenship and nationality
- right of the citizens to determine the authority of government (voting rights)[4]
- right of representation and participation in the government
- right to freedom from press censorship or coercion (freedom of the press)
- right to freedom of opinion and expression (freedom of speech)
- right to freedom of peaceful assembly and association

LEGAL RIGHTS

- right to equal status and equal protection under the law
- right to protection of human rights by the government[5]
- right to petition the government for a redress of grievances[6]
- right to freedom from arbitrary arrest or detention (right to a writ of habeas corpus)
- right to freedom from bills of attainder and ex post facto laws
- right of the accused to be presumed innocent until proven guilty
- right of the accused to a public trial by a jury of peers

---

[3] The definition of *property* includes the knowledge and skills one gains from an education or work experience.
[4] The right of the people to determine the authority of a government establishes that government as an *electoral democracy*.
[5] The recognition by a government of its obligation to protect the human rights of its citizens establishes that government as a *liberal democracy*.
[6] The impartial continuation of this human right requires the government to have an independent judiciary.

An important distinction of human rights is that they pertain to *inalienable* freedoms, and are not claims to *alienable* assets or services.[7] In particular, human rights do not include the "right" of one individual to claim the possessions (tangible or intangible) of another individual. That claim, if enforced, would violate the property rights (a division of human rights) of the second individual, since it would interfere with the freedom of the second individual to use and dispose of personal possessions as he or she desires. For example, a government should be concerned with the lack of food (or water, shelter, medical care, education, etc.) of individuals within its jurisdiction. However, the government's solution to that problem cannot be to "grant" one person a "right" to the food that is owned by another because the enforcement of the new "right" would be in violation of the property rights[8] of the person who owns the food. (In any case, as previously stated, governments do not possess human rights and cannot "grant" human rights to anyone.) The problem with the lack of food or other alienable commodity is the lack of sufficient means to purchase that commodity—a problem of *living standards* (see following discussion), not a problem of *human rights* (see Table A-1).

Living Standards

Living standards describe the economic status of individuals within the jurisdiction of a government. As contrasted with human rights, which deal with equal and inalienable rights, living standards are concerned with *alienable* commodities (goods and services that are bought and sold) and the ability of individuals to purchase those commodities. The following criteria define living standards (modified, from Offenau[9]):

- level of individual disposable income in terms of the government's currency
- purchasing power and stability of the government's currency
- level of individual net worth
- cost of consumer goods and services

Living standards, like human rights, apply to the status of individuals. Specifically, living standards cannot be accurately calculated by dividing the gross domestic product (GDP) of a nation by its population count (GDP per capita). GDP per capita *seriously overstates* living standards because GDP includes the operations of government institutions, which do not contribute to individual net worth, and omits the negative effect of taxes. For example, government-owned

---

[7] If a government makes an accusation against an individual, as in a criminal case of law, and if the accused cannot afford legal aid, he or she has the right to obtain (alienable) legal aid at the expense of the government. In this situation, a threat to the individual's loss of freedom at the hands of the government triggers the conditional right to legal aid.

[8] An important role of government is to protect property rights with legal rights—to enforce contracts and define and record deeds, patents and copyrights through the government's system of courts (i.e., it is necessary to have legal rights in order to secure property rights).

[9] L.V. Offenau, *Science and the Rule of Law* (San Diego, CA: P.C. Press, 1989), p. 28.

military installations, courthouses, museums, jails and libraries are needed to maintain human rights and provide high quality-of-life standards (see following discussion), but they add nothing to individual net worth and, to the extent that the operation of these facilities is supported by taxes, they decrease individual disposable income. While GDP per capita is a convenient indicator of a nation's economic activity, it is an unacceptable measure of living standards.

Quality-of-Life Standards

Quality-of-life standards are the measures of the status of the physical and cultural environment of the people within the jurisdiction of a government. The steps that a government takes to produce a high quality of life will consume resources (i.e., reduce living standards through necessary taxes, fees, etc.), and they may also infringe upon human rights. Thus a government must balance the desire to improve the quality of life of the people against the need of the people to maintain their living standards and human rights. The following positive and negative indices are used to derive quality-of-life ratings (modified, from Offenau[10]):

POSITIVE INDICES

- quality and availability of consumer goods and services
- quality and availability of public use facilities such as parks, museums, libraries, transportation networks, etc.

NEGATIVE INDICES

- incidence of war
- incidence of crime
- incidence of pollution
- incidence of preventable disease, disability and death

The maintenance of high quality-of-life standards (high positive indices and low negative indices[11]) by a government must be supported by taxes and fees, which degrade living standards. The determination of the proper balance between quality-of-life standards and living standards is primarily a task for a government's legislature.

---

[10] Offenau, p. 29.
[11] While it is possible that war can be eliminated with the ascendancy of democracy, it will never be possible to reduce other negative indices, such as crime and pollution, to zero.

Human Rights	Living Standards	Quality-of-Life Standards
Inalienable Freedoms	Economic Environment	Physical and Cultural Environments
Status of:	**Status of:**	**Quality and Availability of:**
• substantive rights • property rights • political rights • legal rights	• individual net worth • ability of individuals to purchase alienable commodities such as water, food, insurance, shelter, entertainment, etc.	• consumer goods and services • public use facilities **Incidence of:** • war • crime • pollution • preventable disease, disability and death

Table A-1. Human Rights, Living Standards and Quality-of-Life Standards: The performance of governments is determined by the status of the human rights, living standards and quality-of-life standards of the people.

Relevance to Laws and Lawmaking

A democracy is obligated to serve the best interests of its citizens in terms of their human rights, living standards and quality-of-life standards. These parameters establish the performance envelope for the laws of government and constitute the measurable quantities by which the performance of governments is derived. They also form the basis for quality programs for laws that will allow democracies to become self-correcting in the direction of optimum performance for the people they serve.

Creativity

Creativity is one of the most ennobling human traits; it allows us to achieve and reflect on our highest aspirations. All humanmade creations—including poems, computer chips, symphonies, sculptures, hot dogs and tennis shoes—are the product of creativity. The humanities (art, music, literature) are primarily concerned with the creation of products that have high aesthetic value and little or no "usefulness." Conversely, the scientific disciplines of engineering are concerned with the creation of useful products, i.e., tools, in which little or no design emphasis is placed upon aesthetics.

Creative Works

All the creative works of humankind may be characterized by their relative content of aesthetics (the work of artists) and utility (the work of engineers), as depicted in Figure B-1.

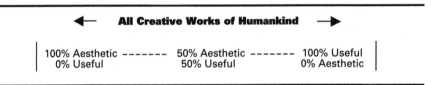

Figure B-1. Scale of Aesthetic and Usefulness Properties of Creative Works: All humanmade creations may be placed on this scale according to their relative content of aesthetics and usefulness.

With reference to Figure B-1, Leonardo da Vinci's *Mona Lisa* and Shakespeare's *Julius Caesar* would be at the far left end of the scale, while computer chips and ampicillin would be at the far right. Sports cars and wristwatches, which combine aesthetics and usefulness in their design, would be in the middle range. A comparison of the aesthetic and usefulness content of creative works illustrates the differences in the roles and responsibilities of creative design efforts. The major differences between aesthetic and useful creations include evaluation standards, limiting factors for new creations, and the nature of their change, or evolution.

EVALUATION STANDARDS

The standards used for the evaluation of aesthetic creations are *qualitative* in nature and are often expressed by adjectives such as "beautiful" or "inspiring." The standards used to evaluate useful products, in contrast, are *quantitative* in nature, e.g., the horsepower and fuel consumption ratings of an automobile engine.

LIMITING FACTORS

The second distinction between aesthetic and useful creations is the nature of the factors that limit the introduction of new creations. For aesthetic creations, the principal limiting factor is the intellect; the next artistic masterpiece will be a function of the genius of the artist who creates it. The creation of a new useful product also depends upon the intellect, but the *principal* limiting factor is scientific knowledge; the next generation of useful implements in every major field (e.g., medicine, energy production, communication, transportation) waits primarily for advances in the *knowledge* upon which the new designs will be based.

NATURE OF CHANGE

The third distinction between aesthetic and useful creations is the nature of their change. Change in aesthetic products is characterized by enrichment rather than advancement. For example, the compositions of the twentieth century composer Maurice Ravel add to and enrich the sphere of music, but they are not necessarily considered an improvement over the compositions of the eighteenth century composer Antonio Vivaldi. In contrast, change in useful products is characterized by advanced problem-solving efficacy; every new generation of useful product features an improvement (greater effectiveness, more user-friendliness, lower cost, less risk, fewer side effects, etc.) over previous generations. In other words, each new work of art is a unique creation that *expands* and *enriches* the cultural environment, whereas each new product of engineering adds an incremental *improvement* in the ability of humankind to solve problems.

Relevance to Laws and Lawmaking

Where do the laws of government belong on the scale of creative works depicted in Figure B-1? A law of government is the product of human creative effort, but who should create laws—artists or engineers? Should laws be artistic or useful? Should the design of laws be based on knowledge? What standards (qualitative or quantitative) should be used to evaluate laws? And should changes in the bodies of laws be characterized by enhanced aesthetics or by improved usefulness for the people?

The answers to these questions should be obvious. Laws are *tools* (the means of government) that are *devoid of* aesthetics; they have less aesthetics than truck tires. Laws are strictly utilitarian and they fall, *perforce*, into the domain of engineering, in which creations are based on knowledge, evaluated by quantitative measures of performance and characterized by improvement from one generation to the next. It is a puzzle, then, that the laws of government have not been recognized for what they are: tools that must be designed, implemented and evaluated by the same knowledge-based engineering methodology and quality standards that apply to all other tools. When such recognition does occur and the creation of laws becomes an engineering discipline, a dramatic improvement in the performance of laws in the service of democracy will become possible.

Control Systems

A *control system* is defined as the means by which a variable quantity is made to conform to a prescribed norm. Control systems are ubiquitous; computers, telephones, automobiles, corporations, governments and biological systems all contain control systems. Although control systems have different sizes and configurations, they all have the same fundamental characteristics: They consume energy and produce an output in response to a prescribed input. There are two types of control systems: feed-forward and feedback.

Feed-Forward Control Systems

Feed-forward control systems are simple one-way command systems composed of input (instructions), controller (the forcing mechanism) and output. In feed-forward control systems, the input is the *independent* variable that operates the forcing mechanism (controller), and the output is the *dependent* variable. The flow diagram of feed-forward systems is depicted in Figure C-1.

Figure C-1. Feed-Forward Control System: Feed-forward control systems are enslaved to the input they receive. They have no inherent mechanism for measuring their output or for adapting to disturbances, and the quality of their output is subject to wide fluctuations. Feed-forward control systems are mostly limited to simple tasks in stable environments, e.g., overhead lights (light = output) that are controlled by wall switches (off/on switch = input).

A traffic control signal at a four-way intersection is an example of a feed-forward control system. The input is the timed sequence for the traffic signal; the controller consists of the power supply, lamps and timing mechanism; and the output is the flow of traffic through the intersection. The traffic signal produces optimum traffic flow when the volume of traffic is equal in both north-south and east-west directions. When the volume of traffic is unequal (for example, when the east-west traffic volume temporarily drops to zero), the traffic signal becomes a hindrance to traffic flow because it unnecessarily stops north-south traffic when it gives the green light for nonexistent east-west traffic. Also, when there is no traffic through the intersection from either direction, the traffic signal continues to operate, consuming energy for no purpose. The controller (the traffic signal) is completely dependent upon the input (the original set of timing instructions), and is oblivious to the output (traffic flow).

For any given 24-hour period, traffic volume and direction through an intersection are variable, and traffic signals controlled by a timed sequence can be expected to produce optimum traffic flow for only a small percentage of time. As this example illustrates, feed-forward control systems are inflexible and of limited utility because the input rather than the quality of the output is used to direct the control process. Feed-forward control systems cannot adapt to changes in their environment, and their output is not measured as part of the system operation.

Although feed-forward control systems are useful for very simple tasks, they are unsuitable for tasks for which optimum outcomes in a dynamic environment are desired. Feed-forward control systems are "dumb" systems that are enslaved to the input commands; they are not adequate for operations for which consistently high quality of output is important.

Feedback Control Systems

To overcome the lack of control over the quality of the output, a "feedback loop" can be added to feed-forward control systems so that the *quality of the output becomes the controlling element*. By this means, the feed-forward control system is converted into a feedback control system, in which the desired output is maintained continuously.

Feedback control systems use information about the output to modify or correct the control system operation. Although the addition of a feedback loop is a simple step, it produces a fundamental and critical change in the operation of the control system: The quality of the output replaces the input as the independent variable and becomes the critical controlling parameter of the control system. The elementary components of a feedback control system are depicted in Figure C-2.

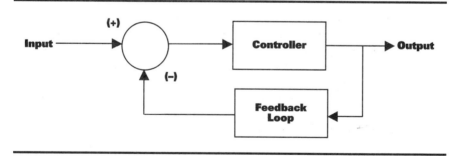

Figure C-2. Feedback Control System: Feedback control systems are "intelligent" systems that are enslaved to the quality of the output (and thus are self-correcting). Feedback control systems are used in dynamic and complex environments where a reliable output is needed.

In the feedback control system depicted in Figure C-2, a desired reference input value is selected. An input signal (+) that is proportional to this value is then delivered to the summing junction (the symbol "O" in Figure C-2) of the control system. The input to the controller is the driving signal from the summing junction, which causes the controller to produce an output proportional to the driving signal. The feedback loop measures the output from the controller and generates a signal that is proportional to the output, but has a negative (–) value. The output signal from the feedback loop is then delivered to the summing junction (O) where it is added to the input (reference) signal. The sum of the reference input signal (+) and the signal from the feedback loop (–) then becomes the independent variable (the driving signal) that drives the controller.

When the driving signal—the reference input signal (+) plus the feedback signal (–)—is greater than zero, the system "speeds up"; and when the driving signal is less than zero, the system slows down. When the reference input and feedback signals are equal, their sum is zero and the system operates at the desired steady-state condition. The feedback control system operation is thus a self-correcting process that is continuously modified by *knowledge of the output* so that the output always corresponds to the reference input value. The significant advantage of feedback control systems is that they can compensate for disturbances and thus reliably maintain the desired output in a dynamic environment.[1]

The cruise control on an automobile is an example of a feedback control system. A desired speed is selected (input) and the cruise control system (controller)—which includes sensors, fuel system, engine, transmission and other drive components—is engaged. The feedback loop of the control system measures the speed of the car (output) and compares it with the desired speed (selected input speed). If there is a difference between the desired (reference) speed and the measured speed, for example when the automobile goes uphill, an error message that is proportional to the difference between the input and the output is delivered to the controller. The controller then acts, through an increase in the throttle setting, to reduce the error message (the difference between the desired and measured speed) to zero, and thus correct the speed to the desired level.

Relevance to Laws and Lawmaking

Since the quality of the output is the critical variable for most control processes, particularly in complex and dynamic systems that are subject to disturbances, feedback control systems are far more effective and are used much more extensively than feed-forward control systems. Of interest, the legislative process is currently a feed-forward control system driven by the input (proposed new laws), and the output (societal effects of laws) is not measured. A significant improvement in the operation of governments will occur when a feedback loop (a quality assurance program for laws) is incorporated into the lawmaking process, thus transforming it into a knowledge-based feedback control system in which the desired objectives of democracy control the operation of government (see Figure 8-8, Chapter 8).

---

[1] See, for example, N. Nise, *Control Systems Engineering* (Redwood City, CA: Benjamin/Cummings Publishing Co., Inc., 1992).

Science

The three principal spheres of human intellectual activity are religion, philosophy and science.[1] Their separate domains and methods of operation distinguish these three activities from one another. In general terms, the domain of religion is spiritual or supernatural belief, and the method for exploring this domain is studying, reciting, interpreting and teaching religious scriptures and doctrines. The domain of philosophy is the constellation of secular opinions and ideas, and its principal method of examination is dialectic. The domain of science is the physical world. Scientists use the "scientific process"[2] to derive knowledge of the physical world and use the problem-solving method to apply that knowledge to useful purposes.

Since the domains and methods of religion, philosophy and science are separate from one another, it is possible for a single individual to believe in a religion, "intellectualize" as a philosopher, and derive or apply scientific knowledge as a scientist or engineer without conflict or contradiction.

The Origins of Science

Until the Renaissance, science was not regarded as a significant field of intellectual inquiry. Knowledge of the physical world at that time was limited and unorganized, and it resided mostly in "practical" fields such as carpentry and masonry. The ascendancy of science began with people such as Copernicus, Gilbert[3] and Galileo,[4] who, in their separate investigations, derived knowledge of the physical world in a manner typical of modern science. In particular, it was Francis Bacon,[5] a contemporary of Galileo, who established the supremacy of observation, experimentation and measurement (i.e., the scientific process) as the only reliable means for deriving knowledge of the physical world. The following anecdote regarding the use of empirical methodology to derive reliable knowledge has been attributed to Francis Bacon:

---

[1] See R. Hutchins (editor in chief), *The Great Ideas: A Syntopicon of Great Books of the Western World*, vol. II (Chicago, IL: Encyclopaedia Britannica, 1952), "Science," pp. 682-705.

[2] Scientists prefer the term *scientific process* to *scientific method* to describe the means by which new knowledge is derived, so the former term is used in this text.

[3] W. Gilbert, *On the Lodestone and Magnetic Bodies*, Great Books of the Western World, vol. 28, pp. 1-121.

[4] G. Galilei, *Concerning the Two New Sciences*, Great Books of the Western World, vol. 28, pp. 125-260.

[5] F. Bacon, *Advancement of Learning, Novum Organum* and *New Atlantis*, Great Books of the Western World, vol. 30.

A group of scholars were speculating about horses' teeth; in particular, how many teeth do horses have? In noting that animals generally have the same number of teeth in the upper jaw as in the lower jaw and also have symmetry between the right and left sides of their mouths, the group of scholars reasoned that the correct number of teeth should be a number that is evenly divisible by four. As a horse needs a certain number of incisor and molar teeth, the scholars narrowed the possible answers to 28, 32, 36 and 40 teeth, and speculated that the correct answer was 36. When Francis Bacon was invited to the discussion, he stated that the way to know the number of teeth was to find a horse, lift its lip, and count the teeth.

This story points out that Bacon's empirical method of observation and measurement, while certainly more dangerous and less aesthetic than philosophical musings, is the only reliable process for deriving knowledge of the physical world.

Bacon also recognized the need to have a society of peers conduct an independent evaluation of the claims of scientific discoveries. Although the earliest scientific society (Academia de Lincei) was formed in Italy in 1603, it was the influence of the writings of Francis Bacon a few years later that stimulated the development and growth of scientific societies, which are essential for the success and growth of science. The most significant contribution to the early development of science came from Isaac Newton, who demonstrated the utility of the scientific process in explaining and predicting the motion of bodies in the solar system according to a few simple, mathematically derived scientific laws.[6] By the end of the seventeenth century, the contributions of Bacon, Galileo, Newton and others firmly established science as a new and separate intellectual discipline.

The Branches of Science

Science has two principal branches: investigative science and creative science (see Figure D-1). Investigative science is the exploration-and-discovery branch that is concerned with the derivation and accumulation of scientific knowledge of the physical world by scientists. Investigative science may be further subdivided into the sciences that study natural phenomena, such as astronomy and botany, and the sciences that study humanmade products and processes, such as aeronautics and electronics. Creative science, or engineering, is the other principal branch of science, which solves problems through the knowledge-based design of useful products (tools, or technology) by engineers (see Appendix E). (While it is convenient to divide science into *investigative science*, the domain of scientists, and *creative science*, the domain of engineers, there is overlap between science and engineering. For example, scientists design experiments to test and confirm their hypotheses, and in that design task they are "engineers." Conversely, when engineers test and measure the results of their creations, they are "scientists." The important distinction between investigative and creative science is in the ultimate *goals* of scientists and engineers: The goal of scientists is to derive new scientific

---

6 I. Newton, *Mathematical Principles of Natural Philosophy*, Great Books of the Western World, vol. 34.

knowledge, and the goal of engineers is to solve problems through the creation of new tools.)

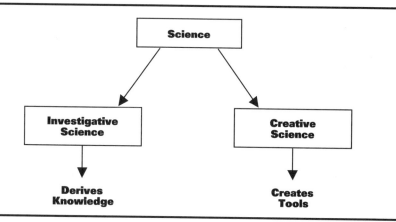

Figure D-1. The Branches of Science: The branches of science are investigative science, which derives knowledge of natural phenomena and humanmade products, and creative science, or engineering, which creates problem-solving tools, i.e., technology.

The Purpose of Science

Investigative science, or simply *science,*[7] may be defined as the scientific disciplines that employ knowledge, tools and the scientific process to derive, record, organize and promulgate reliable knowledge of the structure and mechanics of the physical world. Science is thus the "progenitor and gatekeeper" of scientific knowledge. Every object that exists and every event that occurs within the physical or "real" world, whether natural or humanmade, is a suitable subject for examination by science. The experience of science indicates that there can be no real-world existence or phenomenon that is beyond detection, evaluation and eventual explanation by science.

It is a popular notion that the purpose of science is to produce new "scientific" products such as cancer cures and computers. But that notion is incorrect; the creation of new, useful products, or technology, is the task of engineering not of science. What, then, is the purpose of science? The purpose of science is to end ignorance through the derivation and accumulation of scientific knowledge. Thus humankind's insatiable need for knowledge (i.e., the need to end ignorance) is the motivating force of science: "The desire to know, when you realize you do not know, is universal and probably irresistible....It is impossible to slake the thirst for knowledge."[8] Scientific knowledge is valuable because it provides accurate descriptions of the structure of the physical world and reliable quantitative predictions of the mechanics of the physical world. Science has been an unmiti-

---

[7] For the remainder of this discussion, *investigative science* will be referred to simply as *science,* and *creative science* will be referred to as *engineering.*

[8] Van Doren, p. xxiii.

gated success in its victories over ignorance. Since the ability of science to gain new scientific knowledge is proportional to the knowledge that has been accumulated in the past (a positive exponential relationship), the rate of growth of scientific knowledge, i.e., the successes of science, may be expected to continue to increase in the future.

Science is subject to the axiom that the real world exists separate from the mind and that the real world consists of everything that can be detected and described by the senses and by the extension of those senses with the tools of science, as observed by Einstein: "the concept of the 'real world' of everyday thinking rests exclusively on sense perception."[9] Thus the first and foremost principle of science is that observation (i.e., empirical methodology) of the real world is the final arbiter of scientific knowledge. Since scientific knowledge is based upon sense perceptions, it is always tentative and subject to further refinements that more closely approximate the truth of the physical world.[10] Nevertheless, from these preconditions, science has been successful in deriving knowledge that approximates truth of the real world, and will predictably continue to be successful in the foreseeable future.

The Process of Science

The process of science consists of the principles and techniques that are necessary for the accumulation of scientific knowledge. This process is governed by rules for concept formation, experimentation, observation, measurement and the validation of hypotheses by a society of peers. The scientific process may be regarded as the most important invention of humankind: "Of all the kinds of knowledge that the West has given to the world, the most valuable is a method of acquiring new knowledge—called the 'scientific method.'"[11]

The process of science is a "truth machine" that has the ability to separate fact from fiction, bias and superstition, and to validate or refute hypotheses, thereby deriving scientific knowledge. The compass of science is truth: To the extent that truth of the physical world can be known, the scientific process always and reliably seeks truth, accepts and accumulates truth and rejects non-truth (see Figure D-2). By its ability to discover and accumulate reliable knowledge, the scientific process has caused science to become a dominant sphere of intellectual inquiry and exchange on a par with religion and philosophy.

SCIENTIFIC SOCIETIES

The critical factor that accounts for the success of science is its social structure. In particular, the advancement of scientific knowledge depends on a body of peers—an organization of individuals who have specialized knowledge in a par-

---

[9] A. Einstein, *Ideas and Opinions* (New York, NY: Bonanza Books, 1954), p. 290.

[10] Einstein, p. 266.

[11] Van Doren, p. 184. (As noted, scientists now generally prefer the term *scientific process* to the term *scientific method.*)

ticular field of study. (Science extends beyond national boundaries, and virtually all scientific societies are international cooperative organizations.) The body of peers constitutes a scientific society that establishes and maintains standards for the conduct of scientific activities, judges the work of scientists, and records and promulgates scientific knowledge. Scientific societies give an identity and a focus to the scientific community and provide the forums necessary for the development and growth of the intellectual process of science. These societies are thus the essential structure of science that validates scientific knowledge and assures the freedom of scientific fact from the influence and constraints of outside influences such as superstition, bias and ideology.

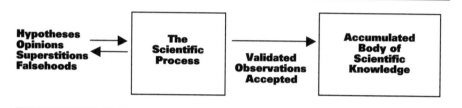

Figure D-2. The Scientific Process: The scientific process is a "truth machine" that evaluates observations, accepts truth, rejects non-truth, and accumulates reliable knowledge of the physical world.

The most important function of scientific societies is the cooperative and consensual validation of scientific knowledge—that is, peer review. Committees of qualified scientists review submitted papers describing scientific research and determine which papers will be published in the journals of scientific societies. The purpose of this peer-review process is to judge whether the experimenter (scientist) used accepted measurement systems, materials, analytical methods, etc. and whether the reported results and conclusions (in the form of a submitted scientific paper) are justified by the data. At the conclusion of the peer-review process, a decision is made regarding the worthiness of the submitted paper for publication in the journal of the society. The reviewers must judge the relative importance of the proposed publication to the advancement of their particular science. If the paper is accepted through the process of peer review, it is published as a tentative scientific fact. But when an experimental observation is particularly significant or unusual, a second form of peer review—direct confirmation by other scientists using empirical methods—is required. Such safeguards are essential in science and must be present in one form or another to maintain the high standards for the derivation of scientific knowledge.

The truth-seeking process of scientific research generates a strict set of work-related values. Scientists are held accountable by their colleagues for the validity of the results they publish, and their careers depend upon a reputation of honesty, integrity, rationality, consistency, cooperation and openness. This set of values must be recognized as a standard for professional behavior;[12] to compromise pro-

---

[12] H. Brown, *The Wisdom of Science* (Cambridge, England: Cambridge University Press, 1986), p. 135.

fessional integrity is to sacrifice one's reputation as a scientist. There are many examples of scientists who have lost their careers for life because they were found to have falsified their experimental data. Thus professional values are essential to the purpose of science and assure its continued, undeniable successes.

The Divisions of Investigative Science

As previously noted, investigative science may be subdivided into the study of natural phenomena and the study of humanmade products and processes. Both divisions of investigative science have the same goal: to end ignorance through the accumulation of scientific knowledge of the real world.

THE STUDY OF NATURAL PHENOMENA

The scientific process for this division of science begins when a scientist observes an unexplained, naturally occurring phenomenon of the physical world. (Scientists frequently derive knowledge of a given subject matter merely for "the sake of knowledge"—for no other reason than the desire to satisfy curiosity.) The scientist then collects and studies all relevant knowledge that relates to the phenomenon and formulates a conceptual model, or *hypothesis*, which is a tentative explanation of the observed phenomenon. The hypothesis is structured so that it can be validated by empirical means and understood by and communicated to other scientists. An experimental procedure is then created to test the validity of the hypothesis in a manner that produces measurable results. A well-designed experiment will control experimental and extraneous variables to produce new unequivocal facts that reveal the accuracy of the hypothesis. In some cases, such as questions of astronomical phenomena that cannot possibly be tested in situ, it is necessary to devise an experiment that simulates real-world conditions. By using accepted empirical methods of observation, experimentation, measurement and analysis, the scientist tests and thus verifies or refutes the hypothesis.

If the results of the experimental procedures do not confirm the hypothesis, the scientist must reexamine the hypothesis and the experimental methodology to determine the source(s) of error that caused the hypothesis to fail. If errors are discovered and corrected, the experimental procedure may then be repeated. If the results of the experiment support the hypothesis, the scientist submits his or her claim of discovery to a scientific society of peers for evaluation. If the methods and materials of the scientist meet the standards of the scientific society and the society agrees that the reported results and conclusions are justified by the experimental data, the society declares that the hypothesis is valid, and the scientist's work is published in the scientific journal of the society. If the society cannot agree that the hypothesis is valid based upon the scientist's submitted report, the scientist's findings and conclusions are not published even if the hypothesis represents a true discovery.

The publication of the results of a scientific investigation represents a statement that the scientist's work and conclusions meet the standards of the society and are accepted as valid. However, published reports are open to further testing and validation—or refutation—by independent investigators. On occasion, hypotheses that were declared to be valid by a scientific society are subsequently determined to be invalid by additional experiments and evidence.

In such cases, the society states that it was in error in its judgment and withdraws its declaration of support for the hypothesis—a process that is self-correcting in the direction of truth. Studies that disprove previously accepted hypotheses are reported as valuable contributions to the scientific literature so that scientists and engineers will not inadvertently use failed hypotheses in their investigative and design tasks. Every hypothesis is subject to the results of additional empirical studies that add credibility to the hypothesis or require either its modification or abandonment. A basic tenet of science is that the recorded facts produced by the scientific process are not absolute truths but tentative and incomplete descriptions of reality. Through the iterative and self-correcting verification of the scientific process, however, scientific knowledge provides ever greater trustworthiness of the sense perceptions of reality, and an ever more probable correspondence with reality. Science does not claim absolute truths, but only the provisional status of "working hypotheses" that approximate the truth. The process of science for the derivation of knowledge of naturally occurring phenomena is illustrated in Figure D-3.

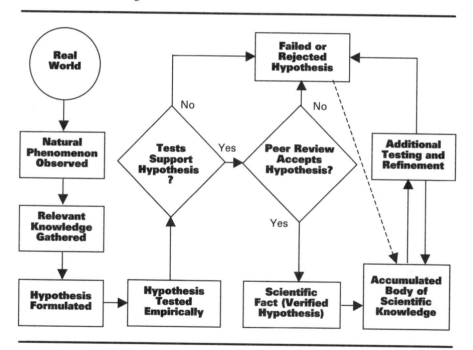

Figure D-3. The Scientific Process for Natural Phenomena: The scientific process is a truth-seeking, iterative process that separates verified facts from failed hypotheses. The result of scientific activities is that the body of reliable knowledge of the structure and mechanics of the physical world (and knowledge of failed hypotheses, as indicated by the dashed line) continues to grow over time.

The process for deriving reliable knowledge of humanmade products and processes parallels the methodology used for deriving knowledge of natural phenomena. When a new product or process with unique properties is created, it becomes a newly observable phenomenon of the physical world that can be evaluated empirically. Relevant knowledge is gathered and, through accepted "proof-of-concept" testing procedures, the structure and mechanics of the new product or process are evaluated by accepted methodologies, and the results are then submitted to a relevant scientific society.

If the peer-review process of the society accepts the results, the proof of concept is reported in the journal of the society and thus becomes incorporated in the accumulated knowledge of humankind. If peer review does not accept the proof-of-concept results and if the society deems its non-acceptance of the results to be significant, that "failed" conclusion is also reported in the literature to inform others that the original claims of the product were not confirmed. By this means, a growing body of knowledge of humanmade products and processes becomes known to the scientific community and the public (see Figure D-4).

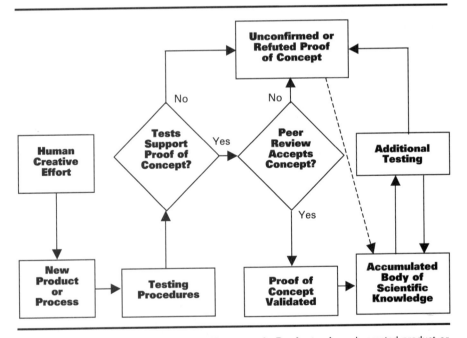

Figure D-4. The Scientific Process for Humanmade Products: A newly created product or process is a humanmade "phenomenon" that is evaluated in a manner similar to that of natural phenomena. The testing and peer-review procedures create a growing body of knowledge that, when combined with increasing knowledge of natural phenomena, is used to create the next generation of products. Note that knowledge of failed concepts (as indicated by the dashed line) is a valuable addition to humankind's store of knowledge.

The inventor of a new useful product may decide to forego the peer-review process and subsequent publication of the design and performance of the product for commercial or other reasons, and public knowledge of the design of the product will thus be delayed or denied. Patent systems, by which governments recognize inventors' exclusive right of ownership of their inventions, protect the commercial rights of inventors while allowing details of their inventions to be published. The advancement of science thus depends to a significant degree on the protection of intellectual property rights (patents), and this protection depends, in turn, on an effective, impartial and independent judicial system that upholds legal rights. It follows that the greatest rate of scientific advances will occur under the jurisdiction of those governments that recognize and secure property and legal rights (see Appendix A).

Relevance to Laws and Lawmaking

Since laws are created by humans and produce changes in the physical world, they are eminently suited to evaluation by science. When the process of science is applied to deriving scientific knowledge of the structure and mechanics of laws, the validity or non-validity of laws in terms of the liberty and well-being of the people will become known. The growing body of scientific knowledge of laws will therefore enable governments to assemble and maintain bodies of laws that optimally serve the purpose of democracy.

Engineering

Engineering is the "creative" branch of science that focuses on the design and optimization of tools. Engineers conceive of original solutions to problems; apply specialized methods, knowledge and tools in the design of new problem-solving tools; and employ feedback procedures to measure and enhance the performance of tools. The hallmarks of engineering are thus creativity, knowledge and the use of tools in a disciplined, self-correcting approach to the efficacious solution of problems. As scientific knowledge grows and as more powerful and sophisticated tools become available, engineering disciplines are able to solve increasingly complex problems, and new engineering disciplines come into existence.[1] In the broadest sense, all useful human creations are the product of engineering, including computers, surgical procedures, pesticides, microscopes, calculus, telephones, governments, accounting systems, etc.

The relationship between the two major branches of science—investigative science, or simply *science,* and creative science, or *engineering*—is synergistic. Both science and engineering use knowledge, tools and their respective methodologies to produce new knowledge (in the case of science) and new tools (in the case of engineering).

As knowledge grows, it becomes possible for engineers to create more sophisticated tools, which, in turn, enable scientists to obtain more scientific knowledge. By this synergistic process, the products of science (scientific knowledge) and of engineering (tools, or technology) continuously grow and improve over time, as presented in Figure E-1.

Science (Investigative Science)
   Knowledge + Tools + Scientific Process = New Knowledge
Engineering (Creative Science)
   Knowledge + Tools + Engineering Process = New Tools

Figure E-1. The Synergy of Science and Engineering: Science and engineering use knowledge and tools to produce more knowledge and more sophisticated tools—a positive exponential relationship. As the reservoir of knowledge and tools grows, the ability of science and engineering to achieve their respective goals increases with time.

---

[1] Aerospace, computer, genetic and software engineering disciplines were created in the twentieth century and new engineering disciplines in fields such as robotics and microelectromechanical systems (MEMS) are emerging.

The Purpose of Engineering

The solution of problems is obviously not unique to engineering; problem solution is the objective of most trades and professions. The key feature that distinguishes engineering from all other problem-solving endeavors is that engineering is the only profession that solves problems by the *creation of new tools*, or solutions.[2] Every other problem-solving profession is restricted to the application of existing products and procedures (that were created by previous engineering efforts). For example, physicians, airline pilots and police officers are required to stay within the boundaries of established norms of operation in their respective problem-solving tasks, whereas engineers have the unique role of creating new solutions to problems and of improving existing solutions. (Physicians, airline pilots, police officers, etc. are occasionally engaged in the development of new problem-solving techniques under controlled conditions—and in those tasks they participate in the process of engineering.) Thus the purpose of engineering is to accomplish the efficacious solution of problems through the creation and optimization of tools.

Engineering has three principal tasks: (1) the optimization of existing tools, (2) the creation of new, more efficacious tools to replace existing tools and (3) the creation of solutions to problems that have never before been solved. The satisfaction of these tasks results in an optimistic scenario: At any given time, problems are being solved by ever-improving means, and problems of the next order of complexity are in the process of being solved. The cycle of engineering problem solution is depicted in Figure E-2.

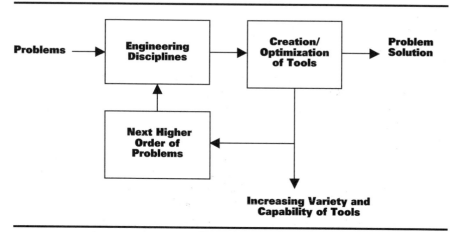

Figure E-2. The Cycle of Engineering Problem Solution: With each cycle of problem solution, the number, variety and capability of tools increase, and engineering disciplines are able to solve increasingly complex problems.

---

[2] Creativity is the hallmark of both engineers and artists. The distinction between engineers and artists is that engineers create useful products whereas artists create works of art (see Appendix B).

Optimization of the performance of useful products, i.e., quality improvement, is a key feature of engineering. The emphasis on optimization results in the rule of engineering: A new generation of useful product is accepted only if its performance—as measured in terms of effectiveness, cost-efficiency, user-friendliness, safety, etc.—exceeds the performance of the preceding generation of product. In other words, the compass of engineering is perfection.[3] The typical result of engineering development and optimization for any given product or process is an "S-curve" of technological improvement, as depicted in Figure E-3.[4]

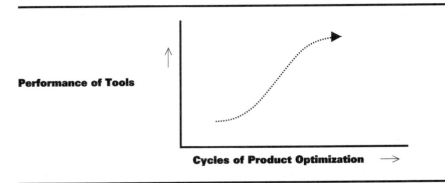

Performance of Tools

Cycles of Product Optimization $\longrightarrow$

Figure E-3. The Rule of Engineering: Each new generation of engineering product is characterized by improvement over the preceding generation, producing a typical "S-curve" of performance, or value, over time.

The Method of Engineering

The method engineers use to create useful products is the knowledge-based *problem-solving method* (see Appendix F). The problem-solving method is not unique to engineering; in fact, with one major exception (the traditional method of law-making—see Chapter 4), this method is the structured procedure by which all complex problems are addressed and solved.

Simple problems such as daily household and occupational chores can be routinely solved without the need to follow a formal, systematic, problem-solving approach. However, the solution of complex problems requires that the rigorous steps of the problem-solving method be observed. It is not possible for the human intellect alone to provide accurate predictions of the dynamic forces and kinematics of systems that have more than two or three interconnected moving parts. How, then, can engineers, by means of the problem-solving method, design a complex product such as a transport aircraft, which has thousands of interacting components? The limitations of the human intellect would seem to preclude the creation of intricate and sophisticated tools. The answer is that engineers have

---

[3] Concomitantly, standards of design expertise for engineers and engineering processes become more rigorous and comprehensive over time.
[4] See, for example, "Closing the TRL Gap," *Aerospace America*, August 2003, pp. 24-5.

three great advantages in the creation of solutions to complex problems: (1) the laws of nature, (2) accumulated knowledge and (3) tools of design.

The first advantage for engineers is that the laws of nature are immutable, quantifiable and predictable.[5] Physical, chemical and biological systems, and electromagnetic, gravitational and thermodynamic forces, etc. all behave according to constant, predictable rules. Laws of nature can thus be described in mathematical terms, such as the rate constant for a chemical reaction, the force of gravity, the modulus of elasticity of a metal alloy, and the oxygen consumption of a human being. As a result of the constancy of nature, mathematical methods such as calculus, differential equations and complex variables can be used to create models of engineering designs and predict their problem-solving performance with a high level of accuracy.[6]

The second advantage engineers have is that scientific knowledge continues to grow through the efforts of investigative and creative science. The ability to solve problems is proportional to knowledge; as knowledge grows, engineers are able to solve increasingly complex problems.

The third advantage is the number, capability and versatility of tools (created by previous engineering efforts) that are available for the creation of new designs. Of particular importance for the design of new engineering products is the digital computer. Computers and their related software programs are powerful instruments that are used for the creation and analysis of engineering models, and they are now routinely used for engineering creations.[7] Also, computers can be linked over long distances so engineers at remote locations can directly observe and interact with a design project throughout every stage of its development. As computers become more powerful and versatile,[8] ever-more complex engineering solutions can be created by means of computer-aided design (CAD) technologies.[9]

Since most solutions to complex problems require human involvement as an essential part of system operation, problem-solving technologies have evolved to include reliable determinants for individual and group capabilities and behavior (human factors). However, the need to analyze systems with such relationships

---

[5] The laws of nature are derived and explained through the scientific process (see Appendix D).

[6] J. Robertshaw, *Problem Solving: A Systems Approach* (New York, NY: Petrocelli Books, Inc., 1978), p. 226: "...when the depth of analysis reaches the point where the relationships have been defined precisely, powerful and sophisticated mathematical techniques can be applied."

[7] Software programs are now able to handle more than one million variables (T. Simpson, "Multidisciplinary Design Optimization," *Aerospace America*, December 2003, p. 38).

[8] Computing power increased by nine to ten orders of magnitude from 1970 to 2000, and it continues to grow at exponential rates.

[9] The principal limiting factor of the solution of many complex problems is the size and speed of computers available for modeling and simulation. Since their inception in the mid-twentieth century, high-speed computers ("super computers") have been used for modeling and simulating natural phenomena and humanmade products. However, there is currently a need for much more powerful computers, and despite continual advances in super computer technology, that need is expected to persist for the foreseeable future. (See K. Greene, "Simulators Face Real Problems," *Science*, vol. 301 [July 18, 2003], p. 301.)

(and the vast amounts of data they generate) remains a significant challenge to both scientists and engineers.

The Engineering Design Process

The solution to a problem involves an applied force that causes a displacement from one condition to another or prevents a given condition from occurring. A solution, then, is a forcible disturbance in the natural order of things that always entails costs and produces unintended side effects. For the creation of a solution to a problem, engineers complete the initial steps of the problem-solving method: the identification and analysis of the problem; the gathering of all relevant, reliable knowledge; the setting of priorities; the definition of measurable goals; etc. If an existing solution is not deemed satisfactory for the solution of the problem being addressed, engineers then proceed with the design of a new solution, which entails (1) ideation, (2) modeling and (3) testing (an expansion of the steps of the problem-solving method—see Appendix F).

IDEATION

Ideation is the formulation of new ideas; it is a key element of the engineering profession. Nothing new would ever be invented without a visionary approach to problem solution. After the first steps of the problem-solving method have been completed and the decision has been made to create a new solution, engineers engage in ideation—the evocation of ideas for a solution[10]—through brainstorming sessions in which ideas flow freely, and even outlandish ideas are discussed and recorded.[11]

MODELING

Of the proposed solution-ideas that evolve from ideation, the one deemed to have the greatest likelihood of success is selected for the first stages of the design process, and a model (formulated description) of the solution-idea and its environment is then created. Models of proposed solutions incorporate the data derived from the problem-model and the solution-parameters model created by the first steps of the problem-solving method (see Appendix F); models are the links between the imagination, where ideas for solutions are formed, and the real world, where solutions operate. Models are less difficult to construct and manipulate than the real-world structures or processes they represent and they

---

[10] The engineering design process and the traditional method of lawmaking both involve ideation. Before a new engineering design is contemplated, however, the first several steps of the problem-solving method must be completed. In other words, the first step of the traditional method of lawmaking is the midpoint of the engineering design process (see Table 7-2, Chapter 7).

[11] E. Krick, *An Introduction to Engineering* (New York, NY: John Wiley & Sons, Inc., 1976), p. 96: "One reason that brainstorming is fruitful is that the rapid-fire flow of ideas is repeatedly redirecting each participant's thoughts into new channels....each person's mind is buffeted about the solution space in random fashion, forcing 'big jumps' to distant points, thus combating the clustering tendency. The probability is high that some of these excursions will lead to profitable ideas."

are the common basis of communication and understanding among engineers during each stage of solution development.[12]

Increasingly, models consist of computer software programs that are created and manipulated by CAD techniques, but they may also be composed of charts, blueprints, written text and miniature-scale structures. Models are essential for the development of complex solutions because the intellect alone cannot possibly analyze and predict the dynamics of a complex system, such as a nuclear reactor or a suspension bridge, without the use of models. A model is a reality check; if a workable model of a solution-idea cannot be constructed, that idea must be abandoned.

Since every product created by engineering is part of, operates within and has an impact upon the physical world, models must accurately depict the structure and dynamics of the proposed solution and its interaction with its environment. Engineers must therefore have access to all relevant knowledge of the structure, forces, costs, mechanics and availability of the components of the product or process they are creating, as well as the physical, social and legal environments within which their product will operate. If a model is accurate in its depiction of real-world conditions, the performance of the proposed solution can be predicted.

Offsetting the desirability for the creation of accurate models is the expenditure of resources required to design a model. It is possible to make design refinements of any model indefinitely, but resources are always limited and the ultimate goal is problem solution, not perfection of the model. As Robertshaw points out: "It is easy to become caught up in useless refinements in order to satisfy...perfectionism....Perfectionism is costly and, in any case, unattainable....'sufficientism'...is the rule for creating a model."[13] Therefore the challenge for engineers is to create *sufficiently* accurate models with a minimum expenditure of money, time, labor and other resources.[14] The creation of a model from the ideation stage of engineering design is depicted in Figure E-4.

---

[12] Krick, p. 170: "most communication [of engineering designs] is through models."

[13] Robertshaw, p. 42.

[14] The ability to create effective models of solutions, leading to the efficacious solution of real-world problems with a minimum expenditure of resources, is termed *design expertise*. Design expertise is the goal of engineering education. It requires the students of engineering not only to have an understanding of the structure and dynamics of their proposed solutions and the environment (physical, human, legal, etc.) in which those solutions will operate but also to create effective models with a minimum expenditure of resources.

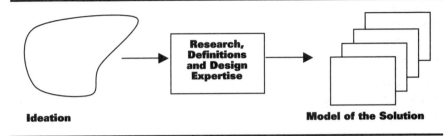

| Ideation | Model of the Solution |

Figure E-4. Creation of a Model of the Solution: After a problem has been defined and analyzed and the decision has been made to create a solution, a model, or formulated description, of the solution is constructed. The model of the solution conforms to the solution parameters derived by the first steps of the problem-solving method.

TESTING

Once a model of the solution has been constructed, it is subjected to a program of testing to verify its design integrity and predict its performance.[15] Testing is used to assure that the solution will be effective, cost-efficient and safe; it provides decision makers with the knowledge needed to commit to the implementation of the solution.[16] Multiple design configurations may be tested until optimum design parameters are identified.[17] This iterative process leads to the evolution of a model that approximates the desired performance of the solution. Then the decision can be made to commit resources to the next stage of problem solution.

If the testing program discloses that a given solution cannot achieve the desired performance, the design process is repeated with adjusted parameters, or a new solution is created. It is just as important to document the results of failed models as to document successes. Reports of both failures and successes are valuable additions to humankind's store of knowledge; failed designs and techniques can be avoided in the future, and successes can be exploited.[18]

If the results of testing indicate that the proposed solution is unable to achieve the stated goal within the specified performance envelope, either the proposed solution is rejected or the goal or performance envelope is modified so that the proposed solution will satisfy the modified performance requirements. For products such as automobiles that are to be produced in large numbers, a working model, or prototype, is created and tested under controlled condi-

---

[15] G. Beakley, *Engineering: An Introduction to a Creative Profession* (New York, NY: Macmillan Publishing Co., 1986), p. 456: "There are five frequently used objectives for engineering tests. These objectives determine: (1) quality assurance of materials and subassemblies, (2) performance, (3) life, endurance, and safety, (4) human acceptance, and (5) effects of the environment."

[16] Robertshaw, p. 41: "The model is a means to an end: decision making."

[17] The utility of a model is obvious when the model fails during testing; the failure of a model is not catastrophic, and models can be repeatedly redesigned and retested.

[18] H. Petroski, *To Engineer Is Human* (New York, NY: St. Martin's Press, 1985), p. xii: "I believe that the concept of failure...is central to understanding engineering, for engineering design has as its first and foremost objective the obviation of failure. Thus the colossal disasters that do occur are ultimately failures of design...."

tions.[19] If the results of testing verify that the predicted performance of the pro-posed solution is satisfactory, the decision to proceed with the implementation of the solution is made, and resources are dedicated to the production and op-eration of the solution.

IMPLEMENTATION, PERFORMANCE EVALUATION AND OPTIMIZATION

After a solution to a problem has been introduced into its real-world environ-ment, it is essential to know if it has been successful in its purpose. A process of measurement and analysis of a solution's performance must therefore be under-taken to determine if problem-solving goals have been reached (see The Study of Humanmade Products, Appendix D). For products and processes that have an impact upon the public well-being, a performance report is prepared. Reports include a description of the effectiveness, costs, reliability, safety and side effects of each solution; any identified flaws in the design or operation of the solution are included or referenced in the report.

The results of performance testing provide decision makers with the knowl-edge needed to continue (or discontinue) using the product and to make design changes that optimize its performance. The follow-up evaluation process of engi-neering products, which is an ongoing process that seeks optimum problem-solving performance, completes the steps of the problem-solving method and leads to the solution of ever-more complex problems.

Characteristics of Engineering Products

The products of engineering are created by humans and are thus susceptible to design imperfections. Tools are intended to be useful, i.e., beneficial for humans, but they entail multiple costs, disturb the natural order of things and produce unintended and unwanted side effects. To satisfy the requirements of usefulness, a tool is accepted only if its problem-solving utility is greater than the sum of its costs and side effects.[20] Although engineering has been highly beneficial for the human condition, there are two negative consequences that stem from the crea-tion of tools. The first negative consequence is that tools can be used as weapons. In particular, chemical, biological and nuclear technologies that have beneficial applications have also been converted to weapons and used to destroy the lives of millions of people.[21]

---

[19] An example of a testing procedure is the flight test program that new aircraft designs must complete in order to obtain a certificate of airworthiness from the Federal Aviation Administration.

[20] To assure that engineering advances are effective and safe, high-quality standards for the design and operation of the products of engineering are maintained by engineering and science professions. See, for example, T. Hunter, *Engineering Design for Safety* (New York, NY: McGraw-Hill, 1992). Quality stan-dards, based upon advances in engineering methodology, are also mandated by law and enforced by government regulatory agencies.

[21] A major challenge for democracies is to solve the related problems of war and the threat of offensive weapons—problems that will need to be addressed by the engineering discipline of laws (see Chapter 7).

The second negative consequence is that engineering advances frequently disturb or even eliminate—through the economic process of "creative destruction"—established and comfortable but outmoded occupations and businesses. While such advances are beneficial for the people as a whole in terms of higher living standards and quality of life, they necessarily produce sociological disruptions. For example, technological improvements in farming resulted in a sharp decline in the size of the agricultural work force in the United States from 1900 (when greater than 40 percent of the national work force engaged in farming) to 2000 (when less than 3 percent of the work force engaged in farming). A similar trend is now occurring in manufacturing,[22] and at some point in the future, all manual labor may be performed by machines.

While technological advances improve productivity and free humans from the need to perform tedious and hazardous tasks, they have negative consequences to the extent that they cause economic dislocations. For example, the development of the polio vaccine was detrimental for the companies that manufactured, sold and serviced respiratory assist devices known as *iron lungs*. A key consideration in the process of engineering, therefore, is to be aware of and minimize the negative societal impact of technological advances.[23] The characteristics of the products of engineering are listed in Table E-1.

- Tools are useful; they are the means by which problems are solved and thus enhance human capabilities.
- Tools are the products of human creative effort.
- Tools are susceptible to design imperfections.
- The application of tools disturbs the natural order of things.
- Tools have multiple costs; they consume and divert resources.
- Tools can be applied to destructive purposes.
- Tools produce unintended and unwanted side effects.
- The performance of tools can be determined.
- The performance of tools can be improved.

Table E-1. Characteristics of the Products of Engineering

Relevance to Laws and Lawmaking

The creative problem-solving process of engineering is highly valuable to the human condition. Although it is an intensely human enterprise and therefore fallible, engineering has been successful in the production of increasingly sophisticated and capable tools. As scientific knowledge and problem-solving technologies continue to grow through the dynamics of science and engineering, problems of ever-greater complexity will be solved, and engineering will thus continue to play a significant and beneficial role in human affairs.

---

[22] R. Doyle, "Deindustrialization: Why Manufacturing Continues to Decline," *Scientific American,* May 2002, p. 30.
[23] The principal engineering challenge to the design of a new supersonic transport aircraft (SST), for example, is not airworthiness, but environmental concerns such as noise and air pollution.

The laws of government have all the characteristics of engineering products; they are *tools*. However, laws are presently created (by means of the traditional method of lawmaking) without the benefit of the knowledge-based methodologies of engineering disciplines. When quality design standards for laws are implemented, a new engineering discipline of laws will come into being and, based upon the experience of all other engineering disciplines, it will be successful in the creation of laws that meet the requirements of democracy.

The Problem-Solving Method

A *problem* is the need or desire for change from a less desirable condition to a more desirable condition, and a *solution* is the forcible action applied to bring about the desired change. Nature supplies humankind with a never-ending series of problems to be solved: hunger, pollution, disease, ignorance, etc. Whenever one problem is solved, a new problem takes its place. Even if all our current problems were to be solved, we would then face boredom, which would be another problem. The following discussion briefly outlines the steps of the **problem-solving method**, which is the only reliable procedure for solving problems.

The problem-solving method consists of a series of steps divided into three sections: (1) problem analysis, (2) selection and implementation of a solution and (3) follow-up evaluation and optimization of the solution. For simple problems, the problem-solving method is not consciously observed. For large and complex problems, each step of the problem-solving method must be observed and documented.

Problem Analysis

STEP 1: PROBLEM IDENTIFICATION

A problem must be known before it can be solved. As an example, suppose that I asked you to help me solve a problem with my bicycle but did not tell you the nature of the problem. What solution would you recommend? Add air to the front tire? Replace the chain? Tighten the brakes? If you advised me to perform any or all of these tasks, would the problem be solved? The answer is unknown because a problem cannot be solved until it has first been identified; you cannot possibly offer me any meaningful solution to the problem with my bicycle if you do not know what the problem is. Also, for as long as the problem remains unknown, your search for solutions will continue indefinitely until time or resources, or both, are exhausted—and the status of the problem will still remain unknown.

The point of the example is simple: If a problem has not been identified, no deliberate process can solve it, and the problem may even be nonexistent. The essential first step of the problem-solving method, therefore, must be to define the undesirable condition that needs to be changed. In the formal solution of problems, a written statement is prepared that encompasses the broad scope of the problem in one or two sentences. The purpose of the statement is to assure that everyone involved with the problem-solving process has a clear understanding of the problem in its simplest form. Examples of problem definition statements might include, "I have a toothache," or "We have insufficient funds." The importance of problem identification cannot be overemphasized; it is the focal point that gives direction to all the efforts that follow. If a problem cannot be defined, its existence cannot be confirmed and no problem-solving efforts on its behalf can be justified.

STEP 2: PRIORITY ASSIGNMENT

After the problem has been stated in its broadest sense, it is assigned a priority for solution. The assignment of a priority to each defined problem with respect to all other problems is an important decision because resources for problem solution are always limited, and logic dictates that the most urgent problems should be solved first.[1]

STEP 3: PROBLEM ANALYSIS

The first step of problem definition was deliberately superficial. The goal of step 3 is to derive relevant and accurate knowledge of the size and nature of the problem so that a prudent decision can be made regarding the next stage of problem solution. The problem definition statement of step 1 described an undesirable condition or situation that needed to be transformed into a more desirable condition. But a closer look at any problem reveals that a problem is not simply an undesirable condition—such as a flat tire, a toothache or a rotten apple—but rather the *separation* or displacement of that condition from a more desirable, or reference, condition. That is, the word "problem" is a *comparative* term that describes the difference between two separate conditions. As illustrated in Figure F-1, a problem is the separation between the less desirable condition, A, and a more desirable condition, B.

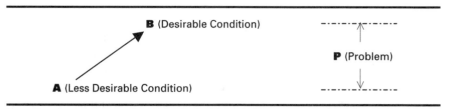

Figure F-1. Conceptual Problem Definition: A problem, **P**, is the **difference** between a desirable condition, **B**, and a less desirable condition, **A**.

Several points become obvious from the relationship between the two conditions:

1. The problem cannot be defined unless *both A and B* are known; ignorance of either A or B precludes problem definition or solution.
2. The problem does not exist if A and B are equal (because there will be no need or desire for change).

---

[1] Robertshaw, p. 4: "If we solve a problem by allocating resources, we must decide which and how much of our resources to allocate. Thus, decision plays a fundamental role in problem solving."

3. The size of the problem is proportionate to the separation between A and B.
4. The difference between A and B only describes the problem; it does not provide any information regarding the means by which the problem may be solved.

The task of the problem-analysis step is to gather, analyze and document all the facts relevant to the *definition* of the problem—points A, B and the displacement between them. The collection and manipulation of data necessary for problem analysis therefore require expertise in the physical measurement of the problem and in data analysis. The investigative techniques used for the competent collection and analysis of data of large and complex problems must meet all established scientific and legal standards—such as efficacy, safety, environmental protection and ethics. In addition, there is a limit to the time and resources available for any project and it is not possible to obtain complete knowledge of complex problems, since that would take infinite time. The challenge for the individuals who perform problem analysis, therefore, is to provide decision makers with *sufficient* knowledge of the problem to make prudent decisions, and to obtain that knowledge with a minimal consumption of resources.

When relevant knowledge of the problem has been gathered, it is organized into a document that presents a *model* of the problem.[2] Models are essential for problem solution because they depict real-world problems in terms that can be understood and communicated by those responsible for solving them. As noted, the problem-definition model needs only to provide knowledge sufficient for prudent decision making, but that knowledge must be relevant and accurate. If the model is inaccurate, the solution will be inappropriate. If the model overestimates the size or severity of the problem, the solution will be unnecessarily large or forceful. If no model (i.e., no collation of reliable knowledge) exists, decision makers will be forced to rely upon anecdotal evidence and their own opinions to understand the problem—a condition of ignorance in which complex problems cannot possibly be understood and effective solutions can never be created.

A typical model of a complex problem may contain descriptive narrative, databases, charts, graphs, mathematical descriptions, diagrams and photographs, all of which are (ideally) organized and presented in a manner that clearly explains the size and nature of the problem. The individuals who collect and analyze data must employ accepted methods and equipment for data collection and have suitable educational and experiential backgrounds for the tasks. They must also be able to communicate their findings in language that can be understood by decision makers, and provide references for all the methods and materials used to create the model. If a solution to a complex problem fails because of an inadequate or faulty model, the documentation of the methods and materials used to construct the model provides a "paper trail" that will assist in the detection and correction of flaws in the preparation of the model.

---

[2] Models are now routinely constructed and tested by means of digital computers.

An example of the expertise required for problem analysis may be illustrated by a hypothetical problem of ground water pollution in a metropolitan area. The construction of a model of the problem would require the following:

- A simple statement of the ground water pollution problem must be provided so that everyone who works with the problem understands the condition that must be corrected.
- A reliable and accurate means of measuring each pollutant must be available.
- The identification and quantity of each pollutant must be defined.
- The environmental significance of each pollutant must be known and described.
- The sources of ground water pollution must be identified.
- The objective of problem solution (desirable condition B) must be defined so that the separation between A and B (the size of the problem) is known.
- Each method and device of measurement and analysis, and the qualifications of the analysts who perform each task, must be established and documented to assure that all scientific, ethical and legal standards have been met.
- The gathering of data and analysis of the problem-model must satisfy scientific and legal requirements of effectiveness, safety, and minimum costs and side effects.
- The written report of the problem-model must be sufficiently clear, accurate and complete so that all involved individuals will be able to understand and make competent decisions regarding its contents.

If in the preceding hypothetical example, the ground water pollutants included chemical toxins, heavy metals, microorganisms and radioactive materials, individuals of many different scientific backgrounds (e.g., biologists, geologists, chemists, medical physicists and statisticians) would need to participate in the preparation of the problem-model. Also, a wide variety of measuring instruments and techniques would be required. This example demonstrates that the problem-analysis step is a knowledge-intensive and knowledge-dependent process; this step must provide relevant and reliable knowledge for the decision-making process of problem solution. For every field of endeavor—energy production, medicine, waste management, agriculture, transportation, etc.—the need for clearly documented, accurate, relevant, knowledge-based problem-models is universal.

STEP 4: REASSIGNMENT OF PRIORITIES

After the problem has been satisfactorily analyzed and the accumulated knowledge of its size and significance has been collated, a decision is made about whether or not to proceed with the search for a solution to the problem. If the analysis demonstrates that the problem cannot be solved with existing resources or technologies, the prudent decision will be to conserve resources by suspending the problem-solving exercise until its solution becomes possible. Similarly, no resources will be designated for the solution of a problem that has been found to be trivial or nonexistent.

If the decision is made to proceed with the solution to the problem, the priority of the problem is reassessed. If the problem-model discloses that the problem is of lesser or greater significance than was originally estimated, it is given a lower or higher priority for solution than was assigned to it in the second step. The value of competent problem analysis is that it provides decision makers with the knowledge needed to optimally assign resources for the solution of the most significant, real and solvable problems.

Selection and Implementation of a Solution

The first part of the problem-solving method was concerned with understanding the problem. The process was one of investigation, or deconstruction, in which the problem was broken down into its individual components for analysis. In contrast, the creation of a solution is a process of synthesis, or construction, in which various solution elements are assembled into an effective solution to the problem.

STEP 5: STATEMENT OF PURPOSE

The solution to a problem is the means by which the translation to the desired state of affairs is accomplished. The beginning point of a solution is the same (less desirable) condition that was defined in the problem-model, and the endpoint is the objective that is sought. The end, or goal, of problem solution must be known before any steps are taken to reach that goal; an objective cannot be reached by any means if that objective is unknown. It is also elementary that the goal must be clearly defined so that no one engaged in the problem-solving effort expends resources on the wrong objective. Therefore the first step in the creation of a solution is to establish an attainable goal of the problem-solution process.[3]

Since the problem has been defined as the separation between points A and B in the problem-model, it is logical to assume that the real-world objective of the solution has already been defined as condition B of the problem-model depicted in Figure F-1. However, this assumption is not quite correct. Why? Isn't the real-world objective the same as the desired condition that was described in the model? The answer is no.

The search for a solution involves a subtle change in the definition of the real-world problem: The conditions A and B that define the problem need to be converted from real-world conditions to the *measurements* of those conditions. The only way to know that the problem has been solved is to use a measuring system that demonstrates that condition B has been reached. Therefore the real-world objective for the solution is not the desirable condition B, but rather the *measurement* of that condition (designated B′), which confirms that the desirable endpoint has been reached. Likewise, the initial condition A is converted to the *measurement* of A (designated A′). The new definition of the problem is now the

---

[3] The establishment of an attainable goal by team leaders is elementary to problem solution. If no goal is established, or if the goal is undefined, the exercise is purposeless; if an unattainable goal is sought, the process is inane.

difference between the measurements of A and B: Problem (P') = B' minus A', as depicted in Figure F-2.

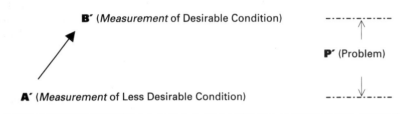

B' (*Measurement* of Desirable Condition)

P' (Problem)

A' (*Measurement* of Less Desirable Condition)

Figure F-2. Actual Problem Definition: A problem is defined as the difference between the **measurements** of conditions **A** and **B**.

The difference between the real-world problem and the measurement of the problem is illustrated by the example of a flat tire. The flat tire is condition A of the problem, and the reference condition B is the fully inflated tire. To solve the problem, an air pump is attached to the tire and air is added until the tire is satisfactorily inflated, that is, when condition B is reached, as shown in Figure F-3.

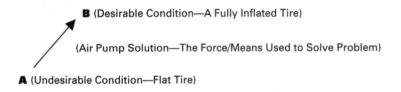

B (Desirable Condition—A Fully Inflated Tire)

(Air Pump Solution—The Force/Means Used to Solve Problem)

A (Undesirable Condition—Flat Tire)

Figure F-3. Conceptual Solution of the Flat Tire Problem: To solve the flat tire problem, an air pump (air pressure force) is used to inflate the tire.

But how does one know when the tire is fully inflated? The answer is to use an air pressure gauge that indicates when a predetermined air pressure has been reached. In other words, the objective for the solution is not the fully inflated tire (B), but rather the *pressure gauge reading* (B') that indicates that the tire is fully inflated. Thus the solution to the problem is to cause the transition from a tire pressure measurement of zero to the desired tire pressure measurement, which will be, for example, a given number of pounds per square inch, as shown in Figure F-4.

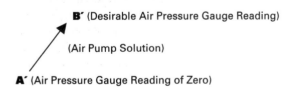

B' (Desirable Air Pressure Gauge Reading)

(Air Pump Solution)

A' (Air Pressure Gauge Reading of Zero)

Figure F-4. Actual Solution of the Flat Tire Problem: The solution of the problem involves the transition from the less desirable air pressure gauge reading to the more desirable reading.

Similarly, an air conditioning system is not activated by the temperature in a room, but rather by the thermometer reading of that temperature, and the cruise control of an automobile does not respond directly to the speed of the automobile, but to the measurement of speed. The important point is that a solution to a problem, no matter how sophisticated, depends on the *empirical method of measurement* used to detect when the objective of the solution process has been satisfied. For the aforementioned reasons, a statement of purpose is issued to specify the attainable and *measurable* objective (B′) that is sought as the end of the problem-solving process. The statement of purpose is typically one or two sentences long, and it provides a simple, clear and concise definition of the *goal* of problem solution. It gives direction and clarity to the problem-solving process and minimizes the possibility that substantive problem-solving forces will be applied without a purpose. Note that the purpose statement does not restrict in any way the method of solution that may be applied to achieve the goal. The statement of purpose produces a subtle conversion of the problem-solving process because it changes the problem to be solved from the original problem that was defined in the problem-model to the challenge of achieving a measurable endpoint, as depicted in Figure F-5.

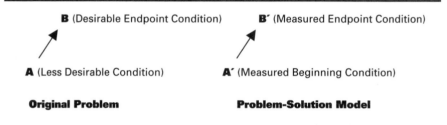

Figure F-5. Comparison of the Original Problem with a Problem-Solution Model: The objective of problem solution is to reach the desired, measurable endpoint or condition.

In the example of the flat tire problem, the purpose statement might read, "The purpose is to attain a fully inflated tire, whose pressure gauge reading is forty pounds per square inch." An important point must be stressed at this juncture. It is a common error for individuals who are unfamiliar with problem-solving techniques to state that the means (the force applied) rather than the end (the measurable objective) is the purpose of problem solution, despite the fact that means and ends are completely different concepts. The problem is that confusing the means with the ends may result in the expenditure of resources on processes that have no objective. For example, the purpose statement of the flat tire problem should never read, "The purpose is to inflate the tire," because inflating the tire is the *means*, the force that is applied, not the *end* that is sought. If one's purpose were "to inflate the tire," then there would be no defined endpoint and the absurd result would be that the air inflation process would continue indefinitely (see discussion of means and ends, Appendix G).

STEP 6: DEFINITION OF PERFORMANCE ENVELOPE

The solution is the forcible means by which the problem is solved. Because all solutions consume resources and produce changes in the natural order of things, the number of potential solutions to the problem is limited by intrinsic and extrinsic constraints that define the limits, or "performance envelope," within which a given solution must operate. Performance envelopes include the functional requirements and external restrictions which, taken together, make up a model of the solution domain, or pathway. *Functional requirements* refer to the intrinsic performance attributes of the solution, such as its effectiveness and operating costs. *External restrictions* refer to such factors as legal constraints[4] and the time and money that can be allocated to the solution. The design effort must identify and specify the maximum and minimum requirements and restrictions that define the performance envelope of acceptable solutions to the problem.

STEP 7: SEARCH FOR SOLUTIONS

After the goal of problem solution has been established and the performance envelope of the solution has been defined, the next step is to search for and identify existing solutions, if any, that are able to solve the problem. All previous successful problem-solving efforts have produced a reservoir of solutions that are available for application to new problems. Since design efforts always consume resources, the selection of a satisfactory existing solution is usually preferred to the design of a new solution. Therefore it is prudent to search for and apply a suitable existing solution, if possible, before embarking on a design effort to create a new solution. A literature search for existing solutions is initiated by consulting information sources such as the computer databases, trade publications and scientific literature that have references to appropriate solutions for the stated goal. For example, a physician may consult the *Physicians' Desk Reference* to find the optimum existing medication (solution) for the treatment of a patient's diagnosed medical problem.

The calculation of the predicted usefulness of complex solutions is often imprecise because benefits and costs are often difficult to quantify and convert into equivalent terms for comparison. In addition, the value of many intangible variables, such as aesthetics (or the lack thereof), and uncertainties, such as the future price of gasoline or insurance, can only be estimated. Nevertheless, all parameters that define performance, including the benefits and costs of intangible and uncertain factors, must be estimated and reduced to equivalent terms (such as the dollar value of each benefit and cost), so that the performance of each solution can be calculated and then compared to the performance of every other solution.[5]

---

[4] Since all solutions must operate within the established framework of laws, it is important that laws are simply stated and have a clear meaning (see Appendix I).
[5] Robertshaw, p. 232: "The essence of problem solving is decision, and the essence of decision is to compare alternatives (not to evaluate each alternative in an absolute sense)."

When the number of possible solutions to a problem is large,[6] the search for solutions and the description of their performance parameters could continue indefinitely; it is possible to analyze anything forever. As a practical matter, the search for solutions is always limited by time and cost restraints. Therefore, it is the obligation of the individuals who conduct the search for solutions to be as thorough, accurate and cost-efficient as possible in deriving the information necessary to reach the best possible decision. Because surveys are rarely complete and simplified assumptions are used to evaluate intangible and uncertain factors, documentation of the sources of information and the assumptions and evaluations used to complete the survey is essential for follow-up evaluations.

A detailed model of the parameters of the solution and its environment is created by the satisfactory completion of Steps 5, 6 and 7. The combination of the problem-model and solution-parameters model constitutes the reference point from which an existing solution is selected or a new solution is designed (see Appendix E).

STEP 8: SELECTION OF A SOLUTION

When the search for solutions identifies multiple satisfactory solutions, the decision can be made to choose the most efficacious one.[7] The selection of a solution, therefore, is an *optimization* process. If several solutions have the same performance, they will be equally satisfactory, and the choice of a solution may then be based upon non-performance criteria such as aesthetics. When a satisfactory solution is found, it is implemented and the problem-solving method proceeds to section three (follow-up evaluation and optimization). Most problems in most fields of endeavor are solved by means of existing solutions. In other words, most problems are initially solved without the need for designers (engineers) to create new solutions. If the literature search for solutions discloses that the performance of existing solutions is inadequate, or that no solutions for the problem exist, then a new solution that conforms to the requirements of the solution-model must be created (see discussion of the steps of engineering design—an expansion of the steps of the problem-solving method—in Appendix E). While the creation of new solutions to problems is not limited to the engineering profession (anyone may potentially create inventions or improvements in existing products and processes), engineering is the only formal discipline capable of efficaciously solving complex problems by the creation of new solutions.

---

[6] For example, what are the possible modes of travel (solutions) that may be selected for transportation between San Diego and San Francisco, California? The list includes automobile, roller skates, submarine, motorized hang glider, jet, sailboat, ox-drawn cart and suborbital rocket, among scores of other possibilities.

[7] A stipulation of the problem-solving process is that the solution selected for a given problem should always be the most useful solution. The optimum choice among alternative solutions for a given problem is the one that provides the greatest benefits and incurs the lowest costs (time, energy, labor, investment, resource diversion, risks, side effects, etc.). Also, the decision to replace an original solution with a new solution is always predicated upon the greater usefulness of the newer solution.

STEP 9: IMPLEMENTATION OF THE SOLUTION

After a solution to a problem has been selected or created and the decision has been made to implement the solution, it is introduced into its real-world environment. Since solutions have an impact on the (legal, human, physical) environment, it is important that the parameters that define its interaction with the environment be identified, and that steps be taken to measure those parameters. For example, if the solution is a transport aircraft, the parameters of the performance of the aircraft—including its impact on the environment—must be defined, and the methods for measuring those parameters must be made available. It will then be possible to derive meaningful measures of the performance of the solution.

Follow-Up Evaluation and Optimization of the Solution

STEP 10: PERFORMANCE EVALUATION

After a solution has been implemented, it is essential to know if it has been successful in its purpose. A process of measurement and analysis of the performance of solutions must therefore be undertaken to determine if the problem-solving goals have been reached. The measurement, analysis and recording of the performance of solutions (see Appendix D) provide feedback used for *quality assurance.* The key requirements of performance testing are the availability of suitable instruments and empirical methods of measurement and analysis, and the ability of analysts to use those tools and methods to derive reliable assessments of performance.[8]

For products and processes that have an impact upon the public well-being, a performance report is prepared. Reports include a description of the effectiveness, operating costs, reliability, safety and side effects of each solution. Any identified flaws in the design or operation of the solution are included or referenced in the report. The results of performance testing provide decision makers with the knowledge needed for the disposition of each solution. The results also add valuable information to humankind's store of knowledge, which may be used to advantage for the solution of problems of greater complexity.

STEP 11: OPTIMIZATION

The periodic re-evaluation of the performance of a solution provides data that can be used to make design improvements in the solution. Through this process of optimization, or quality improvement, design flaws are corrected and design changes are made to increase the solution's effectiveness, safety and user-friendliness.

---

[8] Performance testing is of little or no value if the measuring system is unreliable or inaccurate, if the measurements are meaningless, or if the tests are conducted by individuals who are incompetent or otherwise unsuited to the task of gathering, analyzing and documenting all pertinent data. Also, testing is an expensive proposition; every test must be of value (and a quality assurance program for the testing procedure is therefore necessary to determine that the tests and testing program have acceptable performance!).

After the design changes have been made, documented and implemented, the feed-back process of quality assurance for the solution is then repeated, and problems are thus solved by increasingly efficacious means.

The importance of the problem-solving method in the solution of problems cannot be overemphasized. It is the only reliable method by which problems can be solved. There are no real-world problems that it cannot address, and it will not attempt to solve a problem that does not exist. If a problem cannot be solved by the problem-solving method, that problem cannot be solved. The successful solution of complex problems in every purposeful field mandates that the steps of the problem-solving method be observed.[9] The problem-solving method, which is the process of wisdom (see Appendix L), is depicted in Figure F-6.

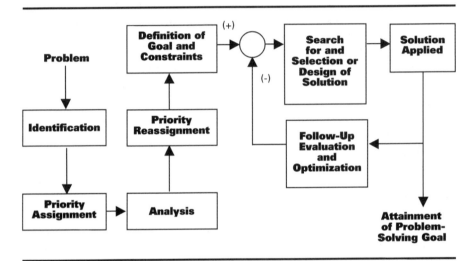

Figure F-6. The Problem-Solving Method: The problem-solving method is a multistep, knowledge-based feedback control system (see Appendix C); it is the only reliable process by which complex problems can be solved.

Relevance to Laws and Lawmaking

The traditional method of lawmaking that currently addresses problems is a law-making rather than a problem-solving process (see Chapters 3 and 4, and Appendices G and J). If the goals of a true democracy are to be achieved, the traditional method of lawmaking must be replaced by the problem-solving method.

---

[9] Since the efficacious solution of problems requires the availability and prudent application of reliable knowledge, it follows that lack of knowledge is the principal limiting factor in the solution of every problem. The biggest problem of all, therefore, is ignorance, and that problem, which should logically receive a high priority for solution by every democracy, can be solved by the application of processes that derive and promulgate reliable knowledge (see Appendix D).

Means and Ends

The *purpose,* or *objective,* of any activity is an endpoint or a condition that is sought, and the *means* is the force applied to reach that endpoint. The relationship between beginning point (A), means (F) and endpoint (B) is illustrated in Figure G-1.

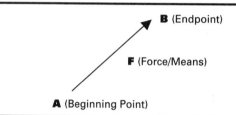

Figure G-1. The Relationship Between Means (Force) and Ends (Goals): A force **(F)** is the **means** that must be applied to cause the transition from the beginning point **(A)** to the endpoint **(B)**.

The difference between means and ends is illustrated by the following examples. Select the correct answer for each of the Questions:

The purpose of a surgeon is to:
1. Perform surgery.
2. Fight fires.
3. Make laws.
4. Drive a truck.
5. None of the above.

The purpose of a legislator is to:
1. Perform surgery.
2. Fight fires.
3. Make laws.
4. Drive a truck.
5. None of the above.

The purpose of a firefighter is to:
1. Perform surgery.
2. Fight fires.
3. Make laws.
4. Drive a truck.
5. None of the above.

The purpose of a truck driver is to:
1. Perform surgery.
2. Fight fires.
3. Make laws.
4. Drive a truck.
5. None of the above.

What is the correct answer for each of these questions? Number 5, None of the above. The first four answers are wrong because they mistakenly state that the purpose is the *force or action* that is carried out rather than the *objective* that is sought. For example, the *purpose*, or objective, of a surgeon is not to perform surgery but to cure disease; surgery is one of the *means* by which that objective is achieved. The purpose of a firefighter is not to fight fires but to attain a safe, fire-free condition by means of firefighting tools and materials such as water and chemicals; and the purpose of a truck driver is not to drive a truck but to assure the delivery of cargo to a specified destination. Similarly, the purpose of a legislator is not to make laws but to accomplish the solution of societal problems by efficacious means.

Imagine the chaos—and the outright hazard and waste—that would ensue if the means of the aforementioned occupations were mistaken for their purposes: Surgeons would never stop cutting, firefighters would spray water continuously, truck drivers would drive forever, and legislators would produce laws endlessly. Unfortunately, the misdirected purpose of the traditional method of lawmaking impels legislators to do just that: Make new laws ad infinitum rather than solve societal problems.

The confusion between the means and the ends for the traditional method of lawmaking is illustrated by the following reports of the actions of the legislature of the state of California, filed within a span of three days in the *San Diego Union-Tribune* :

> SACRAMENTO *The...state Legislature in 1986 passed 1,838 bills and sent them to...Gov. Deukmejian. The governor signed 1,514 of them, most of which took effect today.*[1]

Three days later the same newspaper reported the following:

> SACRAMENTO *When the 120 members of the California Legislature convene in the state Capitol tomorrow to begin their two-year, 1987-88 session, it will be in one sense almost as if they hadn't been away: The same major problems that remained unsolved when the last Legislature adjourned—prisons, toxics, soaring liability insurance costs, allowing out-of-state banking in California—will be waiting.*[2]

For the state of California, the same comments regarding the lack of connection between the enactment of laws and the solution of societal problems could be made for every legislative session since (and before) 1987. In fact the same general comments could be made for every democratic government: Legislatures, under the aegis of the traditional method of lawmaking, are induced to enact laws rather than to solve problems. The result is that large numbers of laws are created without reference to the solution of societal problems (see Table 5-2 and the discussion of Chaos in Chapter 5).

---

[1] *San Diego Union-Tribune*, January 1, 1987, p. A-3.
[2] R.P. Studer, "New Session Offers Legislature a Menu That Can Bite Back," *San Diego Union-Tribune*, January 4, 1987, p. C-1.

Relevance to Laws and Lawmaking

If the purpose of democracy is to be realized, the distinction between the means and ends of government must be understood, to wit: The reason for the existence of a law (means) in a democracy is to attain a beneficial problem-solving objective (end). Democracies will take a significant step toward achieving the status of true democracy when the traditional method of lawmaking is modified so that the performance of legislatures is measured by the problems that have been solved rather than the number of laws that have been enacted.

The Quality of Laws Institute

The Quality of Laws Institute, a California nonprofit corporation, was incorporated in 1995.[1] The purpose of the institute is to foster the development and growth of the science and engineering disciplines of laws.

The Science and Engineering Disciplines of Laws

The Quality of Laws Institute is developing a charter for a scientific society of peers. This society will:

- Define and promote professional ethics.
- Serve as the focus of activities for scientists and engineers dedicated to the derivation of scientific knowledge of laws and the development of efficacious solutions for societal problems.
- Act as the gatekeeper of scientific knowledge regarding laws and lawmaking.
- Provide a forum for the discussion of methods, standards and solutions related to laws and lawmaking.
- Publish periodic scientific journals and arrange annual scientific meetings.
- Invite qualified professionals to become members of the society and serve on peer review committees that will evaluate scientific reports submitted for publication in its journals.

PROFESSIONAL STANDARDS

The disciplines of science and engineering are guided by high standards of professional behavior, such as integrity and competency. These standards are intended to prevent politics, prejudice, moneyed interests and other influences from interfering with the search for and prudent application of reliable knowledge. The institute recognizes that non-truth-directed influences will be significantly greater in the scientific study of laws and the lawmaking process than in other sciences. Therefore the society will carefully define and publish—and rigidly observe—professional standards for the derivation and application of scientific knowledge.

PUBLICATIONS

The institute will use strict professional standards to review existing scientific knowledge that encompasses the interrelated fields of codified law, policy studies, sociology, psychology, economics, software engineering, etc. Existing hypotheses

---

[1] www.qualitylaws.org.

and theories that relate to the performance of laws will be reviewed and documented. This enormous task is essential for the establishment of a foundation of scientific facts. Without this foundation, useful hypotheses cannot be formulated for the development of new, reliable knowledge or for the creation of effective models for the solution of complex societal problems. To promulgate scientific knowledge, the institute will publish an index of abstracts, the *Index Lex Legis*, and journals of scientific reports, the *Journal of the Science of Laws* and the *Journal of the Engineering Discipline of Laws*.

Index Lex Legis

Many valid peer-reviewed articles related to the design, structure and mechanics of laws already exist in the worldwide scientific literature. One of the first tasks of the institute will be to develop and publish a bibliographic listing of references to the scientific literature of laws. This Index, the *Index Lex Legis*, will be made available in printed and electronic form.[2] The institute will develop criteria for determining the validity of studies and reports. At a minimum, these criteria will include accepted empirical methods and materials and scientific peer review. The *Index Lex Legis* will allow scientists, engineers and others access to the worldwide scientific knowledge base of laws.

Journal of the Science of Laws

The society will review submitted scientific reports relevant to the study of the structure and mechanics of laws. If a report meets the society's standards, it will be published in its scientific journal, the *Journal of the Science of Laws*. The journal will be a public document that will make scientific knowledge of laws available to all interested parties. Access to scientific reports will enable legislatures to establish an effective quality assurance program to review the performance of laws. The accumulated knowledge of the structure and mechanics of laws will also be the basis for engineering designs that optimally serve the purpose of democracy.

Journal of the Engineering Discipline of Laws

The society will review submitted reports relevant to the design and optimization of the laws of government such as quality design standards, modeling, computational techniques, networking and software reliability. If a report meets the standards of the society, it will be published in its engineering journal, the *Journal of the Engineering Discipline of Laws*. The journal will make knowledge of law-design processes available to all parties interested in the design of laws that efficaciously solve societal problems.

---

[2] The *Index Lex Legis* will provide access to scientific law articles in a manner similar to existing reference sites for medical literature. See, for example, www.pubmedcentral.nih.gov/.

Relevance to Laws and Lawmaking

The Quality of Laws Institute is working to establish the science and engineering disciplines of laws and thereby meet the need for quality programs for laws and the lawmaking process. When these programs are developed and applied to laws and lawmaking, it will become possible to create laws that consistently and efficaciously satisfy the purpose of democracy.

The Ideal Law of Government

Democracies are highly popular because they serve the best interests of the people as a whole under the rule of law. The problem with the rule of law is that it is wholly dependent upon the quality of laws; if the laws of a government are mediocre or ineffective, the government that enforces those laws must also be mediocre or ineffective. To meet their obligations, democracies must be able to create laws of the highest quality. For this reason it is important to define the *ideal law* as a model for the design of laws for democratic governments.

The ideal law of government has the following characteristics:[1]

IT IS SIMPLY STATED AND HAS A CLEAR MEANING. If the high purpose of democracy is to be achieved, the individuals who enforce and interpret the law and those who are subject to the law must understand both the letter and intent of the law. For these reasons the ideal law is succinct and its meaning is clear.

IT IS COMPLETELY SUCCESSFUL IN ACHIEVING ITS OBJECTIVE. Every law in a democracy has a problem-solving purpose, or objective, that serves the best interests of the people. The ideal law is completely successful in attaining its objective.

IT INTERACTS SYNERGISTICALLY WITH OTHER LAWS. Laws often have an effect on, and are affected by, other laws. The ideal law is designed so that its interaction with other laws is synergistic in the attainment of its problem-solving objective.

IT PRODUCES NO DETRIMENTAL SIDE EFFECTS. All humanmade products, including laws, have unintended side effects that may be beneficial, neutral or detrimental. A law that accomplishes its problem-solving goal is not acceptable if its unintended side effects degrade the established living standards or quality of life of the people, or infringe upon their human rights.

IT OPTIMALLY SERVES THE PURPOSE OF DEMOCRACY. The ideal law imposes the fewest possible burdens on the people in order to attain the optimum positive net benefit of its enforcement.

These characteristics of the ideal law can be attained only by applying quality programs to laws. Quality design standards are needed for the creation of the ideal law; quality assurance standards are needed to determine that the design objectives of the ideal law have been met; and a quality improvement program is needed to

---

[1] Modified from D. Schrunk, "The Ideal Law of Government," *Proceedings of SPACE 2002* (Reston, VA: American Society of Civil Engineers, 2002), pp. 580-6.

maintain the high levels of performance of the ideal law in a dynamic environment. The ideal law is an elegant solution; it solves societal problems effectively in a user-friendly manner with minimum restrictions, costs and side effects, and thus optimally serves the purpose of democracy.[2]

Relevance to Laws and Lawmaking

The ideal law of government serves as a model for the design of laws. While it is not possible to find ideal people to serve democracy in the arena of laws and lawmaking (or any other arena), it is possible to design new laws and to amend existing laws so that they approximate the ideal. A democratic government that is composed of fallible human beings and *ideal laws* will have a far greater likelihood of success in its high purpose than a government that is composed of fallible human beings and *mediocre laws*. A realistic goal for each government is to have all its laws approximate the ideal law.

---

[2] Some problems, such as crime, can never be completely eliminated. The objective of the ideal law is to find the best balance between benefits and burdens so that the societal problem addressed is mitigated in a manner that provides the optimum positive net benefit to the people as a whole.

Solution of Societal Problems: The Limitations of Rhetoric and Dialectic

The traditional method of lawmaking has two steps: (1) the initial design of proposed new laws (bill drafting) and (2) the legislative process. Currently, during the second step of lawmaking, bills are evaluated and subjected to design changes (amendments) by legislators through the mechanisms of rhetoric (persuasive oration) and dialectic (logical argumentation), which are the time-honored methods for manipulating the design of the laws of government.[1] Although rhetoric and dialectic are useful for presenting and examining ideas and, in the case of dialectic, for making decisions, these mechanisms are inadequate for the task of designing laws in a democracy. The purpose of this discussion is to review the utility and limitations of rhetoric and dialectic in the design of laws that satisfy the purpose of democracy.

Rhetoric

Rhetoric is defined as the art of effective expression and the persuasive use of language in speechmaking. The present evaluation is of *political rhetoric* (political oratory), the division of speechmaking that pertains to the design and manipulation of the laws of government as defined by Aristotle:

> *Rhetoric falls into three divisions, determined by the three classes of listeners to speeches. For of the three elements in speech making—speaker, subject, and person addressed—it is the last one, the hearer, that determines the speech's end and object. The hearer must be either a judge, with a decision to make about things past or future, or an observer. A member of the assembly [legislature] decides about future events, a juryman about past events: while those who merely decide on the orator's skill are observers. From this it follows that*

---

[1] Kagan et al. (*The Western Heritage*, p. 302), note that in the medieval time period, skill in rhetoric and dialectic was considered an essential feature of successful government: "The ability to persuade others by clear argument and eloquent prose and speech was the essence of successful government." This observation applies equally well to all present governments, which still rely on the traditional method of lawmaking.

there are three divisions of oratory—(1) political, (2) forensic, and (3) the ceremonial oratory of display.[2]

The key feature of political rhetoric is *persuasion*; its objective in the law-making arena is to persuade a legislature to create laws that advance the interests of the orator. (Political rhetoric is also used to persuade people to vote for candidates for government office; the present discussion is concerned with the lawmaking process.) Consider political rhetoric in contrast with the process of education. The goal of an educator is to increase the knowledge of a group of students, and the measure of an educator's success is the extent to which those students gain knowledge. In contrast, the objective of a political orator is *not* to benefit the audience but rather himself or his cause. The measure of success of the orator, therefore, is not education but *indoctrination*: the extent to which an audience (e.g., a legislature) approves of and acts in accordance with the orator's objectives and beliefs.[3]

The major limitation of rhetoric is that it is not naturally bounded by the constraints of knowledge,[4] honesty or responsibility, and political orators are free to ignore relevant knowledge and manipulate audiences with half-truths and lies without violating any inherent ethical rule of rhetoric. For example, political orators frequently take advantage of the biases of their audience to deliver a persuasive message, as noted by Davies: "Politicians usually design their speeches to confirm audience biases."[5]

It is important to note that the content and meaning of a speech (including the knowledge component, if any) are of little importance as a measure of successful oratory when compared to the manner and style of speechmaking:

...rhetorical spellbinding and the charismatic effect it can induce are produced less by logic and ideas than by emotional stimuli, by words as symbols of more than their literal meaning, in short, by the style of verbal communication.[6]

...a speaker's impact—favorable or unfavorable—is determined by three basic factors: verbal, vocal and visual....Verbal impressions (the actual words spoken) account for only 7 percent of impact. Vocal impressions (tone, range, appeal and "credibility" of the speaker's voice) account for 38 percent of im-

---

[2] Aristotle, *Rhetoric*, Great Books of the Western World, vol. 9, p. 598.

[3] A. Bakshian, Jr., quoting W.B. Yeats in *American Speaker* (Washington, DC: Georgetown Publishing House, Inc., 1994, p. BOD/12): "I always think a great orator convinces us, not by force of reasoning, but because he is visibly enjoying the beliefs he wants us to accept."

[4] For a satirical discussion of the relationship between rhetoric and knowledge, see Plato, *Gorgias*, Great Books of the Western World, vol. 7, p. 258.

[5] Davies, p. 139.

[6] A.R. Willner, *The Spellbinders: Charismatic Political Leadership* (New Haven, CT: Yale University Press, 1984), p. 152.

pact. Visual impressions (the speaker's physical appearance, clothing, gestures, stance, eye contact, etc.) account for a whopping 55 percent of impact.[7]

In other words, successful rhetoric evokes intended emotional responses from the audience by means of impressions rather than truth or logic; it is an exercise of style over substance. Finally, rhetoric is irresponsible in that it has no inherent feedback mechanism that accounts for the consequences, including adverse consequences, of the actions the orator recommends. Thus an unscrupulous orator may, with impunity, obfuscate relevant facts, use half-truths and lies, and ignore potential adverse consequences (i.e., engage in sophistry) to persuade an audience to accept and act upon the agenda of the orator. The use of rhetoric in the law-making process of government is therefore of considerable concern. The limitations and lack of scruples of rhetoric severely restrict its value in the design of laws that satisfy the purpose of democracy, and it is a threat to democracy when it is used to advance agendas that are detrimental to the people as a whole.

Dialectic

Dialectic is defined as logical argumentation, the question-and-answer method of inquiry by which the ideas and opinions of one person are examined by others. The principal value of dialectic is its ability to eliminate illogical concepts and thereby reach the most reasonable conclusion or decision regarding a debatable subject; it is an effective decision-making process and, as such, is an essential element of the problem-solving method (see Appendix F). A significant feature of dialectic is that it does not use empirical methodologies, and relies instead upon logical processes to reach conclusions. That is, dialectic is confined to explorations of the intellect; it is incapable of deriving knowledge of the physical world. For example, a group of hikers may use dialectic to determine that it is in their best interest to travel north but they must use empirical means (e.g., a compass) to determine which direction is north.

There are two forms of dialectic: adversarial and synergistic. In adversarial dialectic the participants are typically divided into two sides that take opposing positions regarding a topic of debate. The goal of each side is to "win" the debate by demonstrating, through logical arguments, that its position or line of reasoning is superior to the position of the other side. The result of adversarial dialectic is that the opinion of the winning side of the debate (and therefore the course of action, if any, advocated by the winning side) prevails over the opinion of the losing side. Examples of adversarial dialectic include the legislative process of governments whose legislatures consist of competing belief systems (ideologies or religions), and the process by which opposing sides in civil or criminal courtroom trials present and defend their positions before a court of law.

---

[7] Bakshian, p. BOD/4.

Synergistic dialectic involves a group of participants who act together to evaluate and reach a consensus regarding a debatable topic. The goal of synergistic dialectic is not to win a debate but to reach a conclusion that represents the collective best opinion of the participants. Examples of synergistic dialectic include the decision-making process that a family uses to purchase an appliance, that corporate executives use in making business decisions and that juries use to weigh the arguments and testimony presented to them in a courtroom trial.[8]

Dialectic is thus a dynamic, interactive reasoning process that critiques, illuminates and provides direction to opinions and ideas. It begins with the presentation of a debatable topic[9] to a group of people (such as a legislature) for evaluation and concludes with a consensus opinion; it is an essential tool for reaching decisions (see Figure J-1).

Debatable Topic ➞ **Dialectic** ➞ **Consensus Opinion**

Figure J-1. Dialectic: Dialectic is a logical decision-making process by which a discussion group evaluates and reaches a consensus regarding a debatable topic.

However, dialectic has three significant limitations: First, it has no regular mechanism for the selection of topics for debate, so a discussion group, however erudite and distinguished, may find itself discussing completely inane subjects. In other words, dialectic requires an external prescreening process to assure that a given subject matter is worthy of serious debate.

The second limitation of dialectic is that it suffers from the same lack of principles that afflicts rhetoric: Unless it is constrained by predefined rules of debate, dialectic is indiscriminate in its treatment of facts, opinions, half-truths and falsehoods in reaching a consensus opinion. Discussion groups are made up of human beings who seek reasonable conclusions, but because humans are fallible, the definition of *reasonableness* may be any presentation, true or false, that "makes sense" or conforms to the preconceived opinions and biases of the people in the discussion group. In reaching what it considers to be a logical conclusion, the group may even give preference to falsehoods over facts if those falsehoods are considered more reasonable than facts. Thus unrestricted dialectic tolerates any means or conclusions, including lies.

---

[8] Synergistic dialectic often breaks down into the adversarial form of dialectic.

[9] A debatable topic is one that has more than one interpretation or conclusion. *Facts* are not debated, since facts have only one true conclusion.

The third limitation is that dialectic, also like rhetoric, incorporates no feed-back mechanism to confirm the validity of the conclusions it reaches.[10] As a result, the participants of the discussion group, unless they are informed by reliable sources of knowledge external to the process of dialectic, remain ignorant of the consequences of their decisions.[11] The participants of dialectic (e.g., the members of a legislative assembly) may then enjoy the "best of all worlds" when they exercise the authority to make decisions but remain unaware of, and therefore take no responsibility for, the consequences of those decisions.[12]

Although dialectic has serious faults, the first two of these can be overcome to a significant degree by confining debate to high-priority topics and to the exclusive use of reliable and relevant sources of knowledge as the basis for reaching conclusions. When it is thus restrained, dialectic can be a highly effective decision-making tool. The third fault of dialectic—the lack of feedback—can be overcome by appending a feedback mechanism that uses empirical methods to measure the consequences of the decisions reached.

The Role of Rhetoric and Dialectic in Lawmaking

Despite their limitations and lack of principles, rhetoric and dialectic continue to be the principal means—by force of tradition—by which legislatures manipulate the design of proposed new laws (bills).[13] However, laws are intended to be the means governments use to achieve their goals; every law in a democracy is created with the intention of satisfying the purpose of democracy.[14] Therefore laws must be purposefully designed to be useful, i.e., to solve problems efficaciously, and that requires that the empirical and analytical steps of the problem-solving method be observed in the design of laws. What are the proper roles for rhetoric and dialectic (neither of which uses empirical methods) in the solution of problems that satisfy the purpose of democracy? To answer that question, the following discussion reviews the ability of rhetoric and dialectic to contribute to the critical steps of the problem-solving method in the creation of laws that satisfy the purpose of democracy.

---

[10] Rhetoric and dialectic, unless they are constrained by external rules, are unreliable in that they are both able, on separate occasions, to reach opposite conclusions from the same premise. Aristotle (*Rhetoric*), p. 594: "No other of the arts draws opposite conclusions [from the same premise]: dialectic and rhetoric alone do this. Both these arts draw opposite conclusions impartially."

[11] Dialectic is a feed-forward control process (see Figure J-1) that produces conclusions but has no inherent feedback mechanism to validate the results of its conclusions (see Appendix C).

[12] Dialectic is the preferred lawmaking process for authoritarian governments, where lawmakers are free to design laws based entirely upon their opinions and do not have to take responsibility for the negative consequences of the laws they enact.

[13] As noted in Chapter 4, bill drafting is the first design step for laws, when an idea for a law is transcribed into a written petition, or bill. The second step is the legislative process, in which substantial changes are made in the design of bills by means of rhetoric and dialectic.

[14] The making of a law of government can be a very simple process when it entails nothing more than the transcription of an order into a written document—a process for which rhetoric and dialectic are more than adequate. However, the efficacious solution of societal problems (the goal of legislators in a democracy) is a far more complicated process (see Appendices E and F).

IDENTIFICATION OF PROBLEMS

The first step of the problem-solving method is identifying societal problems so they can be given a priority for solution by the legislature.[15] The identification of problems requires empirical methods (observation and documentation of real-world phenomena), which are outside the scope of rhetoric and dialectic. (Legislatures are unable, by means of rhetoric and dialectic alone, to identify societal problems; they must rely on the citizenry for the identification of problems.) Therefore rhetoric and dialectic have no role to play in the first step of the problem-solving process for laws.

ASSIGNMENT OF PRIORITIES

Individuals in a society have differing or conflicting values, needs and circumstances, and they inevitably have a wide range of opinions about the need for government action regarding the solution of societal problems. For a democracy to accomplish its purpose, it is necessary for the people, acting through their representatives, to discuss and reach a consensus on the issues that impel government action[16] (to fulfill steps 2 and 4 of the problem-solving method). Therefore, in a democracy, societal problems and their priority for solution must be freely discussed by legislators in an open forum characterized by debate, deliberation, bargaining and compromise.[17]

Rhetoric is used as an adjunct for the presentation of opinions about the comparative seriousness of societal problems (with the caveat that it can also be used to mislead and misinform), but it is not needed for the task of assigning priorities to problems for solution. Dialectic, on the other hand, is the essential reasoning-and-consensus process by which decisions are made, so it has a valid role in the assignment of priorities.

ANALYSIS OF PROBLEMS

When a societal problem has been identified and given a priority for solution by the legislature, accurate measurements and a thorough analysis of the size and nature of the problem must be performed so that an appropriate law-solution may be applied. The accurate assessment of problems requires the use of empirical and analytical processes, and rhetoric and dialectic therefore have no role to play in this step of problem solving.

---

[15] This discussion presumes that the legislature is a representative body (in a republican form of democracy) in which the citizens are represented by elected members of the government's legislature or parliament.

[16] G.W. Hegel, *The Philosophy of History*, Great Books of the Western World, vol. 46, p. 280: "In a democracy it is a matter of the first importance to be able to speak in popular assemblies, to urge one's opinions on public matters."

[17] Mill, p. 361 (see quote in Chapter 7, footnote #4).

DEFINITION OF GOALS AND PERFORMANCE ENVELOPES

The determination of measurable goals and performance envelopes (for the satisfaction of steps 5 and 6 of the problem-solving method) requires the use of empirical and analytical processes that are beyond the scope of rhetoric and dialectic.

SEARCH FOR KNOWLEDGE

The efficacious solution of complex problems requires a literature search and compilation of all reliable knowledge relevant to the problem-solving process. (The search for knowledge involves multiple steps of the problem-solving method.) Since rhetoric is a mechanism of persuasion, not investigation, it has no role to play in the search for knowledge. While dialectic *is* an investigative process, its focus is on the exploration of the intellect—ideas and opinions—not knowledge. When facts are uncovered in the question-and-answer format of dialectic, they are often rendered useless by being commingled with opinions and falsehoods. Furthermore, the process of dialectic permits the exclusion of some or all reliable knowledge if such exclusion facilitates the attainment of a "reasonable" (or predetermined) conclusion. Therefore, neither rhetoric nor dialectic is suitable for gathering the knowledge needed for the solution of problems.

CREATION OF NEW LAWS: IDEATION

The search for, and evaluation of, potential solutions in brainstorming sessions is an exercise of dialectic; it is a critically important step in the engineering design of solutions (see Appendix E). (Note: When quality programs are adopted for laws, these brainstorming sessions will be carried out by the designers of laws, not by legislative assemblies.) Rhetoric is an exercise of persuasion and indoctrination. Although it can be used to *promulgate* new ideas, it has no direct value as a mechanism for *generating* new ideas. (In fact rhetoric is often used to stifle new ideas.)

DESIGN OF NEW LAWS

The design of a law that will efficaciously solve a societal problem entails design expertise—for example, in the efficient application of accepted methods for the creation, testing and evaluation of solution-models for the proposed new law (see Appendix E). Design expertise requires analytical and empirical methodologies that are beyond the scope of rhetoric and dialectic; rhetoric and dialectic therefore have no useful role to play in the design of solutions.

DECISION TO ENACT OR REJECT BILLS

The decision-making process that culminates in the vote to approve (enact) or reject a bill is an essential step in the problem-solving method. Rhetoric can be used as an adjunct for presenting opinions about the merits of proposed new legislation. However, the potential of rhetoric to mislead and misinform decision makers prevents it from having any important role in the vote to enact or reject bills. In contrast, dialectic is the essential process by which decisions are made at this juncture of the problem-solving process.

FOLLOW-UP EVALUATION OF LAWS

In a democracy, after a law has been enacted, it is critical to know whether its enforcement produced the desired problem-solving results. A law that is found to be of no value or to exacerbate societal problems must either be repealed or amended to improve its performance. Thus follow-up evaluation (quality assurance) is absolutely essential for laws in a democracy, just as it is for all other tools that have an impact on the well-being of the public. However, when quality assurance programs are eventually adopted for laws, rhetoric and dialectic will not be used to carry out such programs because these mechanisms are unable to derive reliable knowledge of the mechanics of laws.

OPTIMIZATION OF LAWS

The redesign (amendment) of laws to improve their performance requires the same ideation and design expertise steps that were required for the initial design of laws. Rhetoric has no role to play in this process and, although dialectic is needed for the ideation phase of design, it has nothing to offer in terms of design expertise.

The Limits of Rhetoric and Dialectic

As these points illustrate, rhetoric plays no essential role in the design of laws and, on balance, is more harmful than useful in the law-design process. Dialectic is necessary for ideation and decision making, but is inadequate for the analysis and design tasks that require empirical methods. The useful roles of rhetoric and dialect in the creation of laws that satisfy the purpose of democracy are outlined in Table J-1.

Problem-Solving Steps in the Creation of Laws That Satisfy the Purpose of Democracy	Rhetoric	Dialectic
Identification of Problems	no role	no role
Priority Assignment for Problems	adjunct role	essential decision-making role
Analysis of Problems	no role	no role
Definition of Goals and Performance Envelopes for Proposed New Laws	no role	no role
Search for and Compilation of Reliable Knowledge	no role	no role
Ideation	no role	essential role
Design of New Laws and Optimization of Existing Laws	no role	no role
Acceptance or Rejection of Proposed New Laws	adjunct role	essential decision-making role
Follow-Up Evaluation of Enacted Laws	no role	no role

Table J-1. The Roles of Rhetoric and Dialectic in the Solution of Societal Problems: Rhetoric has no essential role, and dialectic has limited but necessary roles in the creation of laws that satisfy the purpose of democracy.

Relevance to Laws and Lawmaking

A critical point in the ascendancy of democracy will be reached when governments recognize that rhetoric and dialectic (the bases of the traditional method of lawmaking) are not adequate to the full task of creating laws for democratic governments. The path will then be open for the establishment of quality design processes capable of satisfying the purpose of democracy.

College Curricula for the Science and Engineering Disciplines of Laws

Governments have three principal functions: administrative, judicial and legislative. To meet their functional requirements, the administrative and judicial branches of government engage the services of individuals who have appropriate educational backgrounds in management and law. The executive branch of government (bureaucracy) relies upon the graduates of business schools for its management programs, and the judicial branch of government hires and contracts with law school graduates for its adjudication tasks.

But what schools provide students with an education appropriate for the tasks of the legislative branch of government—the design of laws that satisfy the purpose of democracy? And what schools provide students with the expertise needed to gather reliable knowledge of the effects of laws so that legislatures can know if their bodies of laws are serving the best interests of the people? The answer is: none. There are *no* schools that provide an education in the design of law-solutions for societal problems or the accumulation of reliable knowledge of the mechanics of laws. The curriculum of law schools, for example, does not include the design techniques needed for creating laws that solve societal problems. Law schools teach students how to write and interpret contracts (e.g., documents that define the relationships and obligations of parties in a business). However, those skills are far different from the design expertise (e.g., problem analysis, modeling and simulation) needed for the creation of laws that efficaciously solve societal problems, as observed by Gross and Dickerson:

> *Bill drafting has been one of the neglected phases of law-school training. In fact, the legal profession as a whole has done very little to advance the art of draftsmanship....In any case, bill drafting calls for more talents than can be obtained through abstract legal training, no matter how excellent it may be or become.*[1]

---

[1] Gross, p. 191.

In the United States, there is little training in draftsmanship; of that, little is being provided by the law schools. This is especially unfortunate, because today's overburdening of the courts might be significantly alleviated by spending more professional effort to reduce the judicial input generated by substandard legal instruments than in merely lubricating judicial procedure....Although many law schools now recognize the importance of legal drafting, their experiments in trying to teach it have produced, at best, only spotty results.[2]

If the quality-mandated law analysis and design needs of democratic governments are to be satisfied, college curricula for the science and engineering disciplines of laws must be developed and implemented.[3]

The creation of college curricula for the design of laws (the engineering discipline of laws) and for the derivation of scientific knowledge of laws (the science of laws) is a logical process. The design of laws that solve societal problems is a task for engineering, so undergraduate students would major in the new engineering discipline of laws. (Since laws are a form of software, the engineering discipline of laws would be a derivative of software engineering.[4]) Alternatively, students could choose another engineering or science major with a minor in the engineering discipline of laws.

The undergraduate curriculum would include extensive coursework in the sciences (essential because the laws of government operate within and produce effects upon the physical world), software engineering and related mathematical disciplines. In addition, since laws interact with and give direction to socioeconomic activities, courses in the social sciences (with an emphasis on economics and political science) and humanities (with an emphasis on history) would also be necessary. The proposed undergraduate curriculum would provide students with an understanding of the interconnectedness of science, engineering, mathematics, economics, government and humanities—and would thus be the penultimate "liberal education."

For graduate school courses, the science and engineering disciplines of laws would be separated into two distinct entities. Both science and engineering curricula at the graduate level would include courses in the field of law.[5] However, graduate courses in the *science* of laws curriculum would delve into methods for

---

[2] Dickerson, p. 2.

[3] At the beginning of the twentieth century, a college curriculum for aeronautical engineering did not exist. However, when "heavier than air" flying machines became a reality, a significant demand arose for schools of aeronautical engineering. When the first law is created under the auspices of quality design standards, an analogous condition will arise for lawmaking, and academic programs will need to be created to meet the demand for engineers and scientists in the field of law.

[4] See, for example, H. van Vliet, *Software Engineering* (New York, NY: John Wiley & Sons, Inc., 1993); and S.K. Chang, editor, *Handbook of Software Engineering and Knowledge Engineering* (Hackensack, NJ: World Scientific Publishing Co., Inc., 2002).

[5] The interdisciplinary nature of the science and engineering disciplines of laws mandates that their education programs be located at universities that include colleges of science, engineering and law.

deriving knowledge of the structure and mechanics of laws, with emphasis on measurement and analytical techniques, e.g., statistical methods. In contrast, graduate course work in the *engineering discipline* of laws would stress design methodologies with advanced studies of modeling and simulation of law-solutions. Upon graduation, scientists and engineers would join their peers in the accumulation of reliable knowledge of laws and in the design of laws that are efficacious in the solution of societal problems. Lawmaking would thus be transformed into a knowledge industry and governments would be able to assemble bodies of laws that satisfy the purpose of democracy.

Relevance to Laws and Lawmaking

As quality programs for laws are adopted and become more comprehensive, university degree programs in the science and engineering disciplines of laws will evolve. The advent of these programs will be significant because they will lead to the transformation of lawmaking from an opinion-based process to a knowledge-based process, thus enabling governments to make the transition to the status of true democracy.

Wisdom

Humans have an innate and insatiable desire to expand their knowledge and improve the conditions of their existence. The most expedient and reliable means of achieving these goals is through the process of wisdom.[1] *Wisdom* is defined as knowledge combined with good judgment in the use of that knowledge. It is the optimum, knowledge-based, self-critical and self-correcting approach for achieving desired results. Although wisdom is highly desired, individuals and institutions do not always rely upon knowledge and may exercise poor judgment in the use of knowledge.

Knowledge, which is the basis of wisdom, is the body of recorded facts accumulated by humankind over the course of time. The store of knowledge grows continuously through processes such as scientific investigation and event documentation. Since wisdom is a direct function of knowledge, the opportunity for the exercise of wisdom increases, and may be expected to continue to increase, in direct proportion to the expansion of knowledge. The history of civilization may thus be viewed as the slow but inexorable progression from a state of ignorance, in which all decisions were necessarily based solely upon the intellect, to a state of knowledge, in which wisdom is not only possible but routinely practiced.

Since wisdom requires both knowledge and good judgment, the distinction between knowledge and the intellect must be clarified. Knowledge is a recorded *body of facts* that is stored in physical media such as books, journals, videotapes and computer memories. Knowledge is also stored in human memories. The memory of every individual begins with the total lack of knowledge, a condition of ignorance or "tabula rasa" (blank slate) in which no knowledge exists—when wisdom, by definition, is not possible. As an individual matures, his or her store of knowledge grows as knowledge is transferred to the memory through life experiences and education. By this process, the individual acquires knowledge, and the ability to exercise wisdom increases.

The *intellect*, in contrast with knowledge, is defined as an individual's *ability* to learn, reason and make decisions; the intellect is relatively constant over an individual's lifetime. Since wisdom is a function of knowledge (which grows) and intellect (which remains constant), the ability of an individual or a group of individuals to exercise wisdom increases solely in proportion to the growth of knowledge.

---

[1] See Hutchins, "Wisdom," pp. 1102-17.

Good judgment in the use of knowledge, the "action" component of wisdom, is based on the ability of humans to make prudent decisions. Good judgment is a reasoning (intellectual) process that identifies worthy objectives and then selects the most effective, ethical, safe and cost-efficient means of achieving those objectives. Good judgment also mandates that the results of actions be measured and recorded to (1) assure that the objective was achieved (or learn why it was not achieved) and (2) increase the store of knowledge, thus increasing the ability to exercise wisdom in the future. Increasing the opportunities for wisdom is in itself an exercise in wisdom.

Unfortunately, the ability to make good judgments is not a dependable human characteristic because it is a function of the intellect, which can be distracted and influenced by many variables such as emotions, lifestyle, beliefs, circumstances and capriciousness. An argument can even be made that humankind has a propensity for bad rather than good judgments based upon the observed incidences of wars of aggression, human rights abuses and dangerous practices such as drug abuse.

What mechanisms are used to encourage individuals and institutions to be wise, i.e., to use good judgment in the application of knowledge? The moral codes and values of religions, philosophies and cultures are the traditional guides of wisdom. However, the principal means by which wisdom is *enforced* is the body of laws of government. Laws require individuals and institutions to exercise wisdom, that is, to have knowledge *and* use good judgment in the application of that knowledge. For example, the law requires that the driver of an automobile, as a condition of being granted a license to drive, must demonstrate through a written examination and a road test that he or she has knowledge of the "rules of the road." Furthermore, licensed drivers who use bad judgment in the operation of an automobile have their licenses revoked. The use of wisdom in the conduct of human affairs is a major focus of the bodies of law. Laws require that individuals, professions and institutions not only have knowledge of the field of expertise in which they operate but also use good judgment in the application of that knowledge.[2]

The properties of wisdom in an individual are lost, unfortunately, when that individual dies. However, the capability for the exercise of wisdom in enduring institutions, such as scientific societies and universities, is not lost because knowledge of the structure, mechanics and events of the physical world, including knowledge of decisions (good and bad) and their consequences, is recorded and accumulated over time. The outlook for the human condition is therefore optimistic: The conditions required for wisdom grow with time.

---

[2] Thus the irony: Laws of government require the exercise of wisdom for every useful enterprise except lawmaking.

The elements and mechanisms of wisdom are illustrated by the following story: Suppose that you are marooned on a desert island where the only available food is red and green berries. To avoid starvation, you are forced to eat berries. Since it is possible that either the red or the green berries may be poisonous, which type of berry should you choose to eat first? Which choice represents a wise decision? The answer is, there can be no wise decision because you are ignorant of the suitability of either type of berry; without knowledge of consequences, you can certainly make an intellectual, i.e., a "reasonable" decision, but a *wise* decision is not possible, by definition. Now suppose that you decide to eat the red berries and immediately develop stomach cramps, nausea, vomiting and a rash. By this trial, you learn that the red berries are inedible. Suppose that you then eat the green berries and discover that they are nutritious and produce no undesirable side effects. You now have knowledge of the consequences of eating both red and green berries, and have satisfactorily completed the first trial-and-error steps on the road to (berry-eating) wisdom.

Wisdom may now be exercised simply by drawing on your accumulated knowledge. You can make the wise decision to eat only the green berries (knowledge plus good judgment) to maintain a suitable state of nutrition. You also have the option of being foolish by making the unwise decision to eat the red berries (knowledge plus bad judgment). The need to record your newly gained knowledge is critical for the continued exercise of wisdom. What would happen if you forgot which kind of berry was edible? You would then be forced to repeat the berry-eating experiment and run the risk of eating red berries again. In other words, by losing knowledge, you lose the ability to exercise wisdom (an unwise process), and must therefore undergo the time-consuming and potentially unpleasant process of regaining lost knowledge.

As this example illustrates, wisdom is a simple, iterative, self-correcting process that always seeks improvement in the direction of desired outcomes via optimum means and, equally important, records processes and outcomes. Wisdom begins from a state of ignorance and is tolerant of the less-than-ideal consequences that may occur when decisions are necessarily made with little or no knowledge. Wisdom always learns from past successes and failures, and continuously adds to the store of knowledge. Accordingly, wisdom will increasingly dominate, and make improvements in, human affairs.

Relevance to Laws and Lawmaking

Wisdom, contrary to popular conception, is not currently exercised by legislatures in carrying out the steps of the traditional method of lawmaking. For the most part, laws are now created on the basis of opinions, precedents, anecdotes and even falsehoods instead of knowledge (see Chapter 4). Even when knowledge is available, no effective rules exist to prevent that knowledge from being ignored or used to advance the agendas of special interests to the detriment of the citizens as a whole (see Chapters 4 and 5). Furthermore, the results of law enforcement are not measured, analyzed or recorded as an integral and official procedure of the legislative process (an unwise oversight), so in the vast majority of cases, the effects of laws are unknown. Therefore, the traditional method of lawmaking *cannot be a process of wisdom.*

Since wisdom is highly desired for the conduct of human affairs, what steps can be taken to assure that lawmaking will become an exercise in wisdom? All that is required is for legislatures to adopt quality programs as the basis for the design, operation and follow-up evaluation of the laws of government. Quality programs will require the use of reliable knowledge (generated by the science of laws and other sciences) and good judgment in the design of laws (as practiced by the engineering discipline of laws). Quality programs will measure and record the results of law enforcement, add to the store of scientific knowledge of the structure and mechanics of laws, and lead to the repeal of less-than-useful laws. By these processes wisdom will become the basis for the design and operation of laws, and legislatures will then be able to create bodies of laws that consistently and optimally satisfy the purpose of democracy.

aristocracy: An authoritarian form of government in which the sovereign consists of a group of "aristocrats" whose claim to the position of sovereign is based upon wealth, birthright, military rank or other arbitrary factor.

authoritarian government: The category of government characterized by two unequal political classes: (1) the superior, or "elite," ruling class that constitutes the sovereign of the government and (2) the ruled or subject class. There are four forms of authoritarian government: aristocracy, ideocracy, monarchy and theocracy.

bill: A draft of a proposed new law of government presented for approval to a legislative body.

citizen: An individual who is recognized by a government as a political member of that government. In a democracy, the highest unit of political power is citizenship, and each citizen is equal to every other citizen in terms of his or her possession of political and other human rights.

control system: The means by which a variable output is made to conform to a prescribed input. There are two types of control system: feedback and feed-forward.

creative science (engineering): The scientific disciplines that combine knowledge, tools and the problem-solving method to solve problems through the creation and optimization of useful products and processes, i.e., tools, or technology. *See also* **science.**

democracy: The category of government in which the citizenry (the politically equal citizens; the people as a whole) constitutes the sovereign.

dialectic: Logical argumentation; the investigation and evaluation of opinions and ideas through dialogue and debate.

electoral democracy: A government that meets the first requirement of democracy. *See also* **requirements of democracy.**

empirical: Relating to the use of observation or experimentation rather than speculation.

engineering: *See* **creative science.**

engineering discipline of laws: The creative scientific discipline that is concerned with the efficacious solution of societal problems through the creation and optimization of the laws of government. The engineering discipline of laws does not yet exist.

fact: Something demonstrated to exist or known to have existed.

feedback control system: A type of control system in which the system's output directs the system's operations.

feed-forward control system: A simple type of control system in which the input to the system directs the system's operations. A feed-forward control system does not measure or respond to its output.

government: The institution that exercises authority over a society of people. Every government is controlled by and serves the interests of its sovereign. Governments are either authoritarian or democratic.

human rights: The freedoms of action and freedoms from harm that are inherently equal in every individual. Human rights are bounded by two conditions: (1) They are inalienable and (2) the exercise of human rights by one individual cannot interfere with the human rights of any other individual. Human rights include substantive, property, political and legal rights.

hypothesis: An unproven speculation that is tentatively accepted to explain certain observations. Hypotheses are formulated so that their validity can be established by empirical means.

ideal law of government: A law that has five characteristics: (1) It is simply stated and has a clear meaning; (2) it is completely successful in achieving its problem-solving objective; (3) it interacts synergistically with other laws; (4) it produces no detrimental side effects; and (5) it optimally serves the purpose of democracy.

ideocracy: An authoritarian form of government in which the leaders of a secular belief system, or political ideology, constitute the sovereign.

intellect: An individual's ability to learn and reason.

investigative science: The scientific disciplines that employ knowledge, tools and the scientific process to derive, record, organize and promulgate scientific knowledge. *See also* science.

knowledge: The sum of the recorded facts that have been accumulated by humankind over the course of time.

law of government: An order of government prescribed and enforced under the authority of that government.

letter of the law: The entire written content of a law; the fixed arrangement of its words and punctuation.

liberal democracy: A government that satisfies the first and second requirements of democracy. *See also* requirements of democracy.

living standards: The measured level of the economic status of the people within the jurisdiction of a government.

mechanics: The relationship between cause and effect; the linkage between the input and the output of a given process or device.

model: A systemized description, often in the form of a mathematical representation, of a natural or human-created or human-envisioned structure, process or system.

monarchy: An authoritarian form of government in which a "royal" family constitutes the sovereign.

opinion: A belief or conclusion that has not been verified by empirical means.

performance envelope for laws: The internal and external boundaries of a law's range of operations, such as its allowable limits of costs and side effects.

political ideology: A secular belief system that defines the uses of government authority; the dogma of a political party.

problem-solving method: The systematic process by which problems are solved.

purpose of democracy: To accomplish the honorable objectives of the people by honorable means in the best interests of the people. A government must meet the three requirements of democracy in order to satisfy the purpose of democracy. *See also* requirements of democracy.

purpose of government: To accomplish the objectives set forth by the sovereign of government.

quality: The degree of excellence a given entity possesses.

quality assurance (QA) standards: The criteria that are used to determine the efficacy (effectiveness, cost-efficiency, safety, etc.) of products and processes. QA standards are used to identify and eliminate flaws of design and operations.

quality design (QD) standards: The criteria that guide the creation of new products or processes. QD standards emphasize excellence of design methodologies and outcomes.

quality improvement (QI) standards: The quality design standards that apply to design improvements of existing products and processes.

quality-of-life standards: The measured level of the physical and cultural environment of the people within the jurisdiction of a government.

requirements of democracy: The three criteria that governments must meet to satisfy the purpose of democracy: (1) Recognize the citizenry (people as a whole) as the sovereign of government, (2) secure the full complement of human rights of the people and (3) efficaciously solve or mitigate societal problems for the benefit of the people as a whole.

rhetoric: The art of effective expression and the persuasive use of language.

rule of engineering: Each new generation of engineering product is characterized by improvement over the preceding generation.

rule of law: Defined and consistent rule; limited government; the concept of governmental authority that holds that the body of written, duly enacted and codified laws of government is superior to any other directive of government. The rule of law defines the limits of the scope of government.

rule of man: Arbitrary rule; tyranny; unlimited government; the concept of governmental authority that holds that the temporal orders of the leaders of government are superior to any other directive of government. In contrast with the constraints under the rule of law, the scope of government is unlimited under the rule of man, wherein the written laws of government may be arbitrarily enforced, overruled or ignored by the leaders of government.

science: The systematic and principled intellectual enterprise that employs knowledge, tools and peer-reviewed empirical processes to (1) derive, record, organize and promulgate scientific knowledge (investigative science); and (2) solve problems efficaciously through the creation and optimization of useful products and processes (creative science, or engineering). The term *science* is also used as a synonym for *investigative science.*

science of laws: The investigative scientific discipline that derives, records, organizes and promulgates scientific knowledge of the structure and mechanics of the laws of government The science of laws does not yet exist.

scientific knowledge: The recorded facts and theories that have undergone the scientific process and have been judged, by a scientific society of peers, to be accurate descriptions of reality. Scientific knowledge is not regarded as absolute truth. However, it is composed of the tentative and incomplete descriptions of the physical world that have been rigorously tested and judged to have the closest correspondence with reality. It is therefore the most accurate and reliable form of knowledge—the "gold standard" of knowledge.

scientific process (formerly "scientific method"): The principles and techniques necessary for the accumulation of scientific knowledge, including rules for concept formation, experimentation, observation, measurement and the validation of hypotheses by a society of peers.

software: The instructions that direct the operation of a device or process. Musical scores, food recipes, computer programs and laws of government are examples of software.

sovereign: The group of people who control a government.

special interest group: A group of people who share a common belief, goal or circumstance. Special interest groups include corporations, religions, trade unions, schools, political parties, athletic organizations, etc.

spirit of the law: The purpose, or intent, of a law. The spirit of any given law is the hoped-for change, or benefit, that the law will produce from a less desirable condition to a more desirable condition, as predicted by the designers of the law.

statute: A law of government that has been enacted by the government's legislative assembly.

theocracy: An authoritarian form of government in which the heads of a religious belief system constitute the sovereign.

theory: A coherent explanation of a group of related natural phenomena. Theories are not directly observable in their entirety but are supported and refined by a preponderance of facts and ongoing scientific studies. Examples of theories are biological evolution and the big bang theory for the origin of the universe.

traditional method of lawmaking: The lawmaking process of government in which (1) an idea for government action is transcribed into a written petition, or bill; (2) the provisions of the bill are discussed, debated and possibly amended by a legislative assembly; and (3) the assembly enacts (or rejects) the final version of the bill as an enforceable law of government.

true democracy: A government that meets all three requirements of democracy and thus fully satisfies the purpose of democracy. *See also* **requirements of democracy.**

wisdom: Knowledge combined with prudent and just judgment in the use of that knowledge.

Aquinas, Thomas. *Summa Theologica*. Great Books of the Western World. Vol. 20. Chicago, IL: Encyclopaedia Britannica, Inc., 1990.

Aristotle. *Politics*. Great Books of the Western World. Vol. 9. Chicago, IL: Encyclopaedia Britannica, Inc., 1990.

———. *Rhetoric*. Great Books of the Western World. Vol. 9. Chicago, IL: Encyclopaedia Britannica, Inc., 1990.

Bacon, Francis. *Advancement of Learning*. Great Books of the Western World. Vol. 30. Chicago, IL: Encyclopaedia Britannica, Inc., 1990.

———. *New Atlantis*. Great Books of the Western World. Vol. 30. Chicago, IL: Encyclopaedia Britannica, Inc., 1990.

———. *Novum Organum*. Great Books of the Western World. Vol. 30. Chicago, IL: Encyclopaedia Britannica, Inc., 1990.

Bakshian, Aram, Jr. *American Speaker*. Washington, DC: Georgetown Publishing House, Inc., 1994.

Beakley, George. *Engineering: An Introduction to a Creative Profession*. New York, NY: Macmillan Publishing Company, 1986.

Berman, Daniel. *In Congress Assembled*. New York, NY: Macmillan Publishing Company, 1964.

Beutel, Frederick. *Experimental Jurisprudence and the Scienstate*. NJ: Fred B. Rothman & Co., 1975.

Brown, Hanbury. *The Wisdom of Science*. Cambridge, England: Cambridge University Press, 1986.

Byrnes, Nanette, and Louis Lavelle. "The Corporate Tax Game." *Business Week*, Mar. 31, 2003: pp. 80-1.

Chang, S.K. Editor. *Handbook of Software Engineering and Knowledge Engineering*. Vol. I, *Fundamental and Emerging Technologies*. Hackensack, NJ: World Scientific Publishing Co., Inc., 2002.

Chorba, Terence, Donald Reinfurt, and Barbara Hulka. "Efficacy of Mandatory Seat-Belt Use Legislation: The North Carolina Experience From 1983 Through 1987." *Journal of the American Medical Association*, vol. 260, no. 24 (December 23/30, 1988): pp. 3593-7.

Citizens Against Government Waste. *2001 Congressional Pig Book Summary*. Washington, DC: 2001.

Clapp, Charles. *The Congressman: His Work as He Sees It*. Washington, DC: The Brookings Institution, 1963.

"Closing the TRL Gap." *Aerospace America*, August 2003: pp. 24-5.

Constitution of the United States of America. American State Papers. Great Books of the Western World. Vol. 43. Chicago, IL: Encyclopaedia Britannica, Inc., 1990.

Crosby, Philip B. *Quality Is Free*. New York, NY: McGraw-Hill, 1979.

Davies, Jack. *Legislative Law and Process in a Nutshell*. 2nd ed. St. Paul, MN: West Publishing, 1986.

deSoto, Hernando. *The Other Path: The Economic Answer to Terrorism*. New York, NY: Basic Books, 1987.

Dickerson, Reed. *The Fundamentals of Legal Drafting*. Boston, MA: Little, Brown and Co., 1986.

Doyle, R. "De-Industrialization: Why Manufacturing Continues to Decline." *Scientific American*, May 2002: p. 30.

Durant, Will, and Ariel Durant. *The Story of Civilization*. 11 vols. New York, NY: Simon and Schuster, 1935-1975.

Einstein, Albert. *Ideas and Opinions*. New York, NY: Bonanza Books, 1954.

Ezzell, C. "The Price of Pills." *Scientific American*, July 2003: p. 25.

Filson, Lawrence. *The Legislative Drafter's Desk Reference.* Washington, DC: Congressional Quarterly, Inc., 1992.
Francois, Joseph, and Laura Baughman. "The Unintended Consequences of U.S. Steel Import Tariffs: A Quantification of the Impact During 2002." Washington, DC: CITAC Foundation, Trade Partnership Worldwide, LLC, Feb. 2003.
Fuller, J.F.C. *A Military History of the Western World.* 3 vols. New York, NY: Da Capo Press, 1956.
Galilei, Galileo. *Concerning the Two New Sciences.* Great Books of the Western World. Vol. 28. Chicago, IL: Encyclopaedia Britannica, Inc., 1990.
Gilbert, William. *On the Lodestone and Magnetic Bodies.* Great Books of the Western World. Vol. 28. Chicago, IL: Encyclopaedia Britannica, Inc., 1990.
"Global Water Supply and Sanitation Assessment 2000 Report." World Health Organization and UNICEF, 2003.
Goldberg, Bernard. *Bias: A CBS Insider Exposes How the Media Distort the News.* Washington, DC: Regnery Publishing, Inc., 2002.
Greene, Katie. "Simulators Face Real Problems." *Science,* vol. 301 (July 18, 2003): p. 301.
Gross, Bertram. *The Legislative Struggle.* New York, NY: McGraw-Hill, 1953.
Hamilton, Alexander, James Madison, and John Jay. *The Federalist Papers.* Great Books of the Western World. Vol. 43. Chicago, IL: Encyclopaedia Britannica, Inc., 1990.
Hegel, Georg. *The Philosophy of History.* Great Books of the Western World. Vol. 46. Chicago, IL: Encyclopaedia Britannica, Inc., 1990.
Hirsch, Donald. *Drafting Federal Law.* Washington, DC: Office of the Legislative Counsel, U.S. House of Representatives, 1989.
Hobbes, Thomas. *Leviathan.* Great Books of the Western World. Vol. 23. Chicago, IL: Encyclopaedia Britannica, Inc., 1990.
Humana, Charles. *World Human Rights Guide.* Oxford, England: Facts on File Publications, 1986.
Hunt, Daniel V. *Quality in America: How to Implement a Competitive Program.* Homewood, IL: Technology Research Corporation, 1992.
Hunter, Thomas. *Engineering Design for Safety.* New York, NY: McGraw-Hill, 1992.
Hutchins, Robert. Editor in chief. *The Great Ideas: A Syntopicon of Great Books of the Western World.* Vols. I and II. Chicago, IL: Encyclopaedia Britannica, Inc., 1990.
Jefferson, Thomas. The Declaration of Independence. American State Papers. Great Books of the Western World. Vol. 43. Chicago, IL: Encyclopaedia Britannica, Inc., 1990.
Jewell, M., and S. Patterson. *The Legislative Process in the United States.* New York, NY: Random House, 1977.
Juran, Joseph M. *Juran on Planning for Quality.* New York, NY: The Free Press, 1988.
Kagan, Donald, Steven Ozment, and Frank Turner. *The Western Heritage.* 2nd ed. New York, NY: Macmillan Publishing Co., 1983.
Kant, Immanuel. *Critique of Pure Reason.* Great Books of the Western World. Vol. 42. Chicago, IL: Encyclopaedia Britannica, Inc., 1990.
———. *The Science of Right.* Great Books of the Western World. Vol. 42. Chicago, IL: Encyclopaedia Britannica, Inc., 1990.
Kelsen, Hans. *The Pure Theory of Law.* Berkeley, CA: University of California Press, 1967. This is a translation of the second German edition of *Reine Rechtslehre,* published in 1960. The first edition of *Reine Rechtslehre* was published in 1934.
Kernochan, John. *The Legislative Process.* Mineola, NY: The Foundation Press, Inc., 1981.
Krick, Edward. *An Introduction to Engineering.* New York, NY: John Wiley & Sons, Inc., 1976.
Locke, John. *Concerning Civil Government, Second Essay.* Great Books of the Western World. Vol. 35. Chicago, IL: Encyclopaedia Britannica, Inc., 1990.
———. *A Letter Concerning Toleration.* Great Books of the Western World. Vol. 35. Chicago, IL: Encyclopaedia Britannica, Inc., 1990.
Machiavelli, Nicolo. *The Prince.* Great Books of the Western World. Vol. 23. Chicago, IL: Encyclopaedia Britannica, Inc., 1990.

Madison, James, Alexander Hamilton, and John Jay. *The Federalist Papers.* Great Books of the Western World. Vol. 43. Chicago, IL: Encyclopaedia Britannica, Inc., 1990.

Marx, Karl, and Friedrich Engels. *Manifesto of the Communist Party.* Great Books of the Western World. Vol. 50. Chicago, IL: Encyclopaedia Britannica, Inc., 1990.

Maurice, S. Charles, and Christopher Thomas. *Managerial Economics.* 6th ed. Madison, WI: McGraw-Hill, 1999.

McConnell, Campbell R., and Stanley L. Brue. *ECONOMICS: Principles, Problems, and Policies.* 14th ed. Dubuque, IA: McGraw-Hill, 1999.

Mill, John S. *Representative Government.* Great Books of the Western World. Vol. 43. Chicago, IL: Encyclopaedia Britannica, Inc., 1990.

Montesquieu, Charles. *The Spirit of the Laws.* Great Books of the Western World. Vol. 38. Chicago, IL: Encyclopaedia Britannica, Inc., 1990.

Newton, Isaac. *Mathematical Principles of Natural Philosophy.* Great Books of the Western World. Vol. 34. Chicago, IL: Encyclopaedia Britannica, Inc., 1990.

Nise, Norman. *Control Systems Engineering.* Redwood City, CA: Benjamin/Cummings Publishing Co., Inc., 1992.

Offenau, Ludomir V. *Science and the Rule of Law.* San Diego, CA: P.C. Press, 1989.

Petroski, Henry. *To Engineer Is Human.* New York, NY: St. Martin's Press, 1985.

Plato. *Gorgias.* Great Books of the Western World. Vol. 7. Chicago, IL: Encyclopaedia Britannica, Inc., 1990.

————. *Laws.* Great Books of the Western World. Vol. 7. Chicago, IL: Encyclopaedia Britannica, Inc., 1990.

Pound, Roscoe. *An Introduction to the Philosophy of Law.* New Haven, CT: Yale University Press, 1922.

Robertshaw, Joseph. *Problem Solving: A Systems Approach.* New York, NY: Petrocelli Books, Inc., 1978.

Rousseau, Jean Jacques. *The Social Contract.* Great Books of the Western World. Vol. 38. Chicago, IL: Encyclopaedia Britannica, Inc., 1990.

Sandburg, Carl. *Abraham Lincoln.* 6 vols. New York, NY: Harcourt, Brace & World, Inc., 1939.

Scherkenbach, William W. *The Deming Route to Quality and Productivity.* Washington, DC: CEE Press, 1988.

Schrunk, David. "The Ideal Law of Government." *Proceedings of SPACE 2002.* Reston, VA: American Society of Civil Engineers, 2002.

————. "Lawmaking Standards for Space Governance." *Space Governance,* vol. 4, no. 1 (January 1997): pp. 44-7.

————. "The Science and Engineering of Laws." *Proceedings of SPACE 2000.* Reston, VA: American Society of Civil Engineers, 2000.

Serageldin, Ismail. "World Poverty and Hunger—The Challenge for Science." *Science,* vol. 296 (April 5, 2002): pp. 54-8.

Simpson, Timothy. "Multidisciplinary Design Optimization." *Aerospace America,* December 2003: p. 38.

Studer, R.P. "New Session Offers Legislature a Menu That Can Bite Back." *San Diego Union-Tribune,* January 4, 1987: p. C-1.

Style Manual: Drafting Suggestions for the Trained Drafter. Washington, DC: Office of the Legislative Counsel, U.S. House of Representatives, 1989.

Tacitus. *The Annals.* Great Books of the Western World. Vol. 15. Chicago, IL: Encyclopaedia Britannica, Inc., 1990.

2000 Index of Economic Freedom. New York, NY: The Heritage Foundation and *The Wall Street Journal,* 2001.

United Nations. *Universal Declaration of Human Rights.* General Assembly Resolution 217 A (III). San Francisco, CA: 1948.

Van Doren, Charles. *A History of Knowledge.* New York, NY: Ballantine Books, 1991.

van Vliet, Hans. *Software Engineering.* New York, NY: John Wiley & Sons, Inc., 1993.

Weart, Spencer R. *Never at War:Why Democracies Will Not Fight One Another.* New Haven, CT: Yale University Press, 1998.

Willett, Edward, Jr. *How Our Laws Are Made.* Washington, DC: U.S. Government Printing Office, 1990.

Willner, Ann R. *The Spellbinders: Charismatic Political Leadership.* New Haven, CT: Yale University Press, 1984.

Wilson, James Q. *American Government: Institutions and Policies.* 2nd ed. Lexington, MA: DC Heath and Company, 1983.

Aesthetic creations. *See* Creative works
Aesthetics, 114-5
Alienable assets, 111
Amendments, 43-6, 70
Aristocracy, 5
Authoritarian government, 4-9, 93
  assumptions of, 11
  forms of, 5
  instability of, 8-9
  regression to, 51-2, 60, 95
  tactics employed by, 6-8
  and the transition to democracy,
    94-7, 107
Benefits of laws. *See* Law(s), benefits of
Bill drafting, 25-40, 166-7
Bill(s), 24-49
Campaign finance reform, 81
Chaos of laws, 56-8, 62, 70, 83, 101, 107
Citizens/citizenry, 9-16
Committee hearings, 41-3
Committee reports, 42-3, 48
Compass of engineering. *See* Engineering,
  compass of
Compass of science. *See* Science,
  compass of
Computers, for design of solutions, 131
Constitution, U.S., 14, 93
Controller (in control systems), 116-8
Control system(s), 116-8. *See also* Feed-
  back control system(s) and Feed-
  forward control system(s)
Corruption, 54-6
Costs of laws, 31-2, 61, 66-7, 68-9
Creative science
  definition of, 120
  See also Engineering
Creative works, 114-5
  evaluation standards, 114
  limiting factors, 115
  nature of change, 115
Creativity, 114-5
Debate, 40-1
Deception, deliberate, 33-6, 56
  in amendments, 44-5
  bills with irresistible titles, 36
  department bills, 34-5
  "hairy arm" technique, 34
  housekeeping bills, 34

intentional vagueness, 36
omnibus bills, 35
overly long bills, 35
"woodchuck" technique, 34
Declaration of Independence, 10-1
Definition of problem. *See* Problem,
  definition of
Democracy, 9-16
  ascendancy of, 93-105
  assumptions of, 11
  beneficiaries of, 102-4
  constitution of, 14-5
  control system of, 12
  electoral, 14, 94-8, 107. *See also*
    Electoral democracy
  emergence of, 93-8
  history of, 93-5
  judiciary in, 15
  liberal, 14, 93, 96-8, 107
  purpose of, 10-3
  relation to universal peace, 104
  requirements of, 13-6, 107
  structure of, 9
  threat to, 51-60, 159
  transition to, 94
  true, 15-6, 93, 102-5, 107
Department bills, 34-5
Design
  elegant, 28, 82, 156
  expertise in, 163
  imperfections, in bills, 37
  of new laws, 163
Designers, law. *See* Law designers
Detrimental law. *See* Law(s), detrimental
Dialectic, 158, 159-65
  adversarial, 159
  definition of, 40, 159
  limitations of, 159-65
  and the problem-solving method,
    162-5
  role of in lawmaking, 162-5
  synergistic, 159-60
Economic sanctions. *See* Sanctions for
  laws, economic
Educational requirements for law designers.
  See Law designers, educational
  requirements for

Election of legislators. *See* Legisla-
tor(s)/legislature, election of
Electoral democracy
    growth of, 95
    regression to authoritarian form of
        government, 95-6
    transition to liberal democracy, 97
    See also Democracy, electoral
Elegant design. *See* Design, elegant
Empirical methodologies, 119-20, 159,
    161-5
Ends. *See* Means and ends
Engineering, 128-37
    compass of, 130
    definition of, 120
    design process for, 132-5
    hallmarks of, 128
    method of, 130-2
    products, characteristics of, 135-6;
        negative consequences of, 135-6
    purpose of, 129-30
    relationship to investigative
        science, 128
    rule of, 83, 130
    tasks of, 129
Engineering discipline of laws, 73, 76-84,
    137, 152-4
    college curricula for, 166-8
    emergence of, 78
Engineer(s), 128
    advantages for, 130-1
    goal of, 121
Evaluation, performance, 135, 147, 164
    of bills and amendments, 43-4
    of laws, follow-up, 49; need for, 83-4
Evaluation standards
    qualitative and quantitative, 114
Feedback control system(s), 71, 102, 117-8
Feedback loop, 71, 117-8
Feedback mechanism, lack of, 159, 161
Feed-forward control system(s), 52, 71,
    102, 116-7
Gerrymandering, 81, 98
Goals
    failure to achieve, 69
    measurable, 69
    measurement of, 142-4

Government, 3-16
    categories of, 4
    principal functions of, 166
    purpose of, 3
    structure of, 3
"Hairy arm" technique, 34
Haste in law design, 37
Housekeeping bills, 34
Humanmade products, study of. *See*
    Investigative science
Human rights, 95-7, 109-11, 113
    abuse of by authoritarian
        governments, 6
    legal, 110, 127
    political, 110
    property, 110, 127
    substantive, 110
    violation of, 69
Hypothesis, 124-5
Ideal law, 71, 101, 155-6
Ideation, 132, 163
Identity
    of institution that employs
        designers, 65
    of law designers, 25-7, 65, 80
Ideocracy, 5
Imperfections, design. *See* Design,
    imperfections
Implementation of solutions. *See* Solu-
    tion(s), selection and
    implementation of
Inalienable rights, 109, 111
Index Lex Legis, 153
Initiative (direct democracy process), 99
Injustice, 54
Input (in control systems), 116-8
Intellect
    distinguished from knowledge, 169
Intentional vagueness. *See* Vagueness,
    intentional
Interaction of laws, 71, 155
Investigative science (science)
    definition of, 120-1
    divisions of, 124-7
    goal of, 124
    relationship to creative science, 128
Irresistible titles, 36
*Journal of the Engineering Discipline
    of Laws*, 153

Journal of the Science of Laws, 153
Judgment, good
 in the use of knowledge, 170-1
Judicial review of laws, 62-3
Judicial system, independent, 15, 127
Knowledge
 accumulation of, 90-1, 169-71
 definition of, 169
 distinguished from intellect, 169
 lack of in bill design, 28-30, 45-6
 recording of, 170-2
 reliable, of laws, 84
 scientific, 121-31
Law design industry, future, 80-1
Law designers, 25-7
 educational requirements for, 25, 65, 80
 identity of, 25-7, 65, 80
Lawmaking, premise of, 18
Lawmaking, traditional method of. *See*
          Traditional method of lawmaking
Law(s)
 benefits of, 20-1, 57-9, 155
 burdens of, 20-1, 57-9, 155
 characteristics of, 18-22
 constitutionality of, 62-3, 102
 costs of, 19, 20-1, 58
 definition of, 17
 design imperfections in, 37-8
 detrimental, 20-21, 62
 as enforcers of wisdom, 170
 evaluation of. *See* Evaluation,
          performance
 existing, list of, 65-6
 fallibility of, 22
 inefficient, 62
 intent of, 18, 155
 large, complex bodies of, 6-7
 letter of the, 18, 87, 155
 of nature, 131
 performance of, 20-1
 risks of, 32-3
 sanctions for. *See* Sanctions for laws
 side effects of, 19-21, 32-3, 58, 69,
          155. *See also* Side effects of laws
 as software, 18, 78, 167
 spirit of the, 18
 sunset provision for, 70
 as tools, 22, 73, 115, 137
 useful, 20-2, 161
 usefulness of, 59-60, 71
 useless, 20-1, 51-2, 62, 70
Law schools, 76, 166-7

Legal rights. *See* Human rights, legal
Legislative history, 88
Legislative oversight, 63
Legislative process, 40-9
 as a feed-forward control system, 118
Legislative sponsorship, 38-9
Legislator(s)/legislature
 election of, 63
 purpose of, 27
 qualities of, 74-5
 role of in authoritarian governments, 95
 role of in democracies, 74-6, 95, 102
 as trustee, 95, 102
Letter of the law. *See* Law(s), letter of the
Liberal democracy. *See* Democracy, liberal
Living standards, 104, 111-12
Lobbying/lobbyists, 38, 44, 47. *See also*
          Special interest groups
Long bills, 35
Majority rule, 10
Means and ends, 27, 52, 144, 149-51
Measurable goals. *See* Goals, measurable
Mechanics
 of laws, 69-70, 87-9, 127
 of the physical world, 121
Modeling, 132-4. *See also* Problem-model
          and Solution-model
Monarchy, 5
Monitoring methods, 67
Natural phenomena, study of. *See* Investi-
          gative science, divisions of
Omnibus bills, 35, 69
Optimization, 130, 135, 147-8, 164
Optimum condition (number of laws), 59
Output (in control systems), 116-8
Patents, 127
Peer review, 123-7. *See also* Scientific
          societies
Performance envelope
 definition of, 145
 external restrictions and internal
          requirements for, 145
 for laws, 31-3, 113, 163
Performance evaluation. *See* Evaluation,
          performance
Performance report, 135
Philosopher-king concept, 95-6
Philosophy, 119
Political parties, role of in lawmaking, 48
Political rights. *See* Human rights, political
Pork barrel projects, 53, 81, 98
Premise of lawmaking. *See* Lawmaking,
          premise of

Priority assignment for solution of
problems, 66, 162. *See also* Prob-
lem(s), priority assignment of;
priority reassignment of
Problem-model, 140-2. *See also* Modeling
Problem(s)
analysis of, 138-42, 162
definition of, 27, 65, 68, 138-40
failure to address, 68
identification of, 138-9, 162
priority assignment of, 66, 139, 162
priority reassignment of, 141-2
Problem-solving method, 130, 132-5,
138-48
comparison to traditional method of
lawmaking, 78-9, 81-2
Property rights. *See* Human rights, property
Publications. *See* Scientific journals
Purpose, statement/declaration of, 28, 66,
142-4
Purpose of democracy. *See* Democracy,
purpose of
Purpose of engineering. *See* Engineering,
purpose of
Purpose of government. *See* Government,
purpose of
Purpose of science. *See* Science, purpose of
Quality, 61-71
as a political issue, 99
Quality assurance programs/standards
for laws, 68-70, 87-8, 98, 100-1, 155
reliability of, 84
for useful products, 61-2
Quality design programs/standards, 64-8,
81-2, 98-101, 155
Quality improvement programs/standards,
70-1, 98, 155
for existing laws, 82-3
Quality of Laws Institute, 152-4
Quality of life standards, 112-3
negative indices, 112
positive indices, 112
Quality procedures/programs
existing, 62-3
for laws, implementation of, 98-102
for useful products, 61-2
Reasonableness, 160, 163, 171
References used in design of laws, 67
failure to cite, 69
Religion, 119

Requirements of democracy. *See*
Democracy, requirements of
Resources, 51-3, 58, 60-1, 70, 112,
139-41, 145
Rhetoric (political), 157-65
definition of, 40, 157
limitations of, 157-9, 161-5
objective of, 158
and the problem-solving method,
162-5
role of in lawmaking, 161-5
Risks of laws. *See* Law(s), risks of
Role of legislator. *See* Legisla-
tor(s)/legislature, role of in
authoritarian governments; role of
in democracies
Rube Goldberg device, 82
Rule of engineering. *See* Engineering,
rule of
Rule of law, 14-5, 58, 155
Rule of man, 14, 58, 95
Ruling class, 4-9
Sanctions for laws, 19
economic, 7-8
justification for, 66
selection of appropriate, 30-1
Science, 119-27. *See also* Investigative
science
branches of, 120-1
compass of, 122
origins of, 119-20
process of, 122-4
purpose of, 121-2
value of, 84
Science of laws, 73, 84-91, 152-4
college curricula for, 89, 166-8
emergence of, 89-90
historical background for, 85-6
Scientific analysis of laws
mechanics, 88-9
structure, 87-8
Scientific institutions/agencies, 90-1
Scientific journals, 90, 123-6, 152-3
Scientific knowledge *See* Knowledge,
scientific
Scientific method. *See* Scientific process
Scientific process, 119, 122-5
Scientific societies, 78, 85, 90, 120,
122-5, 152. *See also* Peer review
Scientists, goal of, 120-1

Side effects of laws
  actual vs. predicted, 67
  See also Law(s), side effects of
Size of body of laws, 56-8, 60, 100-1
Societal problems, 16, 73, 138
  solution of, 157-65
Society of peers. *See* Scientific societies;
  Peer review
Solution-model, 82, 89, 132-5. *See also*
  Modeling
Solution(s), 132
  definition of, 138
  existing, 145
  follow-up evaluation and optimization
    of, 147-8
  new, 146
  search for, 145-6, 163
  selection and implementation of,
    135-7, 146-7
  testing of, 134-5
  See also Solution-model
Sovereign, 3-4
  in authoritarian governments, 4-5
  in democracies, 9
Special interest groups, 25, 31-6, 39,
    41-2, 44, 54-6, 80-1, 91
Spirit of the law, 18
Standards, professional, of science and
    engineering disciplines, 152
Structural defects of laws, 68-9, 71, 100-1
Structure
  of government, 3-5, 9
  of laws, 68-9, 87-8, 127
  of the physical world, 121
Subject class, 4-9
Substantive rights. *See* Human rights,
    substantive
Sunset provision. *See* Law(s), sunset
    provision for
Testimony, unreliable in committee
    hearings, 41-3
Testing of solution-models, 134-5
Theocracy, 5
Threat to democracy. *See* Democracy,
    threat to
Tools, 78, 87, 128, 131, 135-6. *See also*
    Law(s), as tools
Traditional method of lawmaking, 23-49
  knowledge base for, 28-30
  misdirected purpose of, 52-8
True democracy. *See* Democracy, true
Trustees of democracy. *See* Legisla-
    tor(s)/legislature, as trustee
Truth, as compass of science, 122

Universal Declaration of Human
    Rights, 94
Useful law(s). *See* Law(s), useful
Useful products
  creation of, 121
  evaluation standards for, 114
  limiting factors, 115
  nature of change, 115
Useless law(s). *See* Law(s), useless
Vagueness, intentional, 36, 69
Variable (in control systems)
  dependent, 116
  independent, 116-8
Voting, on bills, 46-8
Voting record, 63
Wars of aggression, 8-9
Waste, 52-3
Wisdom, 46, 89, 148, 169-72
  definition of, 169
  lack of in traditional method
    of lawmaking, 172
"Woodchuck" technique, 34